UNTAMED COAST

AUCKLAND'S WAITAKERE RANGES AND WEST COAST BEACHES

BOB HARVEY

PHOTOGRAPHS BY TED SCOTT

D1451309

EXISLE
PUBLISHING

NEW ZEALAND BEHIND THE POSTCARDS

(Above) **Heading west.** (Opposite) **Fishing is one of New Zealand's most dangerous leisure activities and Flat Rock, Muriwai has claimed its share of victims.** (Front Cover, centre photograph) **Untamed coastline: The Gap, Piha, looking north.** (Back Cover) **Muriwai gannet colony attracts intrepid travellers; Captain James Cook's *Endeavour* log records his sighting of the coast, near Kaipara.**

Dedicated to the late Mr Peter Buffett, historian, author and friend.

© 1998 Robert Anster Harvey
© 1998 Edwin Scott/Fotofile International
© 1998 Exisle Publishing Ltd.
All rights reserved.

ISBN 0-908988-11-7

First published November 1998. Reprinted December 1998. Reprinted January 1999.
Exisle Publishing Ltd
PO Box 8077, Auckland 1035,
New Zealand.
Ph: 64-9-303 3698. Fax 64-9-309 0191.
e-mail: mail@exisle.co.nz
website: http://www.exisle.co.nz

Design and maps by Raymond Salisbury. Cover design by C. Humberstone.
Typeset in Berkeley and Frutiger.
Artwork by Streamline Creative Ltd, Auckland.
Printed by Colorcraft Ltd, Hong Kong.

This book has been published with the generous assistance of the Auckland Regional Council and Watercare Services Ltd. We gratefully acknowledge their support and their continued commitment to the preservation of the Waitakere Ranges and the regional parks.

Acknowledgements: Alexander Turnbull Library; Auckland City Art Gallery; Auckland War Memorial Museum and Institute; Pacific Renaissance Pictures; New Zealand Film Commission; Isambard Productions; *The New Zealand Herald*; Waitakere City Library. National Oceanic and Atmospheric Administration, Washington, DC, for use of Year of the Ocean logo.

No part of this publication may be reproduced or transmitted in any form or by any means, electronic or mechanical including photocopy, recording, or any information storage or retrieval system, without prior written permission from the publishers.

CONTENTS

FOREWORD

Acknowledgements and first steps

(Above) **New Zealand champion surfer Maz Quinn jumping off Nun Rock, Piha.**

THE idea for this book started way back in the mid-1970s as a conservation article about Karekare Beach, when the concept of a coastal highway was proposed by the then Chairman of the Auckland Regional Authority, the late Tom Pearce. Whether Tom was serious about a road linking the coastal beaches and adding a salt water swimming pool to the end of Piha, is now questionable.

The Karekare piece was followed by a series of articles over the years on the glory of Auckland's west coast for *Metro* magazine, and it was while working on these that I met the Titirangi photographer Ted Scott, who also sees the west coast as an asset to be treasured. Like me, he loves the area and believes in its sustainability and the importance of careful tourist and day visitor management. I am indebted to him for his talent and extraordinary patience with me over the years as we developed this project.

To my wife Barbara and our children, my special thanks. Thanks also to my original typist Sarah Williams and to my friend Warwick Roger, who as editor of *Metro* commissioned many of the coastal essays and has been kind enough, on behalf of Australian Consolidated Press, to allow material previously published in that magazine to be used as a source for this book. My gratitude and special thanks to the management and staff of Waitakere City Council, especially my assistant Matthew Bostwick and secretary Lisa Johansen. Ian Rockel of Waitakere Libraries has been generous in his support.

I would like to acknowledge the generous help and contributions of Les Read, Jim Ferguson, Pat and John Shanahan, Sir Edmund Hillary, Alan Gribble, Margaret Clarke, Jack Diamond, Tom Collins, Doug Armstrong, Mary Woodward, Norm Laing and the people of Huia, Gary Taylor and members of the Waitakere Ranges Protection Society, Sandra Coney and her wonderful mother Doris, Dean Buchanan, Felix and Rae Westbrook, Murray Gair, John and Jack Ryder, Diane Dorins Saeks, and special gratitude to Graeme Murdoch, the Auckland Regional Council research historian. Doctor Peter Madison and John Staniland of the Royal Forest and Bird Protection Society. Thanks also to the Karekare Surf Lifesaving Club members, especially Stuart Hammond, Andrew Shaw, Wayne Sendles and Chester Bentley. For information on the Muriwai area, Gordon Ridler and John Thomas. For help with the manuscript, my thanks to Des Dubbelt, Ingrid Dubbelt, Graeme Leitch and Stephen Stratford.

With aroha and the deepest respect I acknowledge the friendship of nga iwi Te Kawerau a Maki, especially Te Warena Taua, Rewi Spraggon, Mary Mem-Jo and the whanau, who have opened up my mind and heart to their heritage.

The following artists have generously allowed their works to be reproduced here: Gretchen Albrecht, Don Binney, Nigel Brown, Dean Buchanan, Ruth Cole, Allen Curnow, Len Castle, John Edgar, Basil Fletcher, John Green, Jean Loomis, Ann Robinson, Maurice Shadbolt, John Walsby, Kate Wells, Zeke Wolf.

Special thanks to the staff of Lopdell House, the Auckland Institute and Museum, the staff of Arataki Visitor Centre, the West Auckland Historical Society for their kind permission to use material from *The West Remembers;* the *Western Leader,* the estate of the late Peter Buffett, Waitakere Libraries, and Anah Dunsheath of Rare Books, who uncovered many amazing old or lost photographs and publications relating to the west coast.

Karekare, 1998

When Bob Harvey and I embarked on this project, I was an immigrant fresh from Britain. I had recently left behind a cottage in a sleepy village surrounded by a tidy landscape developed over thousands of years into the patchwork quilt countryside that is rural England today. What I found in New Zealand was a dramatic contrast to what I had known all my life.

From my very first evening walk at Whatipu I was captivated by this wild coastline. Here were towering cliffs, black ironsand, a primeval forest and a sky that stretched 180 degrees from north to south. The wind whistled around me like ghostly bosun pipes and the Tasman surf boomed. As the sun set, the whole scene glowed red, and the last images I remember of that evening were the lines of kahawai surfing just below the rim of the incoming waves.

Ever since that day, I have tried to record these images on film. I hope that with Bob's words and my photographs we can share with you our love of this special place, too precious to lose. We believe all who live and visit here have a responsibility to protect these treasures. Otherwise this book will merely be a record of what was once the untamed coast.

Titirangi, 1998

BEGINNING THE JOURNEY

Westward to the coast

(Above) **Te Kawerau a Maki gather at Arataki to unveil their history.** (Opposite Top) **Arataki Visitor Centre attracts a million visitors each year.** (Opposite Middle and Lower) **Detail and carving, Te Hawiti, grandson of Maki. Pou whenua, Arataki.**

YOU ARE aware that these hills have scarcely been touched by human feet, although people have been in this area for over a thousand years. The paths through the bush and across these shifting sands have not felt the clamour of civilisation. The fertile valleys of the ranges, although cultivated by Maori, hardly had time to flourish before warfare, disease and despair decimated the tangata whenua.

Compared with the ancient world of the Northern Hemisphere, this land is almost pristine. Now an eclectic mix of baches is scattered along the coastline and although many of these are hardly used, there is always activity in the area at weekends and during the holiday period. The coast is loved by many but used by few, compared with wilderness areas adjacent to large cities in other countries.

Film enthusiasts throughout the world were stunned by the moody, misty backdrop to Jane Campion's acclaimed Oscar-winning film, *The Piano*. The international television series *Hercules, The Legendary Journeys* and *Xena, Warrior Princess* have used many locations on the untamed coast and the bush-clad hills that separate it from New Zealand's largest city .

For Aucklanders, the west coast is still a daunting experience. In winter the westerly gales and thunderstorms darken the skies over these ranges. The heaviest rain always comes from the west. In summer the western skies produce glorious sunsets, and none is more spectacular than the autumn crimson and red-curtained effect of the high cumulus clouds of the coast, providing a back-drop to the Indian summer of the isthmus.

To comprehend the west coast, the string of beaches and the track network of the coastal fringe, your first visit should be to the Arataki Visitor Centre. The inspired architecture of this building, with its breathtaking cantilevered viewing decks and airy indoor display areas, houses a treasury of information on the history, geography and ecology of the area.

Just a few minutes along Scenic Drive from Titirangi village, Arataki, designed by the Karekare-based architect Harry Turbott, was opened in February 1994 by the Auckland Regional Council. The high-roofed structure features a magnificent carved ihi, 11 metres tall, which acts as a guardian to the Centre and to the entire Waitakere Ranges area. It serves to reaffirm Te Kawerau mana in the area and also to remind us of the importance of the natural world and the relationship we all have with it. It also represents the tupuna or ancestors of Te Kawerau a Maki and is one of the largest of its kind in New Zealand.

When finished, the carvings were erected in their present positions and blessed

by Te Kawerau a Maki in a dawn ceremony. The carvers were John Collins, Bernard Makoare, Jack Ewe, Kevin Ewe, John Collins Jr, Rewi Spraggon and Tim Codyne. The project was co-ordinated by Te Warena Taua.

Beyond their visual appeal, the carvings tell of love, war, struggles, legends and hope. The patterns chosen embody part of the life story of each ancestor depicted, all fashioned from two kauri taken from the Great Forest of Tiriwa (Waitakere Ranges). Strict Maori protocol was observed when the trees were taken, carved and dedicated, with appropriate karakia or rituals offered to Tane, the God of the Forest.

Other magnificent carvings throughout the public galleries are a symbol of partnership between Te Kawerau and the Auckland Regional Council. The living presence of all the carvings which depict the early history of the Waitakere Ranges in this building gives it a special significance.

Arataki is a delight to the eyes. Lofty and beautifully finished, the building seems to be perfectly in harmony with its environment. Stand on the wooden decks looking south across a fern valley towards the Lower Nihotupu Dam, Laingholm and Cornwallis, the Manukau Harbour and the Awhitu Peninsula, and you can be forgiven for feeling that you are momentarily suspended in space. Face east across the city and you'll see the distinctive profile of Rangitoto, Kawau, Great Barrier and other islands of the Hauraki Gulf as well as Coromandel on the horizon.

It's quite a place, a fitting venue in which to plan your coastal journey. Maps and photographs, historic and recent, models of contoured hills and the smell of history surrounds you. The staff are exceptionally helpful. Park rangers and voluntary assistants are knowledgeable and welcoming.

Here you can choose your day's adventure on the coast. Pick a track to walk or a beach to wander. But before you leave, allow yourself an hour just to enjoy the spectacular scenery and the warmth and charm of Arataki.

An excellent touch is the native bird sounds. Although recorded, you'd swear they are real, they sound so clear and natural. They are piped through the interior walkway which often has a local craft or painting exhibition. Live insect observatories are built into the south wall.

This place is a favourite weekend haunt of Waitakere locals who continue to return with visitors for the view and the many short nature trails which lead from the Centre. It's time now to step out on our own journey.

THE GLORIOUS RANGES

Out of the blue haze a green paradise unfolds

(Above) **Koru on ponga fern.** (Below) **Remains of Black Rock Dam above the Piha Gorge. (Opposite) Waitakere Ranges on a typical misty winter's morning from the summit of Mt Donald McLean.**

THE Waitakere Ranges guard the western flank of the Auckland isthmus, providing a broad shelter-belt against the prevailing westerly winds from the Tasman Sea. This is the Auckland Centennial Memorial Park, the Blue Mountains of the Auckland region. Its rainforest follows the coastline along the northern shores of the Manukau Harbour from Green Bay to Whatipu and then north as far as Bethells Te Henga. The forested eastern slopes of the Waitakeres can be seen clearly from many parts of Auckland City, providing an appealing backdrop to the sprawling western suburbs.

Although the highest point in the Waitakeres is only 474m (Te Toi o Kawharu, on the Twin Peaks Track up a steep climb from Huia), these ranges are not to be underestimated. There are many good walking tracks, yet every year the media reports lost trampers and day-trippers whose afternoon walks turn into a shivering night. I once joined a search party for a jogger, who had become separated from a group of runners on the Huia Ridge and disappeared in dense bush behind the Pararaha Valley. The police brought in tracker dogs from Henderson and after two days of fruitless searching, reinforcements were called from the Army. Even with what seemed to be a small regiment, we were still unable to find him.

Eventually the man was found alive four days later. In that time he'd walked around in small circles, hopelessly disoriented. He said he'd chewed fern root to keep himself going and eaten wasps, which I thought was rather bizarre and hardly nourishing. What interested me most though, was that when he was eventually found, he was a mere 20 minutes from the track he'd originally strayed from.

I was reminded of this poor fellow's plight when in the late afternoon of an Anzac Day we went for an easy run on a new track that led from Anawhata Road. I'd checked the track on a map and saw it would drop down to Piha via the remains of Black Rock Dam. How wrong I was. The track was excellent and the heavy autumn rains of the Waitakeres had not yet turned the forest floor into a slurry. When we reached the gorge, we crossed the stream and entered the bush on the other side. For 10 minutes we followed the track downwards in the fading light. The track petered out and so did we. Retracing our footsteps only seemed to take us deeper into the hinterland of Piha Gorge and as night fell, it occurred to me with a sickening feeling that we were lost in the very heart of the Waitakeres. Like many hundreds of others over the years, we were so close to home and yet so utterly lost.

It took awhile for us to accept our predicament and admit to ourselves that we were lost. Your own primitive urge for survival kicks in. You have the simple option of staying where you are or attempting to move cautiously in the direction you think safety lies. Turn around once in the New Zealand bush, and it's so easy to completely fool your internal compass. Clad only in running shorts and singlets, we decided to try our luck, moving northwards in the eerie darkness through increasingly dense bush, which at one stage had us crawling on our hands and knees. Occasionally we could glimpse a star or two and then a cloudy night sky through the forest canopy. The night seemed to last forever. We moved towards the peaks, hoping that we might be able to see the radar station searchlight and get our bearings from that. None of these strategies worked.

Just before dawn, we heard the sound of a car on a distant metalled road, in the opposite direction to the way we were heading. We turned and walked in the direction of the sound. As dawn broke we heard another car, and eventually we reached the road, five kilometres from where we had started our run so many frustrating hours earlier. Utterly exhausted and bleeding from cuts and scratches, we lay down on the road with a feeling of sheer relief. Unlike so many others who had got themselves lost in the Waitakeres, we'd survived a night in the open wearing only running gear. Basic survival gear like a parka, map and compass is light and easy to carry, and could save your life.

Every year the Waitakeres host over two million visitors, many of them Aucklanders enjoying a day in the great outdoors. The Waitakere Ranges are visited by more people than any other New Zealand park, drawing greater numbers than better-known scenic attractions such as Milford Sound, Queenstown or Lake Taupo. The Waitakeres is an area with enormous tourist potential, being so close to New Zealand's largest city, and containing a microcosm of many of the features that attract visitors to this country. New Zealand Tourism Board statistics show that the most popular visitor activity in New Zealand is not bungy jumping, trout fishing, jetboat thrills or even going down on the farm to photograph those strange woolly animals that dot the landscape. Bush walking is what visitors to this country want to do most. The Waitakeres have an excellent network of tracks, many suitable for those who are less fit or mobile. There are splendid lookouts, huge and ancient kauri trees, photogenic waterfalls and the focal points of the dams and reservoirs which supply the bulk of Auckland's water.

In 1896 the government of the day added a memo to their agenda, to vote £400 to form a track to the kauri forest in the Waitakeres, and to open up some of the fine scenery in the ranges. It was passed by 99 to 1. It was agreed that the Waitemata County Council would be empowered to do the job, as the Railways Department would be unable to deliver any scoria past Waikumete. It was the beginning of the government's interest in tourism in the ranges.

This magnificent regenerating forest has only recently been recognised for the national treasure which it is. In the 1920s the Waitakeres had been largely reduced to a series of bare hills, with the occasional valley of native bush. It was mainly scrub and burnt-off farmland. Photographs of early Titirangi show a land ravaged by clear-felling and fire following the bush milling days. When the farms failed, quick-growing manuka from the ranges provided firewood for the city. When water from the duckpond in the Domain and then later Western Springs became inadequate for the supply of the growing City of Auckland it

(Top) **Hundreds of streams dissect the hills, flowing south to the Manukau and west to the Tasman Sea.** (Above) **Flax bush.** (Opposite) **Sub-tropical rainforest of the Waitakere Ranges includes the nikau palm, supplejack and many fern species.**

was westward to the Waitakere Ranges that our forebears looked. The saving and restoration of the Waitakeres to its former glory was not initiated for conservation reasons, but for the necessity of securing a ready supply of fresh water. The public was forbidden to enter the catchment areas for 60 years. Under the protection of Auckland City and its water source bill, large areas were left to regenerate. The Waitakeres now provides some of the finest and most accessible areas for bush walking in New Zealand.

In both 1902 and 1904 reports were produced initiating the development of three major gravitational headworks in the Waitakere Ranges. These were built on the Waitakere, the Nihotupu and Huia streams. It was decided by the engineers that they would be built consecutively and in that order. The construction of the original Waitakere Dam began in 1906 and was finished in November 1910. As the first major dam in the Waitakere Ranges, it was built to serve an Auckland population that was then 140,000. It was a colossal project for the times, and was made even grander in 1926 when it was raised a further six metres to its present height. This capping was put to the test following

Cyclone Bola in 1988, when the dam overflowed not only through its spillway but over the top of the walkway. During the night of the cyclone, there were fears that the cap could give way and emergency services prepared to evacuate the Te Henga Valley below. Following the cyclone, the top was screwed to the rock foundation like a massive dental reconstruction.

Nihotupu (now known as the Upper Nihotupu Dam) was planned next, but it had a very chequered career. It was first authorised in 1911 for an August start, but it was not until 1915 that a contract for its construction was let. With the accidental death of the contractor and the First World War intervening, the dam was not completed until 1923. Materials for this massive dam were brought up from the Manukau Harbour at Big Muddy Creek and carried for two and a half miles on a 2' gauge railway, then lifted up 400 feet by a steam winch, and then finally by horse haulage another mile to the dam site. You can walk down to the reservoir and dam from the Piha Road (see page 20), or by track and tramline from Arataki Visitor Centre.

With demand for water continuing to grow, the Auckland City Council lost

(Left) **Waitakere Tramline Society's 'dam tram' to Waitakere Reservoir offers high adventure on a Sunday afternoon.**
(Below) When the original Waitakere Dam **was completed in 1910 to supply water to the residents of Auckland, the city's population was only 140,000.**

(Below) **The Waitakere Falls (107m) are spectacular when the dam is overflowing. Waitakere means 'cascading water'.** (Lower) **Cracked earth at Huia reservoir, during the 1994 drought.**

patience with the construction and authorised the building of an auxiliary dam on the northern side of the Piha Road. The area where they built the dam was the site of the largest kauri in the ranges, including the massive Glasgow tree which had a diameter of 14 feet (4.2m). When it was felled in 1899, it was considered the largest living tree in the Waitakere Ranges. Today, the area is dry. The great plain is regenerating once again to native bush and kauri are already three metres tall.

Historically, the Nihotupu Plain played an important role in bush mill history, for it was here that Frances 'Pop' Mander, father of the writer Jane, engineered the first tramway down into the Henderson Valley, using the unique New Zealand device of a full truckload of kauri going down to pull up the returning empty wagons. This incline was startling, with a drop of 270m achieved in a distance of only 1.2 kilometres, with wooden rails. The drop was just below the Rose Hellaby House, which is one kilometre north of the restaurant and shop near the junction of the Scenic Drive and Piha Road. Now leased to the West Auckland Historic Society, Hellaby House provides a wonderful glimpse of the past including a large model of the Mander bush dam. At the weekend, members of the society, who love dressing in period costume, take over the house, making scones and pouring tea, bringing the past to life. Be prepared to spend a couple of hours with them, as they have plenty to tell you.

Work on the Lower Nihotupu Dam with its magnificent concave spillway was scheduled to start in 1936, but the Depression reduced water demand and made it possible to delay its commissioning. The beginning of the Second World War in 1939 meant that this large project was curtailed yet again. However, water demand rose steeply during the war and all available auxiliary supplies were brought into service, with restrictions being imposed every summer during the war years.

Recently uncovered records reveal that in the

autumn of 1943, all impounding reservoirs fed by the Waitakere dams were depleted to one day's supply and the city prayed for rain. Heavy rains filled the dams over the following four months and by 1948 the Lower Nihotupu Dam was commissioned. The first of the rolled filled dams has beautiful grassy banks, is 25m high and 381m long and contains a lake of 4805 million litres. You can walk out over the double-sided spillway and watch the water cascading in graceful curtains down the spillway on its short journey to the Manukau Harbour.

The Lower Huia Dam was finished in 1970 and stores 6660 million litres of water. It has a large plug-hole spillway with a gantry walkway over the top. It's a fearsome drop.

The Upper Huia Dam was completed in 1929. It is a smaller but still very impressive structure, and became the focus of the local community who all seemed to have had a hand in its construction. You can walk to it from the car-park at the top of the Lower Huia Reservoir, or walk down to it from the Piha Road.

These giant water supply reserves now cover 6800 hectares and the dams draw on a catchment area of 5343 hectares.

The Waitakere Ranges is the wettest place in the Auckland region and although the recording of rainfall goes back to 1915 in Auckland City, it has been officially recorded in the Waitakere catchments only since 1949. There is still some impressive rainfall data to study. The rainfall total for the ranges is generally around 40 percent higher than on the Auckland isthmus. The humid climate contributes to the prolific growth of the vegetation, but when drought or near-drought conditions affect the Auckland region in general, the ranges are dried quickly by the prevailing winds from the west and south-west. This local micro-climate which exists in the ranges gives unexpected weather and climate changes unlike in any other part of the North Island.

In the late 1890s Thomas Chessman began buying up Waitakere land as a public scenic reserve, cheered on by the Auckland City Council. The idea of

(Top, Above and Opposite Top) **The Lower Nihotupu Reservoir and its striking curved spillway.**

BELOW & RIGHT: AUCKLAND PUBLIC LIBRARY

(Top) **City Engineer Mr Bush and council workers inside cut-off trench, Upper Nihotupu Dam.** (Above) **Upper Nihotupu Dam construction, 1923.**

wealthy benefactors giving for the greater good had come to New Zealand via public gifting in Britain and North America. The Waitakere Ranges seemed an ideal place for wilderness gifting; after all, those who could afford it had set up holiday cottages on the ridges overlooking the city. In imitation of the British Raj in India, they had called the area Simla.

In 1924 the Blue Mountain Society was formed, one of the first environmental watchdog groups, which advocated public acquisition of more parkland. The idea took off and prolific writer Earl Vaile and his business associate Dr Kenneth McKenzie started the Waitakere Association, with the sole purpose being that the ranges would become the Waitakere National Park. They found a friend and advocate in Arthur Mead, the waterworks engineer for the Auckland City Council, who from 1929 to 1953 oversaw the building of the dams. Together they decided that they would use the Centenary celebrations of 1940 to give New Zealand and the Auckland region a glorious park whose boundary formed the city's western limits.

They succeeded. The council supported the idea of the ranges becoming a regional parkland and it came into being by an Act of Parliament in 1941. Two-thirds of the funding came from local bodies and one-third from the government. They purchased an area of 3237 hectares for the original park. Over the years donations of land plus other purchases have increased the size of this green wilderness to a parkland area of 5133 hectares. Wesley Spragg, who had a motor garage behind the St James Theatre where the Auckland Public Library stands today, donated 761 acres. He called his donation "a celebration of the glorious ranges". The Cornwallis Park of 1900 acres was given by John McLaren and the 774-acre Goldies Bush area was donated by a former Mayor of Auckland City and father of the famous painter. The enthusiastic Earle Vaile gave 699 acres and Sir William Goodfellow 175 acres and a house. The park continues to expand. In 1987 the Crawe property at Anawhata, a 200-hectare block, was added, followed in the mid-1990s by the Big Muddy Peninsula and the farm block known as Te Henga.

The Auckland Regional Authority was established in 1963 and the control of the park was transferred to it in the following year. Today, the ARC with its professional approach to park management is partnered by the Waitakere City Council with their conservation initiatives, including planting and pest control. Possums, wasps and the plague of the New Zealand bush ginger plant, have all damaged the delicate ecosystem of the ranges. Weeds, creeping vines and prissy ornamentals have all invaded the hills, spreading a carpet of destruction into the bush. These noxious invaders are usually brought in unintentionally or carelessly as when selfish city folk dispose of garden rubbish at the roadside.

There's also an unfortunate irony with wilderness areas, and that is if you build roads and even tracks through areas like the Waitakere Ranges the wildlife retreats. If you overload any park with too many people it simply changes its characteristics to reflect the impact of those visitors. The 'natural' barrier is easily breached. The protection of the Waitakere Ranges is a difficult task, and you will find many of the park rangers more than willing to talk to you about the environmental threats that face these hills and valleys. Fire is still the big fear in the ranges and the large fires of recent decades have generally been around the coastal areas and nearly all deliberately lit. The fire that destroyed bush on the Lone Kauri Road was lit by a Molotov cocktail thrown from a car.

NZ HERALD/AUCKLAND INSTITUTE & MUSEUM

Only quick thinking by locals, helped by the rangers who scaled the cliff to beat the fire back before it flared at the cliff-top, saved the Pararaha Valley. Twenty-eight hectares were burnt at Piha at Christmas 1976, a further five on Waitangi Day 1998 and three massive burnoffs behind Anawhata have left hillsides ravaged and blackened for years.

Despite the increasing numbers of day visitors to this park, bird life is still in abundance, but you have to move or sit quietly to be able to appreciate its presence. Rare birds in the park include the native parrot the kaka and the smaller kakariki. The longtailed cuckoo passes through the ranges on migration. Sadly, the kokako has not been seen here for many years. The weka and the kiwi are also missing and will need to be reintroduced. The kakariki was liberated in the Huia area but failed to survive. On the dams, you will have no trouble spotting the grey and the mallard duck. As you get closer to the coast, look out for the reef heron and the white-faced heron. Above you in these ranges, you may hear the wing beats of the kereru (New Zealand pigeon) and the tui, competing against the possum for berry fruits, flowers and young tender shoots. Poisoning campaigns against this scourge of the bush are conducted annually.

Most of the park rangers have retired in the areas they have worked. Jim Forbes, one of the earlier rangers at Piha, still lives on the Piha Road. John Byers, one of the first protectors of the west coast environment, has worked for years to restore the beach at the Gap.

Bill Beveridge, for many years the Senior Park Ranger based at the Arataki Headquarters, now spends his retirement working for the Friends of Arataki. He has led countless search parties for lost trampers. One of the saddest, he

(Top) **Grand occasion: opening ceremony for the Lower Nihotupu Dam, 1948.**
(Above) **The Waitakeres, paradise for trampers of all levels of ability.**

RYAN PHOTOGRAPHIC

RYAN PHOTOGRAPHIC

BELOW: ILLUSTRATION BY JOHN WALSBY

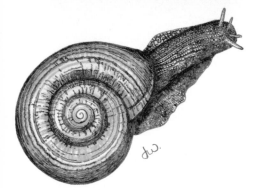

(Top) **New Zealand's endangered native parrot, the kaka, is occasionally sighted in the Waitakeres.** (Middle) **New Zealand's native owl, the morepork, is known by Maori as the *ruru*.** (Above) **The kauri snail is well camouflaged near kauri, with a brown or black shell up to 10 cm across.**

recalls, was organising a search party for a young boy who had disappeared without trace off the Odlin Track. In the four days of the search, 500 people were mobilised to comb the area, but the boy had drowned in a pool near the headwaters of the Pararaha Stream. Not all stories finish so tragically. Keeping their head, many lost walkers bed down for the night in the fern or under a large tree and wait for rescue.

The Waitakere Ranges have had a great champion in the historian Jack Diamond, a remarkable man whose life has kept pace with the 20th century. A bush poet and recorder of early Waitakere history, Jack wrote the classic opus of the ranges, *Once the Wilderness* in 1952. It has been reprinted on six occasions and original copies of the first edition, complete with advertisements to help pay for the printing, sell at $100 or more.

Most of Jack's work has been used extensively as reference for the tracks and their history. His vast collection of photographic negatives is meticulously filed, as are his 27 boxes of West Auckland history and 86 maps. He has donated his extensive collection of photographic glass plates to the Waitakere City Council Library, and his oral history of 135 early settlers is considered one of the finest in New Zealand, and the major reference for the history of the Waitakere Ranges.

Jack Diamond still generously shares his enthusiasm for this wilderness by showing his fascinating collection of photographs and slides to the historic societies. I have talked with Jack over the years about his obsession, the discovery and naming of the gulleys, hills, settlements and isolated places of the ranges, lost and almost forgotten places. No one is better at finding and verifying the original names than Jack. He has also been able to correct a great number of incorrect spellings from the early maps. For instance, Piha was originally Piharau or Pihapiharau, the name Te Kawerau called the lamprey, a delicacy which spawned up the Piha Creek as far as the mill dams. His careful research has shown that Nahana Point and Timiona Stream at Whatipu are in fact named after local Maori who assisted in the rescue of sailors from HMS *Orpheus* and who were later awarded gold medals by the government. Gin Bottle Stream was so named because William Swanson placed bottles along the banks of the stream to be broached during the drive of logs. The Haunted Gully at Huia relates to an incident in 1890 where mill workers returning from a day's toil spotted a fellow miller walking in a clearing before them. When they arrived at the camp, they found their comrade long dead of a heart attack.

Jack and his wife Melville have been members of the Auckland Tramping Club since 1931, and he will drop anything to talk about his beloved ranges. I don't know of anyone who has spent more time researching and reliving the history of the Waitakeres.

Jack Diamond and his old friend Bruce Haywood have spent long hours fossicking through middens, the archaeologists' name for Maori campsites where blackened shells can be carbon-dated to establish their age. They did extensive work on the Whatipu coastline, the highway of spirits. Against the cliffs they were able to locate the sites of fishing settlements from the days when the Tasman Sea rolled right up to the cliffs. Once while walking in the old quarry on the Upper Huia Track, he noticed a rather unusual rock. When Jack picked it up he realised it was a human skull, discoloured and moss-covered. A quick search above the grisly find revealed the remains of an amateur who had vanished 16 years earlier on a fern-gathering expedition.

The Scenic Drive traverses the ranges from Titirangi to Swanson and was part of the grand centennial programme. What a gift it is, offering magnificent panoramas over fern gulleys to Auckland, the harbour and the gulf islands beyond. Don't miss Pukematekeo at the northern end of the Scenic Drive. This was part of a farm in the 19th century, running around 200 sheep. Before it was sold to the Auckland City Council in 1924, there were three farmhouses on the property. In the mid-1990s, the graves of the early settlers were uncovered. A marble plaque was also found in the bush by some trampers. It was cleaned and reinstated over the bush graves. They revealed almost a century of settlement on this often windy outpost.

The easy walk or drive to the top will give you a view that seems to encompass the whole of the Auckland region. You'll glimpse the Kaipara to the north, Bethells to the west, Henderson below, and across Auckland City to Rangitoto and the Coromandel, with the Hunua Ranges to the south-east.

Below you to the south-west is the Waitakere Dam. In winter you will spot the waterfall cascading down one of the highest precipices in the ranges. Puke-matekeo (336m) is the highest point of the Cascade Kauri Park. You can reach the Cascades through the Waitakere Golf Club. It is partly a private road but with easy vehicle access by arrangement with the Golf Club. A short walk over the swingbridge to the left will take you to the gorge, where the Cascade Stream plunges through the cavern at the head of the reserve creating the Cascades. The sound echoes and reverberates in the cavern.

There is also the magnificent Fairy Falls, accessed via an easy walking track from Mountain Road which runs off the top end of Henderson Valley Road. I prefer the walk in from Mountain Road to the steep descent from Scenic Drive, which brings you out above the falls and can be scary for younger kids and those who have no head for heights. Over the years a few have slipped and fallen to their death from the top. I remember a friend videoing the falls following heavy rain. He slipped, the camera flew into space and with a presence of mind which the threat of immediate danger sometimes confers on the fortunate, he grabbed the nearest rock. It was classic movie stuff, and I became part of the action when I took off my belt and used it to help pull him to safety while someone else held onto me. I have been wary of the area ever since.

You will notice the tracks have been well serviced. Many are drained, metalled or rafted. In track maintenance jargon, that means you'll find boards pegged to the ground over soft or waterlogged terrain. On many of the tracks, you'll find boardwalks. These are wooden pathways raised above the water on very muddy terrain. In winter, you'll be grateful for them as it means that you won't have to wear tramping boots, although it always pays to have 'sensible shoes' in rugged country like this. Often you will find large patches of the bush uprooted by pigs. There are still a few there and the occasional family of goats crossing an outcrop of rock. Hunting is strictly forbidden and that is the way it should be.

At the last count, there were 80 official entrances into the Waitakere Ranges Regional Parkland in the 14 districts that make up the Centennial Park. Construction of the Scenic Drive around the ranges was promoted by Auckland City and the Automobile Association in 1936 and opened in June 1939 under its original name The Centennial Drive. This was hardly welcomed by the Waitemata County Council, which was suddenly responsible for its maintenance.

The Waitakere Ranges are a haven of solitude and sheer enjoyment, for the

Many of New Zealand's native trees are found throughout the Waitakere Ranges: (Above from Top) kauri, rimu, ponga (silver tree fern), miro, rewarewa, kowhai, tanekaha.

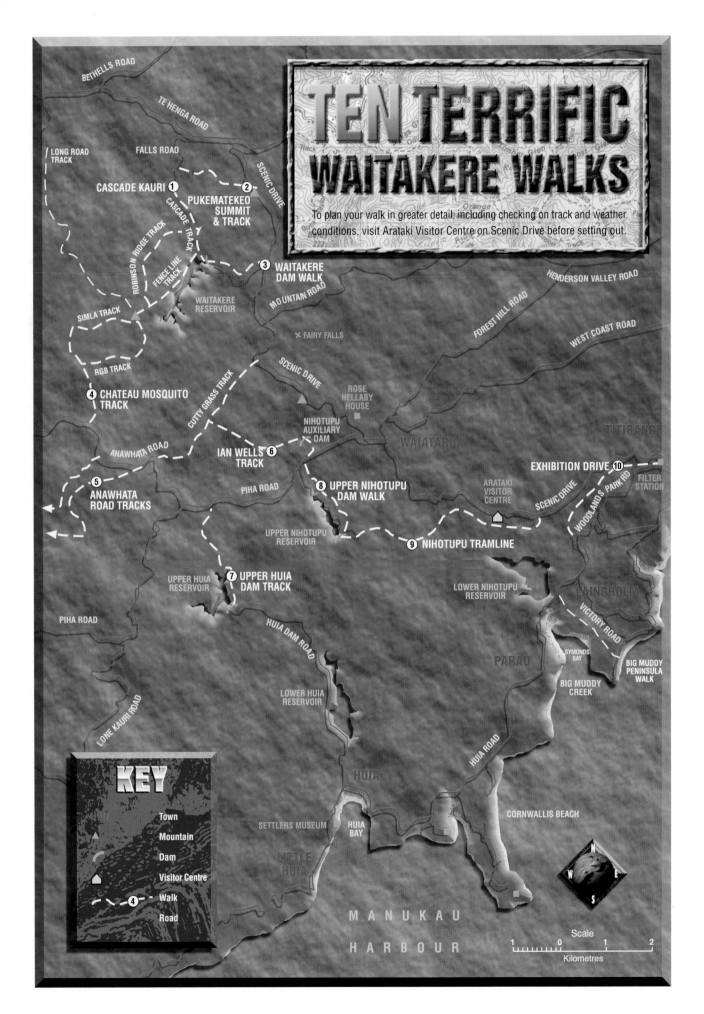

TEN TERRIFIC WAITAKERE WALKS

To plan your walk in greater detail, including checking on track and weather conditions, visit Arataki Visitor Centre on Scenic Drive before setting out.

BETHELLS ROAD

TE HENGA ROAD

LONG ROAD TRACK

FALLS ROAD

SCENIC DRIVE

CASCADE KAURI ①

②

PUKEMATEKEO SUMMIT & TRACK

ROBINSON RIDGE TRACK

CASCADE TRACK

FENCE LINE TRACK

③ WAITAKERE DAM WALK

MOUNTAIN ROAD

HENDERSON VALLEY ROAD

SIMLA TRACK

WAITAKERE RESERVOIR

× FAIRY FALLS

FOREST HILL ROAD

WEST COAST ROAD

RGB TRACK

SCENIC DRIVE

CUTTY GRASS TRACK

ROSE HELLABY HOUSE

④ CHATEAU MOSQUITO TRACK

NIHOTUPU AUXILIARY DAM

TITIRANGI

ANAWHATA ROAD

IAN WELLS TRACK ⑥

WAIATARUA

EXHIBITION DRIVE ⑩

⑤ ANAWHATA ROAD TRACKS

PIHA ROAD

⑧ UPPER NIHOTUPU DAM WALK

ARATAKI VISITOR CENTRE

SCENIC DRIVE

WOODLANDS PARK RD

FILTER STATION

UPPER NIHOTUPU RESERVOIR

⑨ NIHOTUPU TRAMLINE

LOWER NIHOTUPU RESERVOIR

LAINGHOLM

VICTORY ROAD

UPPER HUIA RESERVOIR

⑦ UPPER HUIA DAM TRACK

SYMONDS BAY

BIG MUDDY PENINSULA WALK

PIHA ROAD

HUIA DAM ROAD

PARAU

BIG MUDDY CREEK

LONE KAURI ROAD

LOWER HUIA RESERVOIR

HUIA ROAD

HUIA

CORNWALLIS BEACH

SETTLERS MUSEUM

HUIA BAY

KEY

- ▲ Town
- ▲ Mountain
- 〜 Dam
- ▲ Visitor Centre
- --④-- Walk
- Road

LITTLE HUIA

MANUKAU HARBOUR

N E S W

Scale

1   0   1   2

Kilometres

walker, the jogger or simply for the family to enjoy a wilderness experience by one of the thousand streams that cascade down its marvellous green flanks. What a glorious gift it is.

Ten Terrific Waitakere Walks

1. Cascade Kauri Park
Turn off Te Henga Road at Falls Road and park near the 17th hole of the Waitakere Golf Club. Cross the stream and walk up the kauri-forested ridge on the Cascade Track. This is a tough two-hour climb to the Waitakere Dam. Return via the Fence Line and Robinson Ridge tracks in another two hours. This walk is better suited for seasoned trampers.

2. Pukematekeo Summit and Track
You can make a loop walk of this 336m peak which is located on the northern end of Scenic Drive, by parking your car on Scenic Drive and walking to the summit in 20 minutes, where you will enjoy panoramic views of Auckland City. You can also do a two-hour return walk down the Pukematekeo Track to Falls Road, exiting near the Ranger Station.

3. Waitakere Dam Walk
You will see the sign on Scenic Drive one kilometre north of Mountain Road. It's an easy gradient at first before the steep drop down to the caretaker's house and the magnificent Waitakere Dam. The falls are 107m high, and below the dam face at the weekend you'll see the 2' gauge bush tramway that runs through a tunnel under Scenic Drive to the top of Christian Road. It's one of the most popular attractions in the ranges – you'll need to reserve a seat. Contact the Waitakere Tramline Society or Arataki Visitor Centre for booking information.

Above the dam are two lookouts which are easily climbed by crossing the broad walkway along the top of the dam. There is a network of tracks on the northern and western sides of the reservoir, so you'll need to come prepared if you're planning some longer walks from here. Save some energy for the haul back up the sealed road to the carpark on Scenic Drive.

4. Chateau Mosquito Track
Named after a bushmen's shack on the true left bank of the Anawhata Stream, this track is initially easy. Take the RGB Track which crosses the stream, through to the Auckland University Tramping Club hut, where there is an interesting collection of colourful road signs decorating the verandah. The round trip including a short detour to Simla (323m) takes about three and a half hours.

5. Anawhata Road Tracks
On the left just past the first group of houses of the Anawhata Road settlement, you will see signs indicating the Pole Line Track which links with the Forbes, McKenzie and Home tracks. Heading west, they all go downhill to Piha. Easy to walk in winter or summer, these tracks pass through impressive stands of native trees. If you are doing a round trip, it makes sense to park your car at the bottom of Glen Esk Road, Piha, so that the return journey is downhill. These tracks make excellent Sunday morning runs. Highly recommended.

(Top) **The mighty kauri, king of the Waitakere forest.** (Above) **These spiked boots and handhooks were used to climb kauri trees.**

(Top Left) **Lower Huia reservoir, with the Manukau Harbour and Awhitu Peninsula beyond.** (Above) **Abseiling into the abyss, Lower Huia Dam.**

6. Ian Wells Track

Park your car at the same place as for the Upper Nihotupu Dam walk, but travel two minutes back along Piha Road towards Scenic Drive. Cross the road, and go through the right hand gate down the metal road. It's a 15-minute walk to the empty Nihotupu Auxiliary Dam, which was drained in the 1960s and has more recently been used as the location for the village in the television series *Hercules, The Legendary Journeys*. The remains of the dam are below the road and they were turned into a fortress castle for the first two series.

A short walk in the empty reservoir takes you on a beautiful but damp track of four kilometres, fording the stream several times before you reach the Cutty Grass Track. This links Scenic Drive with the Anawhata Road, crossing wet tablelands as you climb uphill. You may also notice a mining dugout where an early settler known as 'the Fox' possibly resided. If you're fit you'll hardly notice the climb, as the track's gradient is fairly easy. Few people use this track, so enjoy the stillness of the bush. Take survival gear and emergency rations. A round trip via Scenic Drive is about three hours.

7. Upper Huia Dam Track

You'll see the entrance to this track on the Piha Road just before the Anawhata Road turnoff. The track heads in a southerly direction downhill, crossing the Snowy's and Castle streams. It is suitable for a family outing all year. You'll pass through a large grove of rata on your way to the reservoir. To make an adventure

(Left and Below) **Schoolchildren ride the Rainforest Express along the Nihotupu Tramline.** (Lower) **Every year on an April Sunday, hundreds of walkers follow the Upper Nihotupu Dam tramline to raise funds for water projects in developing countries.**

of it, have someone pick you up three to four hours later at the Lower Huia Dam carpark.

8. Upper Nihotupu Dam Walk

Park two kilometres down the Piha Road from the Scenic Drive turnoff. You'll find a small grassed parking area by a green gate. This Watercare Services access road passes a series of waterfalls that were a famous stop-off for early coach trips to the coast. The road skirts the eastern side of the reservoir, surrounded by dense bush, bringing you to the top of the dam in about 40 minutes.

9. Nihotupu Tramline

Below the Arataki Visitor Centre, 11 tunnels were blasted through solid rock and a tramline was laid to build the pipeline from the Upper Nihotupu Reservoir. Hikers normally need a permit to walk along a section of the tramline. In April every year, an organisation called Water For Survival gets permission from Watercare to organise a public walk through six of the tunnels. A donation is requested towards this very good cause, which funds water and health projects in developing countries. The walk is one of the great experiences of the Waitakeres, but be prepared to join hundreds of other walkers. Buses will return you to the Arataki Visitor Centre from the end of the track. Assemble at Arataki between 9 am and 2 pm. Take a torch, hard hat, warm clothes and your camera.

10. Exhibition Drive

We owe this 3.2-kilometre metalled road to the vigorous advocacy of James Parr, Mayor of Auckland, who persuaded his council to form it and name it after the large mining and industrial exhibition in the Auckland Domain in 1913. Park your car beside the Nihotupu Filter Station at the corner of Woodlands Park Road and Scenic Drive. Follow the driveway through the gate and past the Filter Station buildings. Originally a tramline, Exhibition Drive is a level, cool, and refreshing early morning walk to the end which overlooks the Lower Nihotupu Dam. You will pass runners and walkers of all ages. The return journey takes about 90 minutes.

THE ROCKS THAT SPEAK

Intrinsic patterns of time

(Above) **The Waitakere Ranges were born of molten fire.** (Opposite) **Kitekite Falls, a popular 30-minute walk from the Glen Esk Road carpark, and a cool place for a dip.**

FOR THE last 20 years I have enjoyed jogging the bush tracks of the Waitakere Ranges. The network of coastal tracks can be used year-round, whether you are a serious runner or just content to slosh through the winter mud. In warm weather, these tracks are exhilarating. The glorious views from the hilltops are always an inspiration.

In winter the bush cover will shelter you from the wind, but the tracks hold the thick mud and sometimes are more like a watercourse. The high bluffs will often be cloud-covered for weeks on end. But with summer, a day or two of sun and the tracks firm up, and the rich green mantle of the ranges starts smelling with the tang of earth, clay and forest.

During the Lower Miocene (22-19 million years ago) period, volcanic islands became active on the western slopes of a marine basin just off the coast of Piha. As the cooling lava from the volcanoes eroded into rounded casts of andesite, it became embedded in grit and sand, accumulating on the basin floor.

Along the coastline, you will see these conglomerates, sandstone and pillow lavas, layered in splendid streaks when they were lifted from the ocean floor in a new phase of eruptions around 17 million years ago.

Volcanic centres were located along the west coast from O'Neill Beach to Whatipu, and along a major faultline approximating Scenic Drive. Molten lava was forced up through the conglomerate, forming dykes. Earth movements during the Upper Miocene period uplifted the Auckland-Waitakere area again, tilting it north-west. Erosion wore down the soft sedimentary rocks of the Auckland area, leaving the rugged volcanic rocks of the ranges.

You will notice these formations on your coastal walks. Often in the interior of the ranges, you will come across large outcrops of volcanic rock entwined with ancient pohutukawa and rata, suggesting sacred space in ancient times.

Closer to our timespan, during the ice age around a million years ago, the cracking and breaking down of the ranges carved out the great valleys of the coast and the coastal cliffs of today began to take shape. At the same time, the Auckland isthmus volcanoes started their 36,000-year cycle of eruption. Born of fire, the distinctive black coastal sands of the west coast accumulated on the string of beaches from Whatipu to Muriwai.

The Waitakere Ranges consist of a large continuous block of vegetation on an uplifted dissected plateau of resistant volcanic material, across which vigorous short streams have cut gorges. The rainfall for the ranges is generally up to 40 percent higher than on the Auckland isthmus. The annual average for the isthmus is 1219mm, whereas in the ranges the figure varies from 1397mm to

2032mm. The humid climate contributes to the speed of vegetation regeneration here. However, when drought or near-drought conditions affect Auckland, the ranges are also liable to be dry. Because Auckland's prevailing winds are from the west and south-west, the western flanks of the ranges are frequently exposed to strong winds.

In prehistoric times, the Waitakere Ranges were clothed in dense podocarp-broadleaf forest, with kauri on the eastern slopes, pohutukawa on the cliff-faces and kowhai on the rocky outcrops. Today, the vegetation is a mixture of original, cut-over, burnt and completely cleared forest. Around a quarter of New Zealand's native flowering plants, some 420 species, and two-thirds of all ferns and fern allies, over 110 species, are found within the area. They include a wealth of mosses and lichens. The ranges provide a refuge for one endangered plant species, two vulnerable species, three rare and one locally rare species.

If you start to look closely, and slow down your pace, you will be aware that the coastal undergrowth is alive with insects. In fact the ranges form the largest refuge for over 240 insect species in the Auckland region. Common large insects include the Auckland weta, puriri moth, and huhu beetle. Glow-worms can be seen here in damp banks, caves and tunnels.

The myriad of freshwater streams in the Waitakere Ranges provide ideal habitat for 11 native freshwater fish species (about 10 percent of New Zealand's native fish fauna). Koura, long-finned and short-finned eels, banded kokopu, common and red-finned bullies are common. The unique luminescent fresh-water limpet is present in good numbers. The main threats to the freshwater fauna are excessive sedimentation caused by forest clearance, dumping, quarrying and weed invasion, and restrictions to water flow through dam construction.

Three species of frog are found in the ranges. Two were introduced during the late 1860s, but do not compete with the regionally threatened native Hochstetter's frog, which has its own frog tunnel under the Scenic Drive, thanks to a councillor and an Oratia contractor with a sense of fun and community spirit.

My favourite rocks are the cliffs between Karekare and Whatipu. Here the veined strata are clearly delineated on the massive cliffs from Windy Point to the Pararaha Valley. At Karekare, Maori imbued the land formations with special qualities. The rocky promontory on the beach at Karekare, now known as the Watchman, was in earlier times Te Matua or Te Toka Matua, the Parent Rock. Te Matua was parent to two children who wandered too far from their guardians, and were frozen forever in place. They are Paratahi Island off the coast at Karekare and the Split Pin Rock in Union Bay, whose ancient name was Te Tokapiri.

Just over the hill at Mercer Bay sat Rangitoto. According to Maori legend, a tohunga, wanting a better view of the Tasman, cast it from the west coast to its position guarding the Waitemata Harbour. Although this story has a ring of fable to it, its historic and geographical arrival designates its volcanic origin to a time when Maori had settled in the region, and were well aware that the Waitemata Harbour seabed had given birth to Rangitoto. On the other side of New Zealand at Mercer Bay, the watery hole, now filled by the Tasman Sea, bore the name Te Unuhanga o Rangitoto. Above, the towering cliffs held the secrets and legends in their silence.

TITIRANGI AND CORNWALLIS

The village and beyond

COURTESY RAYMOND SALISBURY

(Above) **Formerly Hotel Titirangi, Lopdell House is the dominant landmark on Titirangi Road.** (Below) **Henry Atkinson, immortalised in stone to commemorate his contribution to the district.** (Opposite) **Titirangi, gateway to the Waitakeres.**

IT'S FROM Titirangi that you catch your first glimpse of the Manukau Harbour, New Zealand's second-largest. It is very tidal, shallow and muddy and seems not to sparkle like the Waitemata, yet it is impressive in other ways. Flying into or out of Auckland International Airport, you can appreciate its great expanse: the Manukau covers 388 square kilometres.

Your eye can track the route coastal ships take from Onehunga down the harbour to the high, rugged cliffs of the remote Manukau Heads that guard the entrance. The Heads can also be glimpsed from Titirangi village, before you follow the Huia Road west towards Whatipu.

Before the port settlement of Onehunga was founded in 1847, this harbour had more than 500 canoes shipping wheat, pigs and fish, firewood and kauri gum for a growing Auckland. Maori mills supplied Auckland across the Manukau with flour and bran, flax and wheat. The volcanic soils of Auckland yielded little; the rich fertile Waikato River valley was a land of plenty, and still is.

In the Titirangi area and the nearby portage down in New Lynn, there were busy local Maori communities. The exquisite waka (war canoe) in the Auckland Museum, Te Toki a Tapiri (the axe of Tapiri), that once carried 100 warriors, was based for a while on this harbour. It was spared being burnt in a fire which consumed 21 other waka on the beach at Onehunga, as colonial troops destroyed water transport, when war swept from the Waikato to the outskirts of Auckland in 1863.

Following those savage days, the foothills of the ranges became vast farms and land became everything to the settlers. Firewood was big business and sheep and cattle followed with moderate success. The local school is more than 125 years old, started by the Bishop family, who were early settlers. In 1891, an earthquake struck Titirangi and surrounding areas, toppling chimneys and collapsing roofs. It must have been quite a shake, and it was decided that only substantial buildings should be built in the area. In 1902, Titirangi was covered in a blanket of snow, the first in its recorded history, repeated with a more modest sprinkling in 1968. Today Titirangi is a stylish shopping village. Redevelopment has given the place a trendy reputation and escalating property prices. Cafés and crafts are the new business of the area, and expensive homes are sold and resold by the boutique realtors of the village.

Towering above the village is the Spanish-style Lopdell House. It combines both Lopdell Gallery and a craft shop, Sophora. There is also a bakery and café on the ground floor and a restaurant on the top. The building has had a new lease of life. Below ground is a

HISTORY COLLECTION, WAITAKERE CITY LIBRARIES

(Right) **Bush clearing and fire stripped the early settlement of Titirangi of its green mantle. Early 1920s looking toward Mt Atkinson.** (Below) **Open and ready for business, Hotel Titirangi, 1931.** (Lower) **Section of spiral staircase inside Lopdell House.**

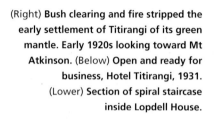

RIGHT: COURTESY RAYMOND SALISBURY / ABOVE: NZ HERALD/WAITAKERE CITY LIBRARIES

small but excellent theatre that seems always to be in production. Lopdell House is the cultural centre of Titirangi, but its recent success masks its chequered past.

In September 1928 a prospectus for the Hotel Titirangi Limited was filed with the Registrar of Companies in Auckland. There were grand plans for a luxury resort hotel in the 'Blue Mountains of Auckland'. Under its Board of Directors, Alec Bishop, James Kemp from Ponsonby, John Ellis of Avondale and Gideon Lunda, a Devonport hotel manager, the company tried to raise £50,000 in £1 shares from the public. The shares were to be fully paid up in instalments within two months of issue.

The directors hoped that a soon-to-be-built concrete road from New Lynn and the expected grant of a liquor licence would convince investors that the hotel could attract sufficient trade to be profitable. Unfortunately for the directors, Aucklanders seeking a return on their investment capital did not share the board's confidence that the plans for a "castle on the fringe of heaven" would prove popular with the tourists or gain a liquor license in a "dry area". The share issue went under-subscribed, despite local support.

They went ahead anyway, commissioning the contractor P.W. Peate to build the tile-roofed hotel complex on the end of the Titirangi Road site for £20,000. Not a bargain, but not expensive either, for the times. Designed by Shortland Street architects Bloomfield and Partners, the hotel was originally envisaged as having four main levels, courtyards, colonnades out the front and arched windows. The building they got was a little less ornate but still noteworthy for its unusual architecture, considering its location.

It was opened on 20 November 1930 by Prime Minister Gordon Coates, in a ceremony attended by local politicians and 300 guests. The same evening at eight o'clock, the hotel staged its most glittering occasion, an invitation-only opening ball, using for the first time the hotel's sprung dance floor. Catering for 63 guests in fully carpeted rooms with attached bathrooms, Hotel Titirangi had drive-in garaging for guest cars, a piped radio/music system to all rooms, an observation roof and furnishings by the same firm that had appointed the Auckland Railway Station which opened the same week.

K. ABERCROMBIE COLLECTION/HISTORY COLLECTION, WAITAKERE CITY LIBRARIES

(Left) **New Lynn's Elim Hall Bible Class picnic on Mt Atkinson, 1938.** (Below) **The local fire brigade demonstrates abseiling on Lopdell House.** (Lower) **Hotel Titirangi Limited share certificate, 1929.**

Included within the hotel was a small shop, tearoom and restaurant. The hotel had a direct Auckland telephone line, a facility not lost on local people who often used it to save on toll bills.

Despite its plush fittings, vacancies outnumbered paying guests in the first year of operation, and in 1934 the hotel closed its register to the travelling public. Without a liquor licence and with trade constricted by the Depression, the accommodation side of the business continued to run at a loss. Weekend business began to pick up in the late 1930s with up to seven tour buses arriving for tea in the afternoons.

The west was still 'dry' during the war years and this was to be the end of the grand Blue Mountain resort hotel. It was the lack of a liquor licence which cramped the hotel's style for most of its existence, and resulted in a prosecution of the management for supplying liquor without a licence to a private club set up in the basement billiard room by workers on a nearby dam project. The workers, finding the city pubs shut by the time they arrived after journeying in from the Waitakeres, arranged for the hotel to buy in their beer, which they sold amongst themselves, raising the ire of a local citizen who reported the management to the police.

In 1942 the building was passed to the Department of Education to use as a school for the deaf, beginning for Titirangi a 40-year association with education.

In 1960 the old Hotel Titirangi was renamed Frank Lopdell House after a former principal of Auckland Teachers' Training College, Superintendent of Education and New Zealand's first director of in-service training. The building became a residential centre for teachers from all over New Zealand on week-long courses, sharing ideas and evolving more efficient methods of teaching and learning. Thousands of teachers attended Lopdell House courses in the 22 years it was open.

In 1982 in-service training transferred to the North Shore Training College and once more the original Hotel Titirangi awaited new occupants. It turned out to be the Waitemata County Council, which saw the potential of the building as an arts centre. After amalgamation in 1989, the area became part of Waitakere City, which now administers this wonderful building.

Titirangi has long been a welcoming haven for the creative spirit. Colin McCahon lived for a time in a cottage at French Bay (Otitori), where he painted his famous Titirangi canvases. The Waitakere City Council is buying the house and the land next door to turn it into an artist-in-residence retreat in memory of New Zealand's greatest painter.

The late Brian Brake, the renowned Magnum photographer, built a spectacular glass-and-timber house above the village in a Japanese style, to house his extensive collection of photographic works and his dazzling Asian art collection. His untimely death took from the village a great local and New Zealand identity.

Len Castle, one of New Zealand pottery's founding fathers, has lived, taught and potted in Tirirangi for most of his life. The novelist and playwright Maurice Shadbolt writes in a simple cottage overlooking the harbour. On the occasion of the local school's centenary, Maurice wrote a foreword that included his homage to the area:

As a suburb Titirangi is the happiest freak in New Zealand. I'm still not very clear why it wasn't razed and bulldozed flat 30 years ago. I do know, though, that up to a decade ago it was still very much a despised place of residence – this is, in the concrete and asphalt wastelands of inner Auckland. Long before I came to live here I remember reading of "the sylvan slums of Titirangi".

If I didn't live in Titirangi, I wouldn't live in Auckland; if I didn't live in Auckland, I probably wouldn't live in New Zealand. So I can blame Titirangi, more than most things, for life as I know it. And life as I know it isn't too bad. I like living with tide and bird, sea and bush; and the bush is no museum piece in Titirangi. The kauri and treefern, the kowhai and pohutukawa, are not local colour; they texture our lives, and make vivid the seasons.

But there is rather more than that to Titirangi. It is still a village, perhaps the only one left in metropolitan Auckland, and looks like remaining one.

Kate Wells, trained in textile design, weaves magical rugs and tapestries of her own design with her partner Simon Grant in their cedar and stone studio gallery under an impressive canopy of kauri trees. You can visit and admire their work here at Breaksea Gallery.

The annual village festival at the end of summer is an opportunity for the whole community to get together. They close the street and rip into it until the early hours.

On the last Sunday of the month, the local Steiner school hosts a large craft and art festival at the Titirangi Library. The stalls are set up by 10 am and the crowds turn up soon after.

Next to Lopdell House is a sombre marble and greywacke statue of Henry Atkinson, the father of Titirangi. He was quite an operator in the Auckland of the late 19th century. In 1915, he built the grandest house in the west, Rangiwai, which still stands above Titirangi village to the east. Atkinson supervised the building of the Auckland gasworks, and was manager for 35 years. Local legend has it that he ordered the workmen to dig a trench from the Auckland Gas Company works in Freemans Bay to Rangiwai. And they did. Auckland's western suburbs can thank Henry Atkinson's private folly for their present-day gas supply. Atkinson had already settled in Titirangi with his family

PHOTOGRAPHS COURTESY DOWSE ART MUSEUM

after arriving on the *Hellvellyn* in 1863. The Atkinsons generously gave a large tract of land to Auckland City in 1900 and 13 years later they also gifted to the city the land from the top of Mt Atkinson to the beach. The locals named the highest hill after him, but it is said he would have rather had a knighthood. They erected the statue to him following his death in 1921, and this stood on Mt Atkinson until it was vandalised in 1983. It is often seen these days wearing the odd piece of clothing, and at Christmas, a Santa hat.

Behind Lopdell House in the carpark is a neo-Classic building that these days serves as a judo centre. It was built at the same time as the hotel, by Frank Peat, a retired Dargaville jeweller. The first name in the visitor book was that of opera star Dame Nellie Melba. Over many years, the jovial Frank had collected thousands of samples of gum and Maori artefacts, which he packed into 'the Treasure House' from floor to ceiling. It formed part of a tourist trail which included the nearby Toby Jug, a quaint tearooms built by Alec Bishop and run by two 'maiden ladies' down on South Titirangi Road. After many owners and changes it is now one of the best wine bars in the west. With its mock Tudor interior and roaring fires, Toby's has found a new life and popularity with locals and visitors. The Treasure House closed during the bleak days of the Depression, its vast collection broken up among New Zealand museums and antique shops.

A short distance from Lopdell House and you are on the Huia Road, at last leaving the city behind and starting to sense the history of the area. There is much of it to see and explore. At the bottom of the Huia Road, standing apart from the new roadway, is a single-lane arched bridge which has been lovingly restored by the local community board, assisted by funding from Astley Tanneries, New Lynn. This beautiful historic bridge carried early settler traffic beyond Titirangi to Roseneath and Huia. Roseneath was the original farm name for Laingholm. Today it is a quiet suburb. The bridge still has an asphalt surface as it served its purpose well into the 1950s. Today it sits silently, spanning a quiet stream as a tribute to the Titirangi settlers of the 19th century.

Ten kilometres along the Huia Road you'll pass the Lower Nihotupu Dam with its massive curved free-form spillway, whose cascading curtains of water are particularly attractive. An observation area gives you a dizzying look into the spectacular moat-like canyon that carries the run-off into the Big Muddy Creek and then into the Manukau.

The Lower Nihotupu Dam, below the Arataki Visitor Centre, lies in what was the valley of the Nihotupu Stream. This was a food gathering area and the lower valley was cultivated. There was a large settlement with numerous kumara storage pits on a small ridge above the eastern side of the dam. This area was associated with a village on the western side of Parau inlet, known as Nihotupu. Parau itself is a mispronunciation of the Kawerau name for the inlet directly below the dam. The correct name is Paruroa, meaning extensive mudflats.

The Big Muddy Peninsula, much of it owned by the Manchester Unity Lodge, was saved from developers and will now be one of Waitakere's newest recreation parks, thanks to the foresight of the Royal Forest and Bird Protection Society, the Waitakere Ranges Protection Society, the Forest Heritage Fund, and the Auckland Regional Council in partnership with the Waitakere City Council. All combined their resources to buy the 140-hectare bush park on the peninsula and develop a series of walkways through the large puriri forest which covers its western side.

(Top) **Past staff and students of Titirangi Primary celebrate the school's 125th reunion, November 1997.**
(Above) **Prolific New Zealand author and Titirangi identity Maurice Shadbolt.**
(Opposite) **From his Titirangi base, Len Castle has produced some of this country's most admired ceramic works, influencing generations of New Zealand potters and craftspeople.**

The Rev. Richard Laishley, minister of the Congregational Church in One-hunga, journeyed to Huia on 19 February 1861 and recorded in his journal a first-hand report of canoe-building at the upper reaches of Little Muddy Creek at today's Landing Road:

The natives not infrequently visit Little Muddy Creek and cut their canoes in the neighbouring forest. I saw one of these fully a half of a mile from the water in an unfinished state. It was probably 40 or 50 feet in length and how it could ever be conveyed through the bush to the shore it was not easy to divine... As the tree, a large kauri, fell, it was cut off below the branches and at once shaped where it fell.

Perhaps as many as 100 natives assemble from a distance to launch the canoe when ready for sea. They bring a large supply of provisions with them, as bread, pigs, etc. When the canoe is launched they feast, while the proprietor of the canoe walks up and down, and in a speech returns thanks to his assembled friends who have aided him to convey it to the sea. The pigs are roasted whole after the S. [South] Sea fashion, in holes in the ground heated for the purpose and the women serve potatoes in little baskets on the occasion. The Maories dance on these occasions but are careful to observe their morning and evening devotions...

The settlers here are partial to the Maories and have never lost anything during their intercourse with them. They speak in the highest terms of their justice and intelligence.

...I saw along the shore some five or six kingfishers, two or three of the *Vanessa itea* butterflies, and about as many of the little moths *Nyeternesa doubledayi*, which are now become scarce... In these woods the large Pigeons and many smaller birds are found and in the more retired parts Parakeets are not uncommon... Three instances have occurred at Little Muddy Creek of the capture of the Kiwi and Mr Brimner's son not only found a young kiwi but also an egg which he said was nearly as large as that of a goose. Mr Brimner correctly described the kiwi, one of which he kept in captivity, as a night-feeding bird making in the evening a strange stir and a peculiar noise.

Symonds Bay and Bokel Bay are also on this peninsula, but they are difficult to reach. The widowed Mrs Symonds farmed here for 10 years before moving on, adrift in a nightmare of despair and sadness like her husband before her. The family name is recalled for posterity as Symonds Street in central Auckland. There is a deposit of stone somewhere around this area which supplied building material for local cottages, but today its whereabouts is a mystery. Two small bays nearby can now only be reached by boat. Swanson Bay was the site of the Woodman's Rest, built on the beach in 1853. Like all early pubs, it attracted a few loyal customers who lived in shacks close by. Duncan Bay had a small mill, but today nothing remains of either building.

You are now at Parau and Armour Bay, a small swimming beach with a grassy reserve and lots of shade. You reach it by a short, dusty, unsealed road, passing the Parau tennis courts and the community house. The courts are named after the late councillor Jo Culley. The house was the first Steiner school in the district. The Manukau Harbour is home to thousands of migratory birds. Before the

(Above) **Kate Wells at Breaksea Gallery, Titirangi.** (Opposite Top) *Lost Moa In Long Grass*, **rug designed by Kate Wells.** (Opposite Lower) *Riding On The Tiger's Back*, **rug designed by Kate Wells. Handtufted rugs made by Dilana Rugs.**

COURTESY KATE WELLS

COURTESY GEOFF MOON

construction of Auckland International Airport at Mangere, vast flocks of these birds used the area as nesting and feeding grounds. I guess that the instinct to return is still in their genes, and every summer the harbour is densely populated with flocks of wading and feeding frequent flyers. In late autumn the Antarctic skua, a carnivorous scavenger, will sweep into the Manukau, often in pairs. Fiercely predatorial, with long, powerful, hooked bills, they will terrorise the colonies of local birds for up to a month.

Next, Mill Bay opens to the harbour with its small picnic area and carpark. At low tide there are usually groups of people wading after shellfish at this spot.

The next road is Pine Avenue. It takes you to the Cornwallis Peninsula, which is a story in itself, a paradise found and lost. These days the long sandy beach, ideal for picnicking and walking, is a peaceful spot. The 1930s squatters' houses have all been removed, with only the odd concrete steps or driveway remaining. Once they lined most of the beachfront. Now it's a verdant park. On a full tide it is one of the Manukau's most beautiful beaches, clean and spacious.

The southern end has an old wharf where generations of kids have fished and dived. Built a whopping 127 metres long in 1927 and now showing its age, it is being restored to its original length. To help with the fundraising of the wharf project, the scow *Jane Gifford*, based at Waiuku on the south side of the harbour, makes regular calls to the wharf on its cruises.

Under her massive canvas sails, the *Janie*, built at Big Omaha in 1908 by David Darroch, is crewed by hearty volunteers who often dress up as pirates, giving you the cruise of a lifetime down the harbour to the Heads. At Wonga Wonga Bay she turns majestically towards the bar and then adds more sail for the run home. The scow served a lifetime on the Waitemata, bringing quarried stone from the Coromandel and finishing life a gutted hulk on the hard. She was given to the Waiuku Museum by the Subritzky Shipping Company and the ASB Trust. Beautifully restored and much loved by her crew, she gives visitors a glimpse of what sail was like on the Manukau in the 19th century.

If you are feeling lazy, drive down the second road to the wharf and you will find a small carpark in the trees by this elegant old structure. If you want to enjoy the long beach, the first road will take you to a large carpark built in the 1980s by the over-zealous Waitemata City. I'm sure you could park a thousand cars here.

At the end of the peninsula, the great Puponga Knoll rises from the Cornwallis saddle. It was near here that Waitemata City's former mayor Tim Shadbolt had his ill-fated timber cutting operation, attempting to make use of the pines. The project was dogged by enthusiastic but unrealistic expectations, and resulted in much criticism for Mayor Tim. The firewood never seemed to reach the target market. It was a worthy attempt to heat pensioners' homes in the mid-1980s. Although well-meaning, in some ways its failure echoed the City Brilliant scheme which dashed the hopes of so many of the original Cornwallis settlers a century before.

As you walk the beach, which was known as Karangahape Beach on earlier maps, you should be aware that this was the location of one of the great con tricks of colonial New Zealand. The beach and the hills behind nearly became City Brilliant, for it was here in October 1841 that the immigrant ship *Brilliant* arrived from Scotland and dropped anchor in the bay. This vessel remains almost forgotten in the annals of New Zealand history, and surprisingly it hardly gets a mention in most accounts of Auckland's past. You can see CITY BRILLIANT on old maps in the Edinburgh Library, as well as the imposing names of the streets and squares, such as Great Queen St, Brilliant Place and Portland St.

The story itself is one of romantic endeavour and utter despair. The Cornwallis scheme was started in England as a possibly genuine attempt by a group of developers to bring settlers to New Zealand. The New Zealand Manukau and Waitemata Company was the brainchild of Major John Campbell, and modelled on Edwin Gibbon Wakefield's New Zealand Company which had been set up the year before.

The company would use as the co-ordinator of the scheme and their man on the spot, an aristocratic young officer of the British Army, honourably discharged and living on Shortland Street, Captain William Cornwallis Symonds, whose title was simply 'agent'. In fact, he was much more. A few months earlier, he had bought from Mary Mitchell the title deed to the land now known as the Auckland isthmus. Mary, a widow, came by the deed from her late husband, who had negotiated with the Ngati Whatua chiefs to put their moko markings on a document that handed over all the land from Otahuhu to the Waitemata Harbour and as far west as the Waitakere Ranges and the west coast beaches. Even for those days, it was a sizeable chunk of real estate, considering that Mitchell had negotiated payment for an unspecified quantity of guns and tobacco. He had died soon after in Sydney at the age of 26.

The deal on the prospectus enticed settlers to voyage to New Zealand and to set up their new life on splendid farmland with abundant timber and fertile soil. There was no mention of the weather. On the maps which were sent to everyone who replied to the advertisements in Scottish and English newspapers, 80 parcels were claimed to have been already sold. The price was £1 an acre, at a time when land in Australia and Canada could be had for only five shillings an acre.

The prospectus was well subscribed and the company's first immigrant vessel the *Brilliant* sailed down the Clyde from the port of Greenock on Christmas Day 1840. Shortly after leaving port, she nearly went aground at Rothesay Bay at the mouth of the Clyde. Two days later, at the port of Cork, the captain, the officers and most of the crew deserted ship. Some passengers also abandoned hope for a new life in the new world. The owners were left to find a new captain (Ritchie) and crew. Difficulties continued and they put into Sierra Leone to offload the troublemakers. In the long, bizarre voyage to New Zealand, the ship made further unscheduled stops at Cape Town, Melbourne and Hobart. At Melbourne, more passengers disembarked, disillusioned and wearied by the journey. On 27 October 1841, after a hit-and-miss finish to the voyage, attempting to cross the bar and enter the Manukau Harbour with an outdated chart, they anchored out from Cornwallis Beach. Given up for lost, the settlers had taken 301 days to reach their new home.

The view of the scrub and the hostile ranges beyond, must have been extremely upsetting to the 27 immigrants. No shelter was visible, no city was being built, no welcome awaited them as they landed on the beach on that

(Above) **Professor Fiddlesticks entertains the crowds at the monthly Titirangi craft market.** (Below) **The scow *Jane Gifford* recalls the great days of sail on Manukau Harbour.** (Opposite) **Titirangi shows its true colours on market day.** (Overleaf) **Once the grandest wharf on the Manukau, this structure at Cornwallis is being restored.**

spring morning long ago. Of the model city that the settlers had invested their savings in from the linen maps in Britain, there was nothing on this bleak landscape. In the harsh winter of 1842, they must have thought they were doomed to spend the rest of their lives here at the end of the world. However, local mission Maori generously helped them by thatching 25 whares. Captain Ritchie would never make it home, dying in Sydney on the return voyage.

Symonds is as fascinating a player as any in early New Zealand. There is only one image of him, a sketch showing him negotating with the Waikato chief Te Waro, but his power in the area was considerable. He was a nephew of Lord Cornwallis, the onetime Viceroy of India, and he knew the Manukau and its surrounding hills intimately. He needed all the negotiating skills he could muster, after the arrival of the *Brilliant* when the settlers were confronted with their situation. First the government-appointed Council of Claims rejected the sale by Mary Mitchell to Symonds. A month later, the Governor's Executive Council by decree published that the Manukau Company's settlers recently arrived from Scotland, would be treated as squatters. The Council then informed Symonds that his clients would not be permitted to cut firewood or timber from any mature trees and that any houses there would be removed at the posting of a month's notice.

Devastated, with their spirits broken, the immigrants looked for help and hope to the Auckland settlement on the Waitemata. It was not forthcoming and within a month Symonds had drowned in a boating accident off Puponga Point.

More ships carrying more conned victims arrived and the situation became worse. It was suggested that large prefabricated houses could be transported

overland from Auckland to the fledgling Cornwallis settlement. They settled for mud, stone and raupo huts and decided to try their luck as millers and timber workers. The brig *Osprey* brought the first of the kitset sawmills, to be situated at Duncan Bay. The new mill was driven by a Cornish steam engine, the ultimate in technology of the time.

Starvation was a real possibility and although the inhabitants of the fledgling settlement improved their prospects somewhat by building the Bird in the Hand, the west's first hotel, customers were scarce. Sadly, by 1843 it was all over. The Bush Mill Company collapsed, cargo on the beach was auctioned and the families who had struggled valiantly through two miserable wet winters moved from the Cornwallis headland beach to Onehunga, Mt Eden and the Waikato.

In 1844, following Hobson's untimely death from tuberculosis, the new Governor Fitzroy, in response to the ill-feeling of the aggrieved settlers, made an offer to appease them: an acre of Crown land for every four purchased in the scheme. Amazingly, the offer was regarded by the settlers' representative as not good enough. Ten years later, following repeated pleas for justice, this time to Governor Grey, the settlers were forced to accept that their case had failed. Grey refused to acknowledge their case, claiming that the land was now uninhabited.

They say the domestic animals were left behind, the houses and hotel rotting in the hostile, wet Waitakere environment. The deception and its aftermath left a bitter taste. Further tragedy followed as recrimination and suicide stalked the survivors. Today only a tall stone monument on top of the peninsula pays tribute to the settlers and their ship. It also commemorates the gifting in 1909

(Above) **The glorious sweep of Huia Bay, looking over Spragg Peninsula towards Paratutae Island and the Manukau Heads.**

COURTESY NORM LAING

COURTESY RAYMOND SALISBURY

This Monument Records the
Arrival of the Ship "BRILLIANT"
In the Manukau Harbour
On 29th October 1841 With A Band
Of Settlers for the Cornwallis
Estate which was Controlled
by the Manukau Land Company
whose Manager was
LACHLAN McLACHLAN
Father of the Donor of this Park
JOHN MITCHELL McLACHLAN
who was Born on the
Estate on 18th October 1842

(Top) The McLachlan Memorial at the head of the Cornwallis Peninsula was struck by lightning in 1934. (Above) Plaque on the monument gives silent testimony to the hardship of the early settlers.

of 1865 acres (755 hectares) as a public park by businessman John Mitchell McLachlan, who was born on the *Brilliant* following its arrival. From the monument you can glimpse Auckland's Sky Tower through a gap in the pine trees, part of the 1.5 million pine plantation established by an early Mayor of Auckland, James Gunson. They are the short, bushy *muricata* pine, never trimmed, good only for firewood or chipboard.

You approach the seaward side of the headland through the Kakamatua Estuary at the bottom of the steep hill half a kilometre on. It's a beautiful walk down the sandy beach, ideally suited for summer strolling at low tide. Wood pigeons are everywhere. The beach is wide and flat and the tide seems to stay in for only a few minutes. Matt Roe had a sawmill below on the Kakamatua Creek. It was later moved up the harbour to Onehunga in the great depression of the late 19th century.

The southern end of this beach is one of the two nudist beaches in the west, safe and hassle-free. The return path leads up a steep embankment to Cornwallis Road and makes an ideal round trip of about an hour.

There is only a walking track up to the Puponga Point summit and the memorial, but a small carpark and turnaround gives a spectacular view of the Huia Bay and the Heads beyond.

These days the Cornwallis Peninsula seems less desolate and forbidding. But it doesn't take much to imagine the winters of the 1840s and the utopian colony of Cornwallis that was never to be.

On Kakamatua Point, the next headland overlooking Kaitarakihi Bay, is the Spragg Memorial. This is another headland park, given by Wesley Spragg in memory of his son who was killed in the First World War. The monument has a simple, moving verse, *Gone West*, inscribed upon it. From this vantage point you look straight out through the Heads to the Tasman Sea over the distant breakers of the bar.

Before Huia is another lookout site that takes in the glory of the entire Huia Bay including Bryan and Foster Inlets below. A track to the left will take you through the bush to a small beach at Orpheus Bay where in summer no togs seem to be the order of the day.

Titirangi and Cornwallis Walks

1. Jubilee Walk

The Jubilee Walkways start from Pine Avenue by the ranger's house and notice-board. The right-hand track is a pleasant, easy walk through manuka and ferns, over a boardwalk to the carpark and the beach. The left-hand track will take you over the headland of Mill Bay. Both these walks can be linked as a loop and it will take you 30 minutes to return to your car.

2. Monument Track

Park your car at the lookout at the extreme end of Cornwallis Road. The track to the summit is clay and can be slippery in winter. The monument, erected by the Auckland City Council in 1918, was struck by lightning in 1934. Lightning conductors were later added both to this monument and to the Spragg Memorial on the adjacent headland. In 1997, the great-granddaughter of John McLaren asked if she could have an escorted visit to the monument and I gladly agreed.

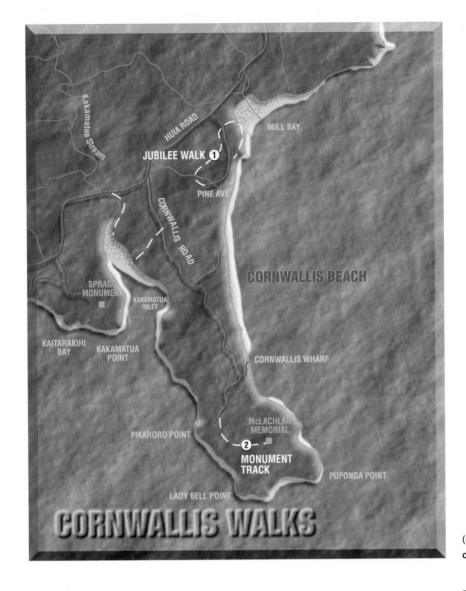

CORNWALLIS WALKS

(Below) **Spragg Peninsula monument tells of courage, honour and a lost son.**

Unfortunately her visit did not eventuate, as she died later that year in Sydney at the age of 92.

The view from the Cornwallis Monument takes in Cornwallis Beach across to Auckland City, and south over the Awhitu Peninsula. Don't be tempted to reach the beaches from this headland, unless you are sure-footed on the steep tracks used by people intent on fishing.

3. Big Muddy Peninsula Bush Track

You will see the concrete strip leading down to the bush on the left, halfway down the steep Huia Road before the Lower Nihotupu Dam. Park at the dam and within minutes you will be enveloped in splendid native bush of truly magnificent puriri, kohekohe and mature nikau. The track is rough but well defined and will lead you through most of this glorious peninsula along the south-east ridge. Large kauri snails are in abundance and protected. This beautiful bush walk is an easily managed introduction to the Waitakeres for visitors to Auckland. Take care with the fragile undergrowth, stay on the tracks and keep your dog on a lead. Round trip back up Victory Road takes about one and a half hours. (See map, page 20.)

TE KAWERAU A MAKI

Te Tangata Whenua

(Above) **The author with Te Warena Taua, Te Kawerau a Maki, following the placing of a rahui banning shellfish harvesting at Karekare Beach.**

THE history of Maori in the Waitakere Ranges has generally been badly served by European historians. In the second half of the 20th century, misinformation has done a great deal of harm and caused great pain to the descendants of this ancient people.

Like many who had heard the legends of annihilation of the coastal tribes by the marauding Ngati Whatua and Ngapuhi, I also grew up believing that these people had been totally callous. Apparently, this is not the case. The survivors of many tribal massacres were taken in by other iwi, shown kindness and given sanctuary and their descendants are now returning to their ancestral homes, where they are recognised and honoured by local authorities.

On the coast there has been a great deal of suffering, enough to last many lifetimes. The Maori belief in the mana of the land and in their self-worth has taken a battering. Many believe they have been betrayed and deprived of their ancestral homes, by both warfare and colonial European acquisition. To a great degree, this is the reality of the situation. In the 20th century, published work on Waitakere Maori has at times borne little resemblance to the truth of the matter. This lack of understanding has been difficult for Maori.

More recently, historians with a better appreciation of the cultural context have, with Maori assurances, pursued the truth, interviewing descendants who have illuminated both legend and fact. All of this is long overdue and it is from these sources that I can see a positive, new beginning for Maori and their future on the coast of Waitakere.

For the first faithful modern recording of the people of the ranges, much credit must go to Graeme Murdoch, the historian for the Auckland Regional Council. Graeme's love of the Maori people of the ranges, his patience and his listening skills, plus his tireless research, have given us a very full picture of the life and times of this iwi. I draw much on his vast knowledge to continue my story.

Te Kawerau a Maki are the holders of the term 'mana whenua' over the Waitakere coastline, the traditional inheritors of the mana and guardianship that dates back to when the legendary Maui first pulled the great fish Ika Roa a Maui, the North Island, from the depths of the Tasman. They have placed the names on the maps and their living legends and traditions are part of the coast and the forests. They have also given names and meaning to the rocks and islands, the surf and the streams, rivers, and the sacred tapu of sites forever in their guardianship.

The tribal name Te Kawerau a Maki has its origin in a migration and conquest that took place in the early 1600s. Maki was a member of the Ngati Awa iwi from Taranaki who had settled at Kawhia. He and a large group of followers migrated northward through the Waikato seeking a new home. They initially settled near Waiuku, then moved north to live near Rarotonga (Mt Smart).

Ultimately, Maki and his people conquered the Tamaki isthmus and land as far north as the Kaipara Harbour, where they settled at Mimihanui near Te Awaroa (Helensville). Maki later fought several battles in the Waitakere Ranges and some of his people settled in the area, intermarrying with the earlier Ngaoho people, giving the descendants of Maki ancient links with the land.

The traditional boundaries of these descendants of Maki stretched from southern Kaipara across the island to Mahurangi and the Hauraki Gulf. Throughout the 18th century, through conquests and intermarriage, their identity merged with other tribal groups and only those at Waitakere and Mahurangi retained the name Te Kawerau. Over time, their tribal domain was diminished around the Auckland isthmus after successive conquests, but their mana was never lost.

When the Wesleyan missionary and surveyor Hansaw Turton, a faithful recorder of Maori land transactions, was travelling through the ranges in 1883, he wrote this remarkable encounter in his journal. My research leads me to believe the events took place in the Bethells Valley area.

When I was travelling over the land of the Kawerau, in company with thirteen chiefs of the Waikato and three of Kawerau, we came to a wahi tapu where the bones of the Kawerau ancestors have been deposited for many generations. By permission of the Kawerau chief, I went alone into the cave, in the midst of which there was built a small house of the swamp reed ornamented with flax of variegated colours, in which were the bones of arikis of the tribe. At the doorway of the house, which measured altogether not more than about five feet by three feet, were the bones of a child, and near them a small canoe; the bones were no doubt that of an ariki child, and the canoe, his plaything, have been taken with him to his long rest. This house contained mats of different degrees of preservation, which I did not touch, and near to a large skull was an ancient Maori shark-hook.

On my return to our camp, I requested to be allowed to take the canoe and fishing hook, which the ariki of the Kawerau permitted; the only condition imposed on me being that in our future progress during the journey, I should be the last man in the line of march, and should carry the two curiosities

(Above) **The author at the gathering of elders of Te Kawerau a Maki celebrating their return to their ancient tribal grounds on the coast.**

myself. This was insisted on, lest the gods of the Kawerau should kill the Waikato chiefs if they followed after me with these things. Again, in the same journey, we caught an uncommonly large eel, measuring six feet nine inches long; and as we were strangers on the Kawerau territory, I waited until the eel was cooked, to see if my friends, the Waikato chiefs, would render the tribute of mana of the land to the Kawerau chief. This, in time was done by them. It is an invariable custom amongst the hapus of the tribes when they are on an eel fishing excursion, to give any eel of uncommon size to the principal owner of the land, and the heads of all the eels eaten while the party is out are laid before the owners of the land on which the eels are caught; this is their mana of the land, and in this instance, when the eel was cooked, the head was first taken off and laid before the Kawerau chief by one of the Waikato chiefs.

In 1836 Kawerau a Maki returned to the Waitakere Ranges under the protection of the Tainui 'Ariki' Te Wherowhero, who had taken up residence at Awhitu near the South Head of the Manukau Harbour. Initially the Kawerau people, who still feared the musket-wielding Nga Puhi, made their home in a bay opposite Awhitu. Their kainga here was named 'Te Kakamatua' in commemoration of both their old home Te Kaka (Te Matua) at Karekare and of the tragedy that had befallen them there. It was a symbolic statement confirming that in spite of the adversities they had faced, Te Kawerau a Maki had once again returned to their ancestral land. In 1837, under the leadership of Te Ngerengere, Te Kawerau moved north to Te Henga (Bethells Beach), their traditional heartland, where they built a musket pa, 'Parawai', beside the lower Waitakere River.

Today, Te Kawerau a Maki are numbered close to 500 and growing with each generation. They are a special people, recognised both by the Auckland Regional Council and the Waitakere City Council as being guardians of the area's mauri (the spiritual essence of the place). For these people hold guardianship over the most sacred tapu areas and although their grieving has lessened with the years, their traditional and emotional links with the coast are recognised at last.

Te Kawerau a Maki's historical link with the land is reflected not only in the placenames, traditions, whakapapa, waiata and tikanga of the area, but in the carved pou that stands guard at the front of the Arataki Visitor Centre and the carvings that adorn the building's interior.

The aim of this account is not an exhaustive history of Te Kawerau a Maki and their traditions, but to honour the tangata whenua of Waitakere and offer a glimpse into this rich and often forgotten layer of our history.

Let me conclude with a waiata belonging to the Kawerau people, lamenting their loss at Karekare, from Graeme Murdoch's history published in the West Auckland Historical Society's journal, *The West Remembers, Vol. II.*

(Above) **White flags carried by children of Karekare signify the community's endorsement of the shellfish ban.**

Aue, aue,

Kei nga wai Karekare

taku huia kua riro, e.

Haere ra a Mana, koutou ko o tupuna.

Waiho ake au ki tihi o Hinerangi,

Kia kite au I nga tai whakatu a Kupe.

Kei Te Kakawhakaara te ipu a Pare, te toki a Nuku.

Aku kuru pounamu, taku ipo kahurangi,

Kua ngaro ki te po e, i

Alas, alas,

my beloved chieftain has gone on

beyond the waters of Waikarekare.

Go on Mana[1], along with your ancestors.

Leave me here, I will remain on the summit of Hinerangi.[2]

So that I may look out to the upraised seas of Kupe.[3]

There at Kakawhakaara[4] rests the sacred calabash of Pare,[5]

and the axe of Nuku.[6]

My treasured greenstone pendants, my beloved jewel,[7]

have been lost to the night.

[1] Mana here refers to the Kawerau ancestor Manaairangi after whom the main village at Karekare was named.

[2] The 'summit of Hinerangi' is the pa 'Te Ahua o Hinerangi' north of Karekare where Hinerangi sat consumed with grief after the death of her husband.

[3] The 'upraised seas of Kupe' are the waters of the Tasman Sea, raised up by the famous ancestor Kupe to throw off a group in pursuit of him.

[4] 'Te Kakawhakaara' – 'the kaka parrot that stands sentinel' is the pa at Karekare often referred to today as 'The Watchman'.

[5] Pare being Parekura the Kawerau ancestress, with her sacred calabash containing fragrant oils for adorning the body, and for ceremonial use.

[6] Nuku being Panuku the husband of Parekura. The sacred ceremonial toko poutangata of Panuku is a symbol of chieftainship.

[7] Here reference to 'my treasured greenstone pendants' and a 'beloved jewel' is to Manaairangi and the other chiefly ancestors who have passed on.

TE HUIA

Misty curtains of a distant time

WEEKLY NEWS/COURTESY NORM LAING

(Above) **Tom Higham and Les Laing, local expert axe and sawmen, cutting 40 ft kauri planks, 1920, Clay Creek, Big Huia.** (Opposite) **Bush poet Basil Fletcher with museum secretary and founder Norman Laing (standing) at the Huia Settlers Museum, open Sunday afternoons.**

IT CAN look like the coast of Ireland or a bay in the Outer Hebrides after rain. Te Huia rolls off the tongue; the words evoke the lushness of the damp bush, the songbirds, the tranquil waters of the still bay. I don't think there is a coastal harbour in the North Island to rival its dramatic beauty, nestled below peaks of dense bush and andesite cliffs, peaceful yet mysterious.

Huia always seems to have a fine mist drifting over the crests, defining more than concealing the rugged terrain, accentuating the folds of the dark green mountain landscape. It has a grandeur unspoiled and uncompromised by development. It was in these valleys that the last kiwi call heard in the ranges was recorded in the 1960s.

In the long, wet winters of the Waitakere Ranges, numerous falls cascade from the bluffs into rockpools, flowing into superb swimming holes before reaching the tranquil Huia Bay. For more than a hundred years, Huia has been a quiet haven for settlers and sea travellers after crossing the treacherous Manukau bar, two kilometres to the south-west. How the place has remained so unspoiled is amazing. Huia is as it was a century ago. Its residents also seem to be untouched by today's technology and frantic pace.

The old kauri cottages and farm homesteads still nestle on the harbourside knolls. The family names on the letterboxes are those of the heyday of sail: Fletcher, Turner, Laing and Barr.

Around the store most days you will find interesting locals with a lifetime of memories – people like Dorothy, now past her 90th birthday, and Phil Sharpe, who used to run the Whatipu store and guest-house, sprightly in his mid-80s. Basil Fletcher, also in his mid-80s, is the local resident poet, and one of the last survivors of the kauri milling days in the ranges. A lifelong bachelor, he is still writing away in a little cottage on a headland above the beach. A puff of smoke from the chimney drifts across the bay in winter and summer.

A big item on the local talk agenda has long been a call to reintroduce the original name of the area, Te Huia, to the maps. Over the years the name has been abbreviated to just plain Huia. On my last visit to the store we all agreed while standing in the spring sunshine, it would be right to call the place Te Huia, no question about it.

But the sad fact is, a few days later at the ratepayers' annual general meeting, the few who turned up voted against the original, romantic name. Sometimes democracy works in strange ways. The people had spoken and the word was that just plain Huia was OK. So be it.

Don't miss the Huia Settlers Museum, one of the most interesting local

COURTESY TIM CHAMBERLAIN

(Top) The tragic wreck of the *Orpheus* depicted in the majestic canvas by Richard Boydges Beechey. (Above) Tombstone in St Peters churchyard, Onehunga, records the passing of one of the 189 victims of the *Orpheus* disaster.

museums in the country. It was the dream of Norm Laing and Jim Nicoll, ably supported by the community, and opened in 1984 after 20 years of planning. The museum's best exhibits are relics from the ill-fated HMS *Orpheus*.

Norm Laing and his team have had treated teak timber sections of the hull as well as a massive anchor dredged from the bottom by the trawlers *Jay Angelo* and *Jay Maree* fishing off the Muriwai coastline. This anchor weighs 18 cwt and is more than three metres long. It was cast at the Royal Naval Dockyard, Plymouth, in 1860 and once hung from a British naval vessel, but no one seems to know which one. It fits the type and size, but cannot be authenticated to the *Orpheus*. The museum's maritime experts say it could well have been carried as a replacement; it certainly fits the vintage. It towers above the other exhibits in the *Orpheus* gallery, which has been added to the museum.

Over the past few years, Norm and I have spent a great deal of time tracking down a painting of the *Orpheus* trapped on the bar in its final hours on 7 February 1863, captured in classic shipwreck style by one of Victorian England's finest seascape painters, Richard Boydges Beechey, R.A. The painting was commissioned by a local squire, Mr Thomas Stillwell Esq, a mere seven months after the wreck. As his informant, Beechey used the ship's carpenter John Beer, who described in detail to the painter the watery death and destruction, floating spars, bodies and survivors. The dramatic painting shows the doomed vessel rearing in the surf as the western sky turns to crimson and the day fades.

I first became aware of this painting's existence while working on his book with the late Thayer Fairburn, an old identity of Titirangi, and brother of the poet Rex. Thayer had spent a lifetime researching this wreck, and indeed when

(Left) **Many strange craft appear on the Manukau during the annual raft race.** (Below) **Cannonball and holder from the** *Orpheus.* **(Lower) Pulley washed ashore from the wreck of the** *Orpheus.*

I met him late in his life, he told me he had a 2000-page manuscript on the subject. Amongst the research items, I found a transparency of this painting, and enlisting the help of Norm Laing, I set out to track down the original. I discovered it hanging on the staircase of a Tudor mansion in England, the home of the Sprake family in Norfolk, on the outskirts of the village of Bungay.

When I visited England, I called on the family and asked if they would consider selling the painting to New Zealand. Initially the response was not positive. It turned out that it was a companion piece to another large seascape which had no interest to New Zealanders. My friendship with the Sprakes grew, and after several months I was delighted to learn that they had decided to negotiate a sale with the New Zealand National Maritime Museum in Auckland. It is on permanent display adjacent to the splendid scale model of HMS *Orpheus*, crafted by Thayer Fairburn in 1927.

The quest is now on to obtain the communion chalice and plate of the *Orpheus*, which were washed ashore following the wreck and ended up in a private collection.

For 80 years, after the beginning of kauri felling and milling around 1860, Huia was serviced from the sea, with sailing vessels of all sizes predominant for half that time. Besides the bigger ships, which carried bulk and sawn timber to destinations outside the harbour, there were cutters and scows making deliveries to Onehunga and the growing farming settlements on both sides of the Manukau Harbour. Old photographs show Huia Bay brimming with logs cut from the kauri forests behind Huia, awaiting towing to Onehunga. Mill operators at Huia built their own cutters to carry timber and for general harbour trading.

John Gibbons operated the Niagara Mill at Huia in 1854 and it ran until well into the 1860s. The mill's strange name came from its giant eight-metre diameter overshot wheel. In 1865, Gibbons was awarded a bronze medal and a government grant for his service to the New Zealand milling industry.

The local families all had longboats that they would row up the harbour to the port of Onehunga and back in a day. Often built on the beach or on the back lawn, these keeled vessels played a conspicuous part in the early times of

COURTESY HISTORY COLLECTION, WAITAKERE CITY LIBRARIES

(Right) The *Weka* berthed at Huia Wharf, 1908, disembarking a picnic party from Onehunga. (Below) Pioneer Huia settlers Maud and Edward Turner, 1890.

COURTESY HISTORY COLLECTION, WAITAKERE CITY LIBRARIES

Huia. The *Seashell*, for example, owned by a number of families but built originally for the Higham family, is remembered by Basil Fletcher as "the boat that carried the body of Bill Barr, nephew of Tom Barr senior, and several shaken men from Little Huia to Onehunga following a shooting fatality. Bill, who had been staying with his uncle, had taken the gun up the hill at the back of the house to shoot pigeons. Tom Barr, doing something in the vicinity, heard a shot and called out, 'Did you get him Bill?' but got no reply. It was in going to investigate that the tragic discovery was made. When they reached Onehunga beach they were met there by the deceased's parents. Emergencies such as this had to be accepted and endured as part of their choice to live their lives in the harbour settlements."

Because Huia did not have the scope for farm development, as on the Awhitu Peninsula on the opposite shore of the harbour, there was insufficient trade between peaks of timber output to attract regular shipping. At such times, the settlers relied on the cutters that came into the bay for rafts of logs or to load firewood for their inward freight and for passage to Onehunga. The record of the sturdy cutters and the exploits of the hardy crews that manned them is deficient. Of the fleet which shared the commercial highs and lows for 40 years with the local people, only a few have left their names in the bay.

The *Betsy*, servicing Waiuku in the 1850s, was an early trader here; with her came the *Dante* and *Williamette*, the latter built by Matt Roe at Onehunga in 1864. A cutter of 28 gross tons, she was wrecked in 1876 south of Manukau Heads.

Well known for years of trading was the *Nautilus*, at first under the command of Pollok storekeeper Peter McInnes, then under his son Johnny, who in later years bought his own vessel, the *Clematis*.

Tom Fletcher's scow the *Ripple*, followed by his cutters *Florence* and *Comet*, in company with Frank Fletcher's *Mary Ann*, were also among those that left the bay laden with flitches from Gibbons' mill at Whatipu.

The upper harbour, in contrast to the fluctuating fortunes of a timber-based community, saw a steady expansion of trade as farms developed. Waiuku was fast becoming a business centre through which surrounding districts maintained

COURTESY HISTORY COLLECTION, WAITAKERE CITY LIBRARIES

(Left) **Huia School, 1928.** The entire school pose for their end of year photograph.
(Below) **Gordon Turner and his son Ken,** proud descendants of the pioneering Turner family, mill macrocarpa from their property at Huia.

their link with Onehunga. This sea lane was to be its lifeline for many years, and as early as the 1860s men of initiative were considering the economics of introducing steam-driven vessels to the run. A number of cutters were fully employed in handling the increasing volume of freight and passengers but, subject to the moods of the weather and the state of the tides, times on the route were uncertain.

The valuable service begun by the small Waiuku Shipping Company was continued by the Northern Steamship Company when it took over in 1906, replacing the *Weka* with the *Waiuku*. Built for the passenger trade with the highest standard of accommodation to be seen on the Manukau, the new vessel offered a daily service to Waiuku, leaving the cargo to two of the company's auxiliary boats, the *Elsie* and *Pono*, which also kept up the run to the lower harbour ports.

The outbreak of war in 1914 was followed by a marked drop in passenger travel and the steamship company had difficulty obtaining the grade of fuel for the *Waiuku*'s kerosene engines. Less frequent sailings were made for a time, then the vessel was withdrawn, leaving the steamers *Elsie* and *Pono* in service. Smaller craft came into competition during this period, further reducing the company's viability.

Brownlee Bros. of Onehunga ran their launch *Mikado* to Awhitu Peninsula ports and Huia, while another vessel, the famous *Te Toa*, started a round that would outlast them all.

In those days the Manukau Harbour was a hive of shipping. Up to 10 vessels a day were taking the bar, and regular services to New Plymouth left Onehunga at 10 am, calling at several Manukau ports before reaching Huia at 3 pm on the way. Ebenezer Gibbons, whose mill at Whatipu was the largest in the area, built the first locally constructed steamship, the 50-ton *Bluenose*, at Onehunga to service his mills and carry timber to Australia and Dunedin.

Both at Huia and Little Huia, wharves were constructed to ship passengers, as well as a vast amount of firewood coming out of the ranges. The wood was destined for the growing number of Auckland homes, decades before electric heating would be taken for granted.

HIGHAM FAMILY COLLECTION / HISTORY COLLECTION, WAITAKERE CITY LIBRARIES

(Right) **The Higham family on the verandah of their house near Big Huia bridge, 1910.** (Below) **Huia boatman and farmer William Higham in 1905.** (Lower) **One-armed Huia farmer-butcher Bob Gordon, photographed in 1920, supplied fresh meat to the district and to the dam construction camps.**

COURTESY HISTORY COLLECTION, WAITAKERE CITY LIBRARIES

AUCKLAND INSTITUTE & MUSEUM

In 1926 the Northern Steamship Company's daily passenger service from Onehunga to the Heads became a weekly service. Later it became popular with the surf lifesavers of the fledgling Karekare Surf Club who would catch the boat from Onehunga for a Sunday patrol and return the same way on Sunday evening. Accomplished captains such as Bill Fletcher, Bert Scopes and Bill Douglas could bring the launches *Te Toa* and *Outlaw* in on any tide and handle the flimsy craft with ease on the turbulent eddies and riptides of the Manukau.

Basil Fletcher recalls a typical arrival scene at the Huia wharf:

Men in oilskin coats climbing down among the passengers to claim their family huddled up against the chill and help them ashore with their luggage. Little children being lifted by strong hands from the heaving deck to others on the wharf, while the lantern being held aloft at the head of the gangway is more for comfort than for the light that shines from its smoky glass. Down in the cabin a man of rough appearance, after kissing his wife and peering for the first time into the face of their newly born, gently takes the little one in his arms and leads the way up the steps.

Someone was always shouting above the noise of the winch engine and the feverish activity for information on the latest timetables. Eager hands grab sacks and boxes, some hurried to the shelter of the shed and some selected by the owners for transhipping to the dinghies tied under the wharf. However dispirited the homecomers may have appeared on arrival, it is obvious that Huia's wharf deck under their feet and the presence of friendly faces has worked wonders in restoring them. There is an appetising smell of fresh baked bread in the shed where loaves are being transferred from the crate to the white flour bags held open to receive them. Nearby, a convivial chatter alternates from the happenings of town to affairs at home, with a general expression for the travellers that it's good to be back again.

The millers and timber cutters are now gone, the bay is deserted and only photographs at the museum recall the days of sail and steam and the bustle they caused in Huia Bay. Today, silt has taken away the channel that led to the wharf, although the ramp and platform remain on the western side of the bay.

It would be hard to understand the history of the Huia settlement without knowing something about the large influence of the Turner family. Maud and Edward Turner, walking down Queen Street in 1890, heard an auctioneer selling properties which had recently come onto the market because of unpaid rates. One was 200 acres (81 hectares) at Huia and they bought it on the spur of the moment, at five shillings an acre. They found paradise, planting an orchard and living in a raupo-roofed cottage within 500 metres of the beach at Little Huia. As their family grew, Maud and Edward built a substantial kauri homestead with large verandahs and spacious gardens. Edward Turner's orchard laid the foundation for the produce market empire which ultimately became one of the largest of its kind in New Zealand, Turners and Growers Ltd. Edward's nine sons all played various parts in the development of the company.

Even before the Turners settled in Huia, there were three sawmills operating in the district: the Niagara sawmill north of the Karamatura Stream in Huia Bay, another by the banks of the Huia Stream, and a third in the Kakamatua Inlet west of the Cornwallis Peninsula. On the banks of Big Huia, between the two streams, stood the first schoolhouse and a store serving the community of around 100 mill workers and their families.

Each of the sawmills was sited on a stream and the water in these was used for holding dams for the kauri logs felled in the hills behind Huia. When these huge timber dams were tripped, the logs raced down with the floodwaters to the sea. It's said you could hear the dams being tripped in Auckland, a sound like distant thunder.

Basil Fletcher remembers the logging days at Huia and the toughness of life in a felling gang. Kauri bushmen usually worked in groups of between 6 and 10, 60 hours a week, from Monday to Saturday. They were paid 'wet and dry' so the Saturday slog was often used to compensate the boss for any time lost through wet weeks in the ranges. When I asked Basil about the bushman's relationship to the great trees that he felled, he referred me to his poem, *The Whistling Rata*:

> Perhaps he mourns for beauty lost
> When crimson blossoms hung
> And songsters from the top-most boughs
> Their joyous anthems rung.
> Perhaps he mourns the fallen friends
> That fire and storm have strewn.

His other workmates were the axes he owned over the years. They were as indispensable to the New Zealand bushman, says Basil, "as a wooden leg is to an amputee."

"From the first morning on the job when the boss presented his axe to him, it was his for better or for worse, till death us do part. Whenever he went through his hours of work, his axe was within an arm's reach.

"A man's axe was exclusively his own. Only in a case of emergency would he use his mate's axe. Each man usually sharpened his own on the grinding stone, though to help a mate one sometimes 'took the rough off it', leaving the owner to effect the finish he desired. On taking possession of a new axe, some men

(Below) **Huia pioneer storekeeper and harbour boatman Alfred Hill.** (Lower) **Tom Barr, an early member of the Kauri Bushmen's Association, was the resident saw doctor at Huia.**

COURTESY NORM LAING

COURTESY NORM LAING

(Above) Between Goat Hill and Jackie Peak, Cornwallis Peninsula appears out the early morning mist, viewed from the summit of Mount Donald McLean.

liked to remove the head from the handle (not liking the manufacturer's fit) and, just as important, to file the sharp edge of the eye of the axe."

Other local families, such as the Barrs, neighbours of the Turners, have been at Little Huia for more than a century. The Bryans and the Kilgours, two old families who first lived alongside the mill wharf, later moved to Fosters Bay, tucked away on the north-east of the big harbour and reached by a small narrow road before it drops down to the Huia store at the bottom of the hill.

This old store has one of the great kauri counters in the country. Milled locally, it's been shortened a bit over the years to get in the modern freezer cabinets, but the building, with its wooden interior, still has a turn-of-the-century feel about it. A small antiques section often has a rare find. The present Huia store proprietors carry on a long tradition of close friendship with the community. They know everybody in the bay. After all, everyone used to come to the store for mail. The Huia Post Office was established in 1886 and was situated at the Higham's farmhouse on the reserve. The large Norfolk pine on the foreshore marks the spot.

Next to the store is the first storekeeper Alfred Hill's homestead, a grand house completed in 1908 from local pitsawn boards. It has an ornate, stately exterior, large rooms with beautiful, decorated plaster ceilings and a large verandah.

In a studio above the bay, Ruth Cole paints the coastline in strong, thick swirls of colour. She has been painting this harbour and the coastal beaches since she returned from Europe. Her oils are readily snapped up by the dealer galleries throughout New Zealand.

Across the road from the domain which flanks the bay, is a short tunnel dug in a clay bank in 1925 by Tom Higham during an attempt to produce bricks from local clay. The scheme never succeeded, so the tunnel was used to store meat and butter and was later used as a convenient smokehouse for large catches of mullet from the bay. The tree next to the cave was for many years the roosting place for native bats. Huia is one of the few places in New Zealand where they are known to breed. They could be seen hanging upside down in rows on the branches right up to the late 1940s.

On the foreshore of the bay, behind the grove of pohutukawa trees, the Auckland Regional Council Parks Department has established an excellent picnic and playing area on the 'home paddock' of the Higham farm. Before the bridge there were stepping stones which the locals had to cross at low tide. At high tide, a boat was used to cross the creek.

Toward the coast is the Hinge residence, one of the oldest houses in Huia, sited on a commanding position with a magnificent view over the bay and harbour beyond. It was built around 1890 for the manager of the Manukau Timber Company's sawmill which operated in the bay below. Today it's little altered from its original form and is in an excellent state of repair. After the closure of the mill around 1900, it passed to a Mr Kennedy who had been the mill company's carpenter. Several local families occupied the house until it was eventually purchased by the Hinge family in 1922. In 1972 they sold the property to the Auckland Regional Authority, which renovated the house and turned the old orchard into a paved courtyard ringed by accommodation blocks. Today it serves as a centre for youth groups.

COURTESY NORM LAING

(Right) **Supplies were unloaded for the lightkeeper's house at the Marine Department wharf, Destruction Gully.** (Below) **Between the 1830s and 1940s most of the kauri in the Waitakeres were extracted, then sawn into timber in the 23 mills that operated at different times.** (Opposite) **Regenerating kauri in Destruction Gully, looking west towards the original signal hills, Paratutae Island and Wing Head.**

COURTESY NORM LAING

Further on past the museum and hall is the old Huia School, opened in 1894. For more than 80 years it had a roll which fluctuated between 20 and 30, but in 1961 dwindling numbers forced its closure. It is now Huia Lodge.

The ARC maintains an excellent park reserve at Karamatura. Many tracks lead from here into the ranges, but a short loop track with some beautiful bush lookouts can be enjoyed on an easy two-hour walk. A reconstructed miller's whare is on this track. The double-storeyed Niagara Mill stood derelict for 10 years at the mouth of the Karamatura Stream before being demolished. It was believed to be haunted until some brave local lads staked it out. Instead of ghosts, they found wild goats using the top storey as a bunkhouse. I often run this loop track in winter, starting and finishing at the Huia Museum carpark.

To reach Huia Bay from Titirangi, the road twists and winds around the northern shore of the Manukau. Locals remember the road as a clay bush track. All this ended when work began on the two great Huia dams in the massive catchment area in the hills behind the bay, in the 1920s. It was the Auckland City Council which originally decided to build a large concrete dam where the two Huia streams converged. The construction of the Huia Dam was an epic undertaking for any community. Apart from the actual structure, a wharf was required, as well as a railway from the Huia settlement and a large quarry and crushing plant two kilometres past the dam site. Then a pipeline to Titirangi was built, over numerous trestles and through six tunnels.

The Huia wharf was built in 1908 by an agreement between the Turner family and the Waitemata County Council. At that time the government had responsibility for the Manukau Harbour (the Auckland Harbour Board did not take it over until 1913). To help persuade the parties to build the wharf, the government transferred 1000 acres at Whatipu and some land at Huia. Part of the deal was that the Northern Steamship Company was exempt from charges or levies for the first four years. This wharf and landing was the lifeline of the dam project and handled the loads of sand, cement, timber and equipment brought in by scows or towed up in punts from Onehunga. A large steam crane was mounted at one end of the landing and supplies were unloaded directly into the railway wagons to be taken to the dam site.

Even today, the enormous effort required for the construction is apparent. The whole face of the mountain was quarried from top to bottom, involving hundreds of labourers working in shifts. Cuttings were hacked through the ridges, embankments laboriously built by pick and shovel and two tunnels were blasted through sheer rock. Some of the bridges towered more than 12 metres high. Sleepers were cut and split on the spot from the surrounding bush. Steel rails were laid at a gauge of 1.15 metres; two bush locomotives operated round the clock carrying the materials.

Some old-timers at Huia still remember the middle campsite, set up at the junction of George's Creek, and the top camp, on the hillside just below the main dam construction site. At the top camp, during the building of the dam, there was a large self-contained community with numerous houses for married men and their families, single quarters, a cookhouse, dining room, social hall and a small school. There was even a sealed tennis court, carved out of the side of the hill. The bush socials held there are still talked about. A special train would be run up from Huia to bring the residents and visitors to join in the fun; boats would bring entertainers, jugglers, singers and small orchestras from Onehunga. For a time there was plenty of money as well as hard work.

The big metal quarry and its rail line were worked to capacity, the crusher going day and night as slowly the dam rose from its foundations deep in the bedrock of the stream to reach its full height of 36 metres. The dam was officially opened in December 1929, with the reservoir full and the surplus water cascading down the concrete steps of the overflow face. Back down the line went all the equipment used over the five years of construction; roofing iron and windows were stripped off the houses and the rest burnt. Hundreds of people and families had lived and worked in the area, but a simple caretaker's house, installed at Huia, was all that remained. It's said that all the local men and their sons worked on the project in some capacity, either directly or by providing a support service, such as the use of a bullock team, a horse and dray, or a boat.

The line between the dam and Huia remained in use until 1960, when it was ripped up and replaced with a road. It makes a great Sunday walk and is well signposted; it is a catchment area and permission should be sought from Watercare Services before venturing past the locked gates on the way to the top camp. During the 1994 drought, with the dams at their lowest level ever, the 'short tunnel' covered by the waters of the Lower Huia Dam for 70 years emerged out of the lake, as did the remains of wharves, decks and platforms, reminders of the time when Huia echoed to the sounds of construction.

What was for so many decades a long, tiring journey by sea is now a short drive from the city. There is talk of a new section of road to cut off the Marama Stream ford at Little Huia, but it has not yet come to anything. If you discover something as idyllic as Huia you want to leave it as it is.

Nature has a lot to say at Huia. The misty curtains drift over the peaks, the bay shimmers and smoke rises from the cottages. Everyone seems content and at peace with the place and themselves. At the weekends, Norm Laing comes down and opens the museum for visitors. Basil Fletcher, at his kitchen table, writes another epic poem of days gone by. Chickens leisurely cross the road by the Hinge farm. Nothing moves very fast, including time.

To visit Huia is to take a trip back into the past, to the New Zealand which used to be and which some of us wish still was.

Huia Walks

1. Huia Dam Road and Big Kauri Track

Drive to the face of the Lower Huia Reservoir. The road is sealed to the top of the dam. Park and walk westward. As this is a water catchment, please observe the No Dogs rule. The road goes through a locked gate along the edge of the reservoir. After about 3 kilometres a small sign indicates a kauri – follow the track for five minutes until you see rearing above you this colossus of the Waitakeres. In fact there are two, as there is a smaller tree about 10 metres along the ridge.

If you wish to continue your journey, follow the road through the tunnel leading to the top dam. Watercare, which operates these dams, asks you to wear a hard hat before entering the 40-metre long tunnel. Best just to see the tree and return, which will take you around one hour.

2. Twin Peaks Track

A muddy track through dense bush on the way to the Waitakere interior or the coastal walks above Karekare. This route traverses the highest point of the ranges: Te Toi o Kawharu (474m), though there are no views from here. Use a good map and don't wander from the tracks: many day trampers have been lost in this area. Time: two and a half hours to reach the Huia Ridge Track.

(Above) Huia Bay is now heavily silted. The old shipping channels are no longer navigable by boats of the size that used to ply the harbour. Jackie Peak is at top centre of the photograph. (Opposite Page From Top) Relics in Huia Settlers Museum: One end of a two-man cross-cut saw; Kauri 'dogs' were used to haul the fallen logs to the mill; Camp oven; Axes for felling large trees typically had wide heads. The broad axe (lower) was used for squaring off the log so it would not roll over.

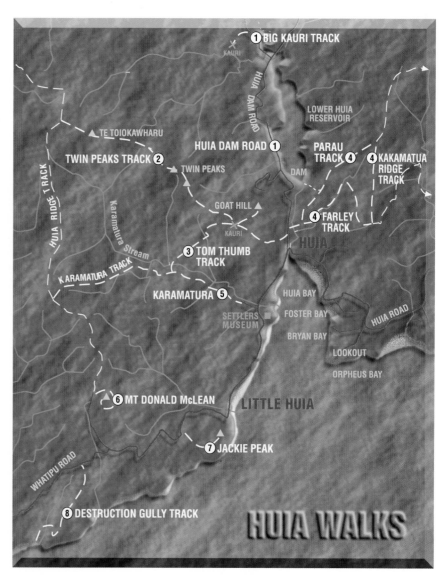

HUIA WALKS

1. BIG KAURI TRACK
KAURI
HUIA DAM ROAD
LOWER HUIA RESERVOIR
TE TOIOKAWHARU
TWIN PEAKS TRACK 2
HUIA DAM ROAD 1
PARAU TRACK 4
4 KAKAMATUA RIDGE TRACK
HUIA RIDGE TRACK
TWIN PEAKS
DAM
4 FARLEY TRACK
Karamatura Stream
GOAT HILL
KAURI
HUIA
3 TOM THUMB TRACK
KARAMATURA TRACK
KARAMATURA 5
HUIA BAY
FOSTER BAY
SETTLERS MUSEUM
HUIA ROAD
BRYAN BAY
LOOKOUT
ORPHEUS BAY
6 MT DONALD McLEAN
LITTLE HUIA
7 JACKIE PEAK
WHATIPU ROAD
8 DESTRUCTION GULLY TRACK

(Below) **Huia Bay's tranquillity belies its busy colonial past.**

3. Tom Thumb Track

The track to the stubby Tom Thumb kauri is one hour return from the Karamatura Loop Walk, accessed from the Karamatura picnic area opposite the Settlers Museum. Alternatively, park by Huia bridge, a few metres up Huia Dam Road on the left, and follow Twin Peaks Track for an hour. Well marked and easy at first, then steep but worth the climb. Opposite the tree, you'll find a track leading to the top of Goat Hill, where you can look back into the interior of the Waitakeres, down to Huia, or south to the Hunua Ranges.

4. Farley, Kakamatua Ridge & Parau Tracks Loop

From near the swing bridge below Lower Huia Dam, walk along the Farley Track to a small waterfall. Climb up to the Kakamatua Ridge Track and follow the ridge north for half an hour. Take the Parau Track to return to the bridge. A short detour leads to the top of the dam. Total time: one and a half hours.

5. Karamatura

A camping area and regional park, beautifully kept by the Auckland Regional Council Parks Department. Entrance is opposite the museum by the ranger's house. Take lunch and walk to the headwaters of the valley where you will find swimming holes fed by two waterfalls. Camping is allowed by permit.

6. Mount Donald McLean

This peak, two kilometres from Little Huia, is named after Sir Donald McLean, whose career took him from timber worker to Chief Land Purchasing Commissioner under Sir George Grey. Early on a clear morning you may see Mount Taranaki across the Tasman Sea to the south, and Rangitoto, the Sky Tower and Coromandel to the east. Below are the raging waters of the Manukau bar. This is one of the most breathtaking coastal views in the country. Drive up the mountain to the large carpark near the top, and a short, easy walking track will take you to the summit (390m). The drive can be tricky, especially on the steep and corrugated road to the carpark.

7. Jackie Peak, Te Komiki

A steep but easy walk, with a spectacular view over Little and Big Huia and a memorial seat at the top (148m) on private property. Permission is needed. Care and consideration is required by visitors. An English expatriate, John Wade, whose Maori name was Jack-a-Marama, lived below the peak on the harbour side with his Maori wife and large family. Wade ran a canoe water-taxi in the 1860s from Huia to the pilot station, and he guaranteed a landing under any conditions. Said John Gibbons: "Wade appeared to be more Maori than pakeha."

8. Destruction Gully Track

The track begins on Whatipu Road and descends to a small rocky bay. After a steep drop, you reach the site of the old lightkeeper's house. This house was situated rather precariously close to the steep cliff above the boulder-strewn beach below. Supplies of provisions and fuel for the lighthouse lamp came by boat from Onehunga and were unloaded at the small wharf which has since been washed away. The name Destruction Gully comes not from shipwrecks but from ancient hostilities on this beach.

(Below) **View down Karamatura Valley to Huia Bay, Kaitarakihi Point and Cornwallis Peninsula.**

BARNSTORMING THE COAST

High flying sons of Karekare

COURTESY DUDLEY BADHAM

(Above) **Dudley Badham at 16 with Gypsy Moth. Dudley and his brother Wally were soon soaring above their beloved west coast beaches.**

IN THE 1920s, the drone of the small plane was first heard over the roar of the surf. The Mangere aerodrome was the training ground for young aspiring pilots, and none was more enthusiastic than Dudley and Wally Badham. They were sent off for week-long live-in instruction and returned to Karekare, both with their pilot's licence. And that was just the start of it.

Whenever they had a spare moment, they would race back to Mangere and borrow their favourite plane, ZK-AAL, No. 866. Taking turns, they would climb over the Manukau, bank towards the Manukau Heads, and with their altimeter showing 3000 feet, would start to lose altitude for a low run over the roof of the Whatipu guest-house. Then, gaining height to clear the Pararaha, Wally would make a tight turn and buzz the Karekare guest-house. If the tide was out, they would land on the beach, taxiing into the wind before gently bringing the craft to a halt in the soft sand.

Karekare and Muriwai made great landing strips, and they often planned for a weekend excursion to these deserted beaches. It was not unusual for 20 visitors from the guest-houses to be given a joyride over the surf and the headlands. To give them the thrill of their lifetime, they would get a larger plane, an Avro 504 K, a splendid three-seater, often captained by two famous First World War pilots, Captain Brake and Captain Hewett, instructors from Mangere. Stunting was also a big plus for the passengers, looping the loop and impressing the ladies with their bravado.

The first airmail to be delivered on the west coast was on the morning of 30 May 1932, when Hewitt and Badham dropped a bundle of mail and newspapers onto the lawn of Winchelsea House.

Wally remembers his first two passengers were his grandmother, aged 76, and her boyfriend Rob Shaw, 84. They'd seen a lot of changes in their lives, but the thrill of flying over the west coast in the new aeroplane must have topped them all.

Still unable to obtain a licence to drive a car, at 17 Wally Badham was now the resident pilot and local hero of the untamed coast. In his diary in the spring of 1932, he recounts vividly a flight along the coastline:

I now started to lose altitude for a low run over the roof of the guest-house and my cousins at Whatipu. They got a surprise and came running out waving tea-towels as I circled round again before heading along the beach past Pararaha. I now spotted a horseman between Windy Point and Pararaha, and kept over the breakers so as not to frighten the horse. As I looked down I could see it was my Uncle Wally on a white horse. I then looked down on the tunnel at Pararaha and thought of the many times I had gone through it on foot and horseback over the years and now at 17 I am flying past it. Then came Mt Zion at 900 feet and I was just 100 feet above it.

When I was opposite and with Paratohi under my port wing, I did a right turn to go over the Black Rocks and then left to pass over the house and the Flax Gully. Then between the Watchman and Fishing Rocks before coming round in another circuit. By now they were all out waving tea-towels and ZK-AAL in red and cream checks with silver wings must have looked quite a sight in the morning sun. With a waggle of my wings I then went back down the coast to Whatipu and passed over Wally Farley again, still making his way along the beach. At Whatipu I roared over the house again and then circled round to climb up to 3000 feet for the trip back up the Manukau Harbour to Mangere.

(Above) **Flying goggles and leather helmet were essential equipment and part of the romance of the barnstorming Badhams.**

Above the Tasman swells these tiny aeroplanes were used to spot sharks and toss lifebuoys to those in distress. As the golden age of flight passed, the Badham boys lost interest. Today the Whatipu sands are directly below the flightpath of widebodied jets carrying over 400 people. As you climb through the clouds out of Auckland International Airport at Mangere, you can glimpse the landmarks so lovingly described in Wally Badham's diary.

THE WHATIPU WILDERNESS

Bleak, black and beautiful

(Above and Opposite) **The Whatipu coastline offers endless possibilities for reflection, alone or with company.**

AT THE entrance to the Manukau Harbour is a remote and remarkable landscape where time, legend and history are interwoven. It's here that the overwhelming sense of place staggers the senses. Its sheer grandeur is unsurpassed on the west coast, yet few visitors dare the journey on the rough, unsealed, cliff-hugging road over Mt Donald McLean to savour its splendour. I always think it is the beach for winter, when the bar gives Whatipu its dramatic seascape and the sand swirls and spume skudders around your legs.

The first recording of Europeans at Whatipu was in 1821, when a group of missionaries, led by Samuel Marsden of the Christian Missionary Society, walked the coastline, biding their time while waiting for Marsden's schooner the *Active* to arrive in New Zealand. Having a few days, they decided to explore the coastline of the Waitakere Ranges, coming over to the Manukau in the hope they would catch up with their ship, should it sail into the harbour. It didn't, but we are left with a record of the first known European contact with the west coast landscape, from the Rev. John Butler's journal. From his writings, we get a feel for the local people and the warm hospitality afforded to these pale, overdressed strangers:

...as soon as matters could be arranged and natives procured to carry our necessaries, we departed by land for Manukow... We arrived about five o'clock pm, and were, as usual, received with every mark of gratitude and respect. No Europeans had ever been here before, and everyone, young and old, was eager, if possible, to touch the hem of our garments. The natives are numerous, the land good, the timber fine, and the little naked children ran about like rabbits in a warren. This would be a good place for a missionary settlement...

We remained in this place one day and two nights, during which time we engaged in a great deal of interesting conversation with the natives.

The River of Manukow runs into the ocean on the west side of New Zealand, and is separated only by a narrow neck of land about half a mile wide, from Mogoia [Tamaki] River on the east side, and also from the Wye-te-Matta on the north-east side, by the same extent of land.

During our stay, we went down to the heads of the harbour of Manukow, but, as the distance is about twenty miles from the town [Onehunga], we had not sufficient time to say much about the entrance. It appears to be a bar harbour; we sounded inside, and found from four to ten fathoms.

The name of the head chief of this place is Kowow. He appears to be a man of a bold disposition and a good countenance. He furnished us with pork and potatoes, and did everything he could to serve us during our short visit; and

offered his services, and as many of his people as we needed to conduct us to the Kepero [Kaipara]; this offer we gladly accepted.

We left Manukow on Saturday for Kepero; our party consisted of about twenty persons. As we passed along, we came to a large volcano mountain down which the path led. When we had ascended the summit, we sat down a little while both to rest and take a survey of the country.

On this elevated spot we had the opportunity of observing the entrance of Manukow Harbour to the western, and the River Thames on the eastern side of New Zealand.

Later we will rejoin these travellers as they journey up the coast to the Kaipara Heads.

To reach Whatipu, take the Huia Road past the small Huia settlement, over the hill to Little Huia along the road which skirts the harbour. After the ford at Little Huia, the road rises steeply from the valley floor towards the domed face of Mt Donald McLean, the grand beginning of the Waitakere Ranges.

At the top of the hill, you glimpse Whatipu laid out before you, with its view of the Manukau bar stretching 10 kilometres out into the Tasman, still one of the most treacherous of all the west coast bars. Even on calm days the sea around and over the bar is never still.

(Above) **Timeless transition of sea, sand and sky looking north across the Whatipu wilderness.**

Here is New Zealand's Atlantis. The landscape, destroyed in the great storms of 1836, extended many kilometres out into the ocean and was covered in lush bush, manuka and flax; there were small fishing villages dating back to Kupe's time, around 925 AD. Called Paorae (forever rich in seafood), the whole area is now engulfed in boiling surf, the land long vanished under the incessant rollers. The surviving sentinel is the Ninepin Rock, Toko tapu a Kupe (the sacred rock of Kupe), which stands solitary in the centre of Whatipu beach.

On his epic first voyage of discovery, Kupe, Polynesia's legendary navigator, is said to have made a sacrifice on this rock for the continuance of the journey. Just what the sacrifice was, remains unknown, but it seems he was travelling with family members, crew and slaves and it would not be unrealistic to assume that it was a human sacrifice, common in ancient Polynesian societies.

It was also near this rock on 7 February 1863 that a longboat of the HMS *Orpheus* brought ashore some of the ship's records before returning to the doomed vessel, hopelessly stuck and without any chance of survival on the extreme tip of the middle bank, three kilometres from the present steep beach.

Around this tragedy local legends have grown – it's long been held that the longboat carried some bullion, gold to pay the soldiers in the ongoing Waikato land wars. A box of bullion, or 'specie' as it would have been entered in the ship's records, is still reputed to be buried in the sand near the rock.

During this tragic afternoon the 1700-ton, 21-gun steam corvette, powered by a combination of sail and steam and launched in June 1860, became a total wreck as huge swells swept its deck, toppling the masts and drowning 189 of its officers and crew. During the crossing of the Tasman, it was agreed by the

officers and Commodore William Burnett, that they would save a few days' journey by entering the Manukau Harbour and crossing overland to Auckland to pay their respects to Governor Sir George Grey. This decision was to cost them their lives.

The Kawerau people tell me that this disaster was foretold as one of their most sacred trees had been axed by settlers on Puketutu Island. This ancient tree was used by women for centuries as a spiritual influence to assist pregnancy, and therefore had huge significance in Maori life. This legend and the tragedy that followed, is still discussed today.

The wreck of the *Orpheus* remains New Zealand's worst sea disaster. The following morning, the stump of the mast seen above the surf and the coastline strewn with bodies and wreckage would record the ship's passing.

Charted a while ago by an Air Force Orion, the iron-clad hull of the *Orpheus* lies close inside the Heads, near Destruction Gully. It has moved continuously eastward in the currents. As it rolled in its death throes, the guns would have been toppled from their mounts into the surf, where they rest on the bottom. Although divers still report sightings of guns off the bar, no heavy weapons have been recovered. The 9.1-metre main mast floated towards the Kaipara, where it was washed ashore following a storm in 1950. The Baltic pine topmast was recovered in 1992 in the South Kaipara Head lagoon by farmer Malcolm Waller, who moved it to the Huia Settlers Museum, where after careful preservation, it is displayed in the courtyard under a canopy.

So what's on the bottom? For starters, there are two six-ton bronze propellers, each 16 feet in diameter; four anchors 12 feet long weighing in at two tons

THIS PLAQUE MARKS THE GRAVES
OF THREE UNKNOWN SAILORS OF
THE QUEEN WHO LOST THEIR LIVES
WHEN H.M.S. ORPHEUS FOUNDERED
AT THE MANUKAU ENTRANCE ON
FEBRUARY 7TH 1863
UNKNOWN FRIENDS WHO RECOVERED
THE BODIES FROM THE SEA BELOW
LAID THEM TO REST IN THIS QUIET PLACE

(Top) **The turbulent Manukau bar has claimed numerous ships and lives. The site of the wreck of the ill-fated *Orpheus* is in the lower centre area of the photograph.** (Above) **Headstone at Kakamatua Inlet to three drowned seamen from the *Orpheus*.**

apiece; 16 muzzle-loading cast-iron broadside guns at three tons each; four 40-pound Armstrong guns, eight feet long and each weighing 28 hundredweight; and one 110-pound seven-inch Armstrong breech loader weighing four tons. It's believed that the sand will have packed the hull, holding much intact, including the four boilers. The *Orpheus* bunkers held 300 tons of coal, and little was used in crossing the Tasman. Divers finding coal strewn across the sea-bed will know they are onto the wreck.

Many vessels would founder over the years on the Manukau bar, casting wreckage and bodies along the strip of coastline known as Taranaki Bay. Relics of these wrecks still surface today, so look carefully for teak beams, copper bolts, nails and rigging pulleys. Many found on this stretch of beach are on display in the Huia Settlers Museum.

Bodies were buried where they were found at Karekare in Union Bay. At Piha a full-length skeleton of the assistant sailing master of the *Orpheus*, Mr W. Taylor, was found years later with his jacket and boots still attached. Children playing in the dunes noticed the boots sticking out of the sand. On this coast the drowned drift north.

The seascape at Whatipu is always dominated by the white-capped bar for as far as the eye can see from the beach. As coastal vessels move slowly down the middle channel, they appear as in a mirage to be sliding through the black ironsand dunes that border the northern side of the harbour entrance.

In the summer of 1987 I was one of three swimmers who crossed the Manukau Heads, from South Head to Destruction Gully, probably the first Pakeha crazy enough to do it. The Maori would have done it because of necessity – flight or

fight. There would be no other sensible reason for such an act. Admittedly we picked the right tide, if there is ever such a thing at the Manukau Heads. The force and the fury of the water in the middle channel was unabating, its sense of menace unforgettable. My friends Karel Witten-Hannah and Stuart Hammond and I had been planning the swim for a year or two, and with the help of our surf club boat crews we entered the water at South Head on the last few minutes of the outgoing tide. We quickly moved out towards the bar – then as if a giant undersea eggbeater were at work, the tide turned and we were swept toward the northern side. It took less than an hour. Not a recommended swim for beginners.

(Above) **Memorial plaque on Paratutae Island, placed in 1976, 113 years after the** *Orpheus* **wreck, where the flagstaff stood in 1863.**

At Whatipu, swim only on the calmest days, staying close to the beach. The bay delivers a fine surfable wave on high tides. It's a well-kept secret, but don't expect anything over two metres, and never on a low tide. Beware the coastal sweep northwards.

To greet you at the road's end is the Whatipu Lodge, on the grass bank to the right above the carpark. This establishment dates back to the 1860s. The main section was built by the Gibbons family, who also built and ran the mill in the lush valley behind the house. A new wing was added in 1910. The pit-sawn kauri boards are, of course, all local and weathering well, considering their age.

The lodge has a small shop where you can buy bait and refreshments after the dusty trip over the hill from Huia. The proprietors Neil and Mary Roberts left their respective careers – he was an engineer and she a nurse – years ago to run the lodge, which is one of the great getaway places within an hour's drive of the city. With 18 small timbered, neat rooms, it sleeps 35 people and the rates

WING OF THE MANUKAU

Harbourmaster and navigator extraordinaire

COURTESY T. B. BYRNE

(Above) **Captain Thomas Wing, harbourmaster, mariner and surveyor.** (Below) **Official drawings of various maritime signals which Edward Wing used to communicate with the** *Orpheus* **from his signal-station atop Paratutae Island.**

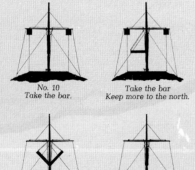

No. 10
Take the bar.

Take the bar
Keep more to the north.

No. 14
Keep the vessel more off shore

No signal.

COURTESY T. FAIRBURN

IN HIS 80th year, my father-in-law Geoff Pollard recalled how as a young man he and his family returned to Whatipu to help his grandmother, Emily Wing, visit for the last time the site of her old home, the signal-station and pilot-house of the Manukau harbourmaster on Wing's Head. The signal-station is now across on the other side. In the last century, this was the home of one of the most important seafarers in New Zealand, Thomas Wing. His nurturing influence helped shape New Zealand maritime history.

Even by today's standards, Captain Thomas Wing of the Manukau is one of New Zealand's most remarkable mariners. He was also a harbourmaster, cartographer and pilot. Born in Essex, England, he began his sea experiences from the port of Harwich. Studying hydrography, he sailed first on a convict vessel to Sydney and then later as first mate on the *Fortitude* from England to the Bay of Islands in 1832. In 1834 he became the master of the *Fanny*, making charts of the Tauranga, Kaipara and later Manukau harbours.

In 1839 he returned to England to marry Lucy. The marriage produced five children. After periods of trading around the New Zealand coast he returned to charting, including both Stewart Island and Bluff Harbour.

Before Wing made some sense of the bar and the channels, the Manukau Heads were sketchy notes on the sea charts. As a result of Wing's endeavours, the entrance gained serious consideration as a major coastal shipping channel.

Thomas was well supported by his wife Lucy Wing. She felt the 10 years that the Wing family spent at Whatipu were the happiest years of their lives, their five children enjoying the isolation and splendour of the area. The comfortable house on the signal hill was warm and welcoming. They had many well-known visitors, including Thomas Bracken, who penned *God Defend New Zealand*, and the English novelist Anthony Trollope. The famous German geologist Hochstetter, whose pen-and-ink rendering of the Manukau Heads is shown opposite, visited the Wings in 1857. All were very impressed by the warm welcome they received while at the Wing homestead.

Clearly Wing was greatly affected by the wreck of the *Orpheus* and its aftermath, with the official enquiry. He and his son Edward, who was on duty and first saw the ship moving towards the bar, were exonerated. Commodore Burnett, standing on the deck when she struck, was fingered, along with the incorrect charts, for the loss of the vessel.

Wing spent a great deal of his latter life reacting to criticism of his actions and discussing the circumstances of that fateful day in 1863. He continued both as pilot and harbourmaster for many years as well as assuming the role of patriarch of the Manukau Harbour. The shipping traffic was declining on

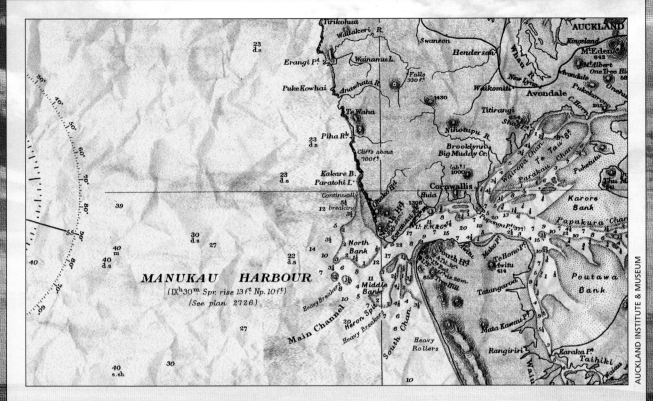

AUCKLAND INSTITUTE & MUSEUM

COURTESY T. FAIRBURN

COURTESY T. FAIRBURN

the Manukau as the 19th century came to an end. At 77 years old, Captain Wing was still frequently out in all weathers supervising maintenance at the harbour entrance. Lucy and Thomas moved to Onehunga, where he died in 1888, age 78. He was survived by Lucy who also rests in St Peters churchyard in Onehunga. A simple headstone is inscribed 'Captain Wing, late Harbour Master, Manukau'.

Wing's legacy is his amazing contribution to the exploration and extensive surveying of both the Kaipara and the Manukau harbours. His descendants include my wife Barbara and the renowned yachtsman Sir Peter Blake.

(Top) **Section of 1905 map showing detail of the treacherous entrance to Manukau Harbour. (Above Left) Eight survivors of the wreck of the *Orpheus* pose in an Auckland studio soon after the fateful day. (Above) Commodore William Farquharson Burnett, aged 48, who was held responsible for the disaster. (Below) Hochstetter's drawing of the Manukau Heads.**

(Top) **Whatipu wilderness with Whatipu Lodge in centre foreground.** (Above) **Longtime Lodge proprietors Mary and Neil Roberts.**

are very reasonable. It also comes with its own ghost, the Pink Lady, a shady apparition which appears flitting between the rooms. Many guests claim to have glimpsed her over the years. She's a bonus to a most welcome and restful weekend retreat. If you're planning to stay at Whatipu Lodge, you'll need to book, as it's popular with surfcasters and beachcombers.

Charles Blomfield painted a superb oil of the Whatipu bush mill, which is now in the collection of the Auckland City Art Gallery. You can still see the site about half a kilometre up the Whatipu Valley. This mill, owned by Nicholas Gibbons, a Nova Scotian, dates from around 1887 and the high earth wall is still intact today. At one time Gibbons also owned the Pararaha Mill, and the family name is remembered with the Gibbons Track.

Some people have been coming back to the Whatipu Lodge for 30 years. For those who prefer to rough it, there's a camping ground close by, which over the Christmas period takes around 60 people. Because the Whatipu fishing is still worthwhile, you'll find up to 20 people camped there year-round. The Whatipu Lodge held the world record of a 37 lb (16.8 kg) snapper in the 1930s. A cast of this magnificent catch is in the Auckland Museum. The good news is they're still pulling them in today, although they're nowhere near the record weight. Diving for crayfish and mussels is popular but unfortunately, drowning fatalities are all too common in the fierce underwater currents and tidal rips.

From the 1800s until 1916, the Whatipu sands area was one of the great timberyards of New Zealand. Acres of sawn timber were stacked along the beach waiting for transport up the Manukau to Onehunga, or to be taken by scow or barge to build the cities of Wellington, Christchurch and Dunedin.

COURTESY HISTORY COLLECTION, WAITAKERE CITY LIBRARIES

Behind the beach, the Waitakere Ranges were still clothed in a vast green forest. Rising sheer above the landmass were the great kauri. And kauri was king in these forests when these awesome trees held up the sky.

From the Karekare mill, snaking along the sea-cliffs, came the daily bush tram, loaded with sawn timber. Constantly battered by Tasman rollers and operational only at low tide, the bush mill's rail fed the Whatipu wharf landing site. Now only the odd sleeper and rusty spike mark the track to the wharf.

In the late 1970s, a group of well-meaning rail enthusiasts from South Auckland attempted what appeared to many historians and environmentalists to be one of the coast's most bizarre schemes: to recreate a working slice of bush mill history and rebuild the bush tram rail system from Whatipu to Karekare. Paying scant heed to local outrage, they continually battled to obtain permission and funding for their venture. The idea was to use the project as a tourist attraction, and link it with a scow, the *Tally Ho*, which they planned to build. Over the years they built many of the proposed rail junctions and sections of the trestles to carry the rail over the sea gaps. When the company collapsed, they cut up the half-built scow and scrapped the rail iron.

All that is left today of the original Whatipu railhead is the remains of the old wharf, cut from the sheer cliff in the northern bay just inside the Manukau Heads. The wharf under the great rock Paratutae was built by Nicholas Gibbons and William Foote in 1870. Nature, at its wildest in the Whatipu area, ensures that virtually nothing man-made lasts for long. The constant moving sand always blowing in the slightest breeze will inevitably cover the tracks of everything.

The potential of the black ironsand of Whatipu more than interested the

(Top) The barque *Njord* loads timber at the Paratutae wharf, 1909. (Above) The wharf has long gone from Paratutae Island, but coastal shipping still negotiates the ever-changing Manukau shipping channel.

(Right) **The author flanked by Stuart Hammond and Karel Witten-Hannah after swimming the Manukau Heads, 1987.** (Below) **Relics of the old Whatipu wharf at Paratutae Island.** (Opposite) **Desolate landscape of the Whatipu wilderness area has a stark, elemental beauty.** (Overleaf) **Surfcasters try their luck from the sandspit at Whatipu.**

minds of the early mineral entrepreneurs. A small smelter using high-grade iron ore on the Puponga Peninsula was the first step and in 1883 the New Zealand Iron and Steel Company was registered for the purpose of dredging the ironsand from Whatipu to Piha. The company leased Whatipu Beach and the coastline, employing a Mr Jones, a mining engineer from Philadelphia. The plant and furnace was built to Jones' specifications in Onehunga and within a month was operational. The end result was much praised and a set of grand gates commissioned for the mansion of brewery baron Sir John Logan Campbell set the standard. I'd like to know where the prized gates are today.

The venture ground to a halt a year later when Jones shot one of his bricklayers in the leg in a dispute outside the Onehunga Hotel. He was given 10 years' hard labour in Mt Eden and behind bars his expertise was of little use to the company. His successor died on the job and others could not work the complex foundry equipment. The directors wound up the company in 1886. In 1920 the black ironsand lured another group of investors with an innovative smelting process. The West Coast Iron Sand Smelting Company was registered and gained a licence, but never started to dredge. The last licence was granted in 1956.

Paratutae stands guarding the northern Whatipu shoreline and it once had on its topmost crown a signal mast. It was to this rock that Edward Wing ran to signal the ill-fated *Orpheus* not to take the bar. For many years ships loaded Waitakere kauri from the wharf. The cutters that serviced the timber run were capable of carrying around 12,000 super feet of sawn timber, which is about a truck-and-trailer load. Their names, romantic as they are, the *Dante*, *Rose Ann* and *Tay*, are all but forgotten. They shipped from this rock to Onehunga where overseas cargo was loaded on schooners like the *Fiery Cross*, *Atlanta*, and the brigs *Derwent* and *Syphyn*.

At high tide the rock becomes almost an island. Gone is the wharf, the wooden makeshift pen which used to hold cattle awaiting shipment and a small weather-board shed which served as a booking office and occasional post office. It's now a shower and toilet at the lodge. These days the annual Head to Head Triathlon starts from under its massive flank.

At Whatipu you can enjoy a great winter walk, with awesome views of the Manukau, beginning from the carpark by the lodge. Cross the Whatipu Stream and head straight up Wing Hill. On the top, the house of the Wing family was sited, chained to the ground to hold it against the roaring westerlies.

Near the cliff-top stood a flagpole which was cut down during the land wars by warriors from a raiding Waikato war party, who crossed the harbour during

(Top) **A lonely remnant of the lost land of Paorae. (Above) Whatipu offers excellent diving if you are prepared to risk the dangerous currents.**

the night to give the signal-station a touch of what was to come. Lucy Wing had shown kindness in the past to members of the warrior's whanau. This act of charity probably saved their lives, preventing a midnight massacre.

The old house foundations can be traced and in spring the garden surrounding the cottage blooms with wild flowers. The westernmost point is Burnett Head, named after Commodore William Farquharson Burnett, CB, commander of the Australian naval station, whose seniority in the British Navy gave him command of the corvette HMS *Orpheus* as it steamed towards destruction directly out to sea from the lookout. A bronze plaque was unveiled on Paratutae Rock in November 1976, 113 years after the wreck.

There is something very appealing about the Whatipu wilderness. You'll return to the city refreshed, with a sense of having discovered a very special place. Dress warmly and pick a day with patches of blue, with the wind roaring from the Tasman Sea across the bar. Take the dog, the kids and a kite.

Whatipu Walks

1. Pararaha Valley Track

The Pararaha Valley is accessed from behind the giant sand-dune at Pararaha Bay, halfway between Karekare and Whatipu. Some walking through water is

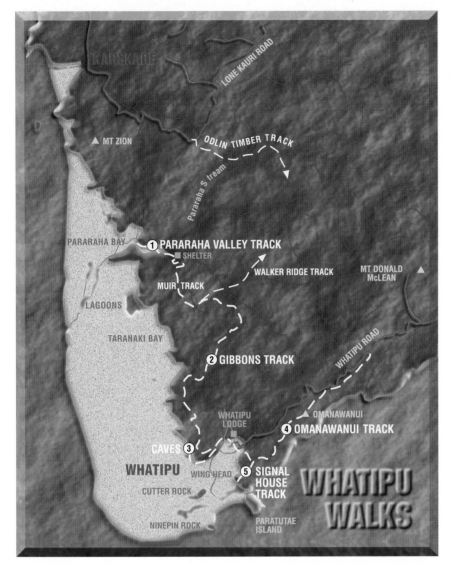

(Top) **The Whatipu wetland is a botanist's paradise.** (Above) **Violent storms lashing Auckland's west coast transformed these depressions in the sand at Whatipu into small lagoons.**

necessary, and it's possible to lose the path if you're not careful. At the junction with Muir Track there is now a campsite and shelter. For the adventurous, the Pararaha Gorge reveals a dramatic kauri log-jam of felled forest giants, rendering further damming impossible. Trampers need to negotiate this log-jam, then do some tricky scrambling around waterfalls to gain the upper levels of the gorge. The route emerges at a campsite beside the Odlin Timber Track, within an hour's walk down to the Karekare carpark at the bottom of the Lone Kauri Road. Pick a fine day for your five-hour tramp.

2. Gibbons Track

From the carpark, walk alongside the campground fenceline, cross the Amphlett Stream (named after an officer from the *Orpheus*), and up the Gibbons Track which runs along the cliff-top, following the old logging road. This excellent walk takes you inland, around the head of the Taranaki Stream, then back to the coast. From the cliff-tops on a clear morning, you may spot Mount Taranaki on the southern horizon. Below you will see the outline of the old beach railway. Allow two hours to reach the junction of Muir and Walker Ridge tracks.

3. Giant Cave

From the carpark, head right over the Whatipu Stream and through the first

(Right and Below) **Whatipu's Cutter Rock, once surrounded by Tasman surf, was popular with abseilers until the Regional Council, fearful of accidents, restricted the sport at this location.**

lagoons, keeping close to the cliffs. The first large cave (Giant Cave) is 600 metres from the carpark. From the cave, move out towards the main beach where you'll soon find the old rail embankment, partly obliterated by sand but still discernible.

Up to the late 1970s, you could find wild cattle wandering through the valleys and the swamp area. I was told that they could well have been descendants of the cargo of livestock that made it ashore from the wreck of the barque *Orwell* in March 1848. The Farley family, who moved down the coast to run the guest-house at Whatipu in the late 1920s, found a wandering dog which had been lost overboard from a scow. They named it Neptune's Gift. A local legend at the lodge, the dog lived another 15 years. Keep walking to the Pararaha Stream and Valley. Enjoy the great sand-dune and Tunnel Point to the north, once a small fortified pa site. Camping is allowed here by permit. Return via the beach.

4. Omanawanui Track

Three kilometres before Whatipu, you will spot the sign for this track. It leaves Whatipu Road and follows an undulating ridge above the Manukau Harbour entrance. The view across to South Head shows the volcanic strata. Sometimes you can see orcas in the harbour below. Take care, as it's steep. Dropping down to the Whatipu carpark will take about two hours. Climb the metal road back up to your car.

5. Signal House Track

The climb up Wing Hill will last about 30 minutes; it's not particularly difficult. Follow the ridge down to the site of Captain Wing's house above Paratutae Island. It's an easy 20-minute walk back downhill to the carpark. At the top you can also turn north-east, up through a bushline track towards the towering cliffs of Omanawanui for a superb view of the harbour below.

This is a great track for an afternoon walk. These are the peaks at the Manukau Heads that you can see from all over the Auckland isthmus. The track is in good condition and safe for children over 10. Omanawanui, 'the place of long suffering', is said to be yet another legendary lovers' leap. You can believe it.

If you wish to continue, the track will take you higher and higher through the bush following the cliff's edge, and then along the ridge-top to the road at the head of the valley.

WRECK OF THE UNION

A footnote in history

THE *Union*, a schooner out of Sydney carrying a cargo of coal, was not insured and from all accounts, was somewhat unseaworthy. Hindered by violent mid-winter gales, the ship was caught for four days off the Manukau Heads trying to take the bar. Some time around 20 July 1860, the captain attempted to run the vessel onto shore in a bay north of Karekare. It is my belief that in doing so, the *Union* clipped Paratahi Island and broke up. To me, this is one of the most fascinating shipwrecks on the untamed coast.

The finding of wreckage 10 days later was reported to Governor Grey through the Auckland marine authorities by Thomas Wing, the harbourmaster at Manukau. His son Edward had found sails and wreckage strewn along the beach. However, no bodies could be found.

The lack of any bodies surprises me. But local Maori reported no sightings of survivors or drowned seamen. The mystery is compounded by Edward Wing's log notes of a single, imperfect imprint of a boot by the main wreckage.

In his official report, Captain Wing sites the wreck in "a bay north of Karekare". Could this be Mercer Bay? It fits Wing's description as he writes of a small bay "with numerous straggling rocks abounding". It's certainly not to the south, which is the broad beach of Taranaki Bay, that even in those days would not have had rocky outcrops.

However, near the end of his life Wing wrote in his personal papers with a shaky hand that the *Union* came ashore in a small bay a little to the south of Karekare. If this then is true, the bay in which the wreckage was found would be Whakaruro Bay, which lies inside Paratahi Island. By 1880 Union Bay, north of Karekare Beach, had been named. Today it is an extension of the main beach, but in those days the surf would have come up to the cliffs, giving the impression of two separate bays.

(Above) **A single bootprint in the sand adds a further touch of mystery to this tragic sea tale.** (Below) **Signature of Captain Edward Wing, who discovered the wreckage, from his official report.** (Lower) **Excerpt from newspaper story.**

E. T. Wing.

AUCKLAND INSTITUTE & MUSEUM. FROM THE NEW ZEALANDER

AUCKLAND, AUGUST 8, 1860.

WRECK OF THE SCHOONER UNION,

Through a letter received from Mr. Pilot Wing, dated Manukau Heads July 31st, we derive the following melancholy particulars relative to the wreck of that ill-fated vessel, which he supposes to have taken place about the 22nd ultimo. From the state of her sails, he is of opinion that they must

ESTER,
he 14th

board,

WHATIPU TO KAREKARE

Highway of the spirits

COURTESY HISTORY COLLECTION, WAITAKERE CITY LIBRARIES

(Above) **One of the classic early photographs of the west coast shows the** *Sandfly* **framed by the Kawakawa tunnel. (Opposite) The tunnel is used frequently these days by trampers on their coastal journeys.**

THE WIDE black sand beach stretches in a shimmering carpet north-ward. The Tasman Sea once came to the very base of the high sea-cliffs but in the 20th century it receded almost three kilometres. In autumn, sea-mist often sweeps inland, blurring the headlands. Sand-dunes now rise from the coastal plain, trapping mini-lakes of clear rain and spring water. Grasses and swamp marsh grow in profusion; lupins, flax and native cabbage trees thrive in this damp sub-tropical climate. It can rain here almost every day for six months, as the westerlies whip onto these hills. The precipitation in the Waitakeres gives the bush a rainforest quality and a lushness and density that is found nowhere else in the Auckland region.

Legend has it that the spirits of the Maori journey the length of Aotearoa's west coast, crossing the Manukau Harbour to Whatipu and then continuing north to Cape Reinga, on their way to mystic Hawaiki to join their ancestors.

At Whatipu, to stand on this immensity of beach is to feel the body diminished, the soul enlarged. It feels like a very special place.

The sand stretching before you as far as you can see comes from Mt Taranaki. It was eroded first, then crushed by the sea and is one of three black sand coastlines in the South Pacific. The beach is littered with shells but the most common is the free-floating violet snail (Janitha) and the tiny spiral shell of the small squid (Spirula). Up close, they make the sand sparkle.

If you just want to stay around Whatipu for an afternoon stroll, take the northern track, skirting the camping ground over the footbridge, following the old mill rail track north, hugging the cliffs towards the Pararaha Valley and distant Karekare. About a kilometre on, you will find a number of small sea caves at the headland. They are a day caver's dream. Some caves extend into the rocks almost 30 metres. The great ocean cave is the pick of them all. Now high and dry, the largest sea cave on the west coast once had a laid kauri floor for mill dances.

Stories have it that during a dance in the 1920s a large wave rolled in from the sea during the midnight hour and put a damp finish to the evening. The hooks for the lamps are still there, but the wooden floor has long since been removed. To get to the cave you will need to traverse the freshwater lakes of the area.

Since Cyclone Bola in 1988, the Taranaki Bay area has become a myriad of small lakes with lush vegetation patches. Ducks and wild geese now populate the whole area. Herons and bitterns are everywhere as the Whatipu wetlands have become a rich and exotic bird sanctuary.

COURTESY HISTORY COLLECTION, WAITAKERE CITY LIBRARIES

(Right) **A steam locomotive, built in 1906 and nicknamed the *Sandfly*, crosses a trestle bridge on the beach tramway.** (Below) **This painting of the Pararaha mill in full production, 1880, is credited to Charles Blomfield but may have been executed by an amateur artist. The mill was destroyed by fire in March 1881.** (Lower) **Engineplate from the *Sandfly*.** (Opposite Top) **Battered by surf at Windy Point, and rebuilt many times, the track on this stretch of coastline eventually caused the logging company financial ruin.** (Opposite Lower) **If you look for them, you can find relics of the railway from Karekare to Whatipu.**

COURTESY J. DIAMOND

On this wild and isolated coastline you can find yourself again. Away from the stresses of urban life, in the secluded groves, cliff caves and small beaches, you can let nature heal your city wounds. As we journey up this coastline, there are many places of solitude and special significance that I believe could be used to increase awareness of the spirituality of the land and how to contemplate it.

In the past, this has been a busy human highway, from Whatipu along the sands to Karekare. After the dances in the big cave at Whatipu, there would be up to 20 horses and the odd coach, lanterns swinging in the darkness heading home along the beach. From the early days of the motor vehicle, when the Karekare Point could be traversed, cars and trucks would belt along the hard sand, the Farley's Dodge, Model T and Essex racing to drop passengers at the Whatipu wharf. If they made a mistake with the tides, as the Farleys found out in 1922 when their brand-new Dodge got stuck in the soft sand round the point, nothing would budge it. It was salvaged at the next low tide, stripped down and totally washed in kerosene. It remained a familiar sight in the area until the 1950s. Well-known beach racer Wizard Smith used to practise on this stretch of coast, achieving speeds of 75 miles per hour in his 1922 model speedster.

If you start walking north from the Whatipu carpark around Sargent Point and into Taranaki Bay, above you are the towering cliffs, 226 metres high, the result of the tearing apart of this coastline 20 million years ago when New Zealand was shattered by the collision of the Pacific and Indian tectonic plates. Then followed the eruption of the great volcanoes rising out of the Tasman Sea to form the Waitakere Ranges. A mere seven million years ago these massive upheavals produced the beginning of the Manukau Harbour. Its grand entrance of rock and lava on the North Head is so different from the South Head's sandstone and soft form.

Towards the bar you will see Cutter Rock and the Ninepin, once well out to sea and now surrounded by freshwater lakes and swamp vegetation. This area is known as the Whatipu Sands; it has always had special significance for local Maori, who have used it for centuries as a strategic pathway. Also delineating the western boundary of the Kawerau a Maki tribe, these rocks are regarded as

COURTESY HISTORY COLLECTION, WAITAKERE CITY LIBRARIES/ALEXANDER TURNBULL LIBRARY

tapu. They are collectively called Te Kupenga o Taramainuku, the rocks of Kupe. The area was known for a thousand years as Waitipu and formed a link with the main inland walkway to Te Rau o Te Huia, an area of strategic importance protected by four pa at Whatipu, which you will see on the headlands as you pass. Two are above the Whatipu Lodge and another is at the entrance to the Pararaha Valley. It's a steep climb to the summit of Ohaka Head (254 metres) where you will find the cooking pits and the base structures of the pa that once guarded this important headland settlement.

Below is the Pararaha Valley, one of the most impressive gorges in the ranges. In recent years it has become popular with trampers and day-trippers. The Pararaha Stream flows out of the ground above the Lone Kauri Road and is joined by a number of tributaries to form a decent flow over several waterfalls and through a gorge dominated by an impressive kauri log jam from the milling days. The entrance of the valley was farmed up until the 1930s. The Muir Hut, a cottage on the farm, was used by tramping clubs for many years. The Auckland Regional Council has since built an open shelter for walkers to enjoy their lunches and a well-earned rest.

Even after the closure of the mills at Pararaha and Whatipu in 1881, the Kawerau people still used the coastline to harvest their food resources and more importantly, to visit and pay their respects to the sacred areas, caves and ledges which were being increasingly desecrated by mill workers and visitors. The Maori were dejected and disillusioned by the outcome of the Land Wars, which had brought much grief to their relatives on the northern shores of the Manukau. As colonisation breached the ranges, the Kawerau people lived in

(Top) **Freshwater lakes of Whatipu, trapped by sand-dunes, are a haven and breeding ground for wildlife.** (Above) **Walking the ancient highway of the spirits to Karekare.** (Opposite Top) **The unmistakable shape of Mt Zion on the coastal skyline.** (Opposite Middle) **Tunnel Point, Kawakawa and the abandoned boiler from the Pararaha mill.** (Opposite Lower) **Catalogue illustration, 1884, of Tangyes Cornish Steam Boiler.**

cultural isolation at Te Henga and at Piha. Although they maintained good relations with their pakeha neighbours, they spoke little English. About this time, they abandoned the Wesleyan Church, which had converted them in 1845. They now became firm adherents of the King Movement, Pai Marire, which they follow to this day.

If you sense Maori history in the Pararaha Gorge you would be right. The historian Joan Lawrence suggests the valley may have supported 84 people, calculated by the number of storage pits. There are many caves of refuge used by Maori close to the stream and high up the cliffs, and it is my belief that they were probably used extensively in times of conquest. The valley entrance is dominated by the huge domed cliff-face known as Old Baldy.

At the entrance to the Pararaha Valley, the largest sand-dune on Auckland's west coast is a treat for jumping off or rolling down. To the north is a small headland pa site, Te Kawakawa or Tunnel Point, jutting towards the coast. In its grassy flank is the 10-metre tunnel cut through by Charles Murdoch to bring the cut timber from the Karekare mill to the Whatipu wharf. Beside the tunnel lies the rusting mill boiler which proved too large to pass through. All the way from Tangyes Works in Birmingham it came. Now it lies like an iron Ozymandias beside this highway of spirits.

The headland is an ancient pa site, fortified and able to give warning to the coastal communities. It is terraced to the north, with three major ridges. There appears still a small spring on the lower rock-face, and even in summer there is a trickling of fresh water flowing from the crevice. Te Kawakawa commands a vantage point of significance on this stretch of coast, and it's easy to imagine the

sounding of the great war trumpets, pukaea, reverberating against the cliff wall stretching to the Pararaha Valley. In summer on the southern slopes by the tunnel there is a large rainwater lagoon, home to a million frogs. In the swamp land around the entrance to the Pararaha Valley, the giant kapokapowa dragon-flies whiz urgently about their business in the swamp grasses. Close by, there are a number of caves. In their lofty dark caverns live the puratoke glow-worms. There is an eerie stillness here and the odd dinosaur would not seem out of place.

Despite the sad decline over the past 30 years in the numbers of New Zealand dotterel on the west coast of the North Island, there are still three or four pairs nesting around Tunnel Point and Cutter Rock. Trapping of wild cats and a ban on dogs, two of their main enemies, have allowed this very special bird to hang on in this area. If you're lucky you might also spot the smaller banded dotterel, although their numbers are much healthier elsewhere in New Zealand.

Back on the beach the surf swells give fine left-handers coming off the bar. This area is known as 'Wastelands' by surfers. In winter majestic swells peeling from the back of the island give a one-kilometre ride. You'll find local knowledge invaluable if you want to try these waves. You'll need to take your board over the rocks, around Karekau Point from Karekare to Whakaruro Bay and enter the water about a kilometre from the southern rock. It's worth it, even if you need to walk the whole length of the beach.

In the natural suntrap of Whakaruro Bay, there is a

magnificent grove of ancient pohutukawa which climbs up the steep face. Two small waterfalls cascade down the rock formations, which include a massive section of andesite which has slipped, while remaining upright, from the cliff. The surf reverberates off this gigantic rock-face. The Maori referred to it as Pari Whakaruro, or the Rumbling Cliff. It resembles the interior of a volcanic blow-hole, and creates a surf sound-shell.

In the summer of 1968 a cliff walkway was chipped and blasted over the Gut before Karekare. This almost superhuman effort was carried out by park rangers Bill Beveridge and Jim Forbes, hanging from ropes and a makeshift platform. The Gallery, as it is now called, enables walkers to reach Karekare Beach at any tide. Before the path was cut you had to make a dash for it between the surging waves, or wait hours for the tide to recede.

The Gallery is quite high, but safe. It also gives a superb view of Paratahi Island (called Parera on the old maritime and survey maps). On a moonlit night when the high surf on the point is streaked with light and phosphorescence and the echoes of the waves are in your ears, you may still hear the music of the Turehu fairy people venturing out to guide the spirits home.

For me, Karekare Beach has enormous power and spiritual presence and I believe that many people who go there sense this too. I remember

after dinner one evening in mid-winter, walking the beach with a full moon illuminating everything, talking with an old mate about last summer's waves. In the moonlight, the surf could be seen pounding the beach's outer sandbank. As we approached the water, our breath vaporising in the chilly air, we were suddenly stunned by an utter silence. On this coast, the sound of the surf is constant. The sheer disbelief that we could not hear the surf left us somewhat prickly with unease. The closer we approached the sea, the more unreal the situation became. The more we strained to hear the pounding surf, the more the silence overcame us. To keep the story straight, I should confess we'd been drinking a little. Unbelieving, we walked into the freezing water, trying to pick up the surf's roar. There we stood, two people before a huge movie screen on which was projected a massive and thrashing ocean, a silent film of gigantic proportions.

Next day, we returned to the beach to retrace our footprints, indeed to convince ourselves we'd actually been there the night before. Everything was back to normal. The natural world reveals itself to us in unexpected ways.

(Top) **Parents and children from Lone Kauri School head for a day's adventure on the sands.** (Above) **Day trippers in the Pararaha Gorge.** (Opposite) **Lunch break in the Pararaha for Titirangi's Orpheus sea-scouts.**

SEAPLANE RESCUE AT KAREKARE

Surf lifesaving from the skies

COURTESY D.R. BRICKELL

(Above) **Hazel Bentham's nursing graduation photograph.** (Opposite Top) **Newspaper photograph showing the epic rescue in its early stages when surf lifesavers attempted to reach Hazel through the breakers. Paratahi Island at top left of picture.**

SUNDAY, 3 February 1935 was a beautiful summer day at Karekare. The water was warm and inviting to the campers and day visitors. The beach was isolated by an extremely rough, poorly developed road through the Waitakere Ranges. There were only three resident families, no facilities, no surf club and, of course, no surf rescue helicopter. For all that, it was a favoured spot of west coast enthusiasts. The surf was generally good and the beach inviting. What matter if the road was a nightmare?

On this particular day, adults and children were enjoying the warmth and water as they swam, paddled or sunbathed. The surf, though boisterous, was now ebbing and gave no hint of the dangers that are ever-present there.

Suddenly, the peace and calm was rudely shattered. For the next four hours a young woman fought for her life as those on shore watched helplessly. Unnoticed, the tide had turned and was ebbing fast, so that by mid-afternoon a strong undertow had developed. A young nurse named Hazel Bentham had entered the water with her friends shortly after two o'clock and for the next quarter of an hour they played on their inflatable rubber mattress as they enjoyed the rough and tumble of the breakers. At some point, in the surf, the mattress and Hazel parted company. She continued in the rip, out past the breakers to the open sea. Hazel was a strong and confident swimmer, but the rip proved too strong and she was pulled into the swells beyond the surf line.

It was decided to send a message by runner over the hills to the Piha Life Saving Club to ask for help. The Piha team, seizing the moment, stacked their new reel on a truck and chugged over to Karekare with four of their top swimmers. It was an exhausting swim and the beltman could make no progress. The cotton surf lines of the day became waterlogged and only the strongest swimmer could drag 440 yards (400m) of it out through the surf. The segmented canvas and cork belt was a hindrance as well as being a potential death-trap as there was no release pin. Two hours had now elapsed.

When the rescue efforts seemed to be failing, somebody remembered that one of the young men of the Farley family had a pilot's licence and had landed a Tiger Moth on the beach. Wally Badham (the son-in-law of boarding-house owner Charles Farley) remembers the incident well. He was trying to start the generator when he heard people shouting. He thought it would be worth trying to raise the airbase at Hobsonville, to ask if the seaplane was operational. He remembered seeing it a few months before. He phoned the base, which was in those days contactable only through the Muriwai exchange, and the news was all good. Flight Lieutenant Wallingford agreed

COURTESY EVENING POST

to attempt the rescue from the sea. With Wallingford, leading aircraftsman J. Palmer launched the Fairey 111F, a large single-engined biplane with open cockpit and a 3m climb from the floats to the controls through a maze of guy-ropes. The base commander, Squadron Leader L.M. Isitt (later Sir Leonard), decided that he would oversee the operation from a Gypsy Moth.

In normal times this seaplane took over an hour and 15 men to launch it. On this occasion, the Air Force reports show, a record was set by eight off-duty servicemen. Out on the coast the ocean swells rolling in from the Tasman towards Karekare were pushing three metres. Meanwhile the Fairey slid down the concrete slipway of the base into the calm waters of the upper Waitemata, where it took off and headed towards the west coast.

The rocky headland was now crowded with anxious spectators. Within 20 minutes the plane was over the beach. They spotted the exhausted Hazel, still floating on her back 300m beyond the breakers off the cliffs and the Cauldron. Ignoring the potential hazards, the pilot skilfully landed the floatplane on the heaving water and taxied towards the young woman. She was quickly hauled on board where, though semi-conscious and shaking with cold, she responded to treatment. The pilot then taxied seawards before lifting off and flying his patient to Hobsonville for medical care and eventually, full recovery.

The month following the rescue, a meeting was called at the YWCA and the Karekare Surf Life Saving Club was founded.

As for Hazel Bentham, popular rumour at Karekare was that the shock of the ordeal sent her crazy and she died soon after in a mental institution. Not true! Soon after the rescue she married one of her companions of that day, Les Shaw, and lived a normal life in Hawkes Bay and later Auckland, dying in 1977 at the age of 72.

History also records that Hazel Bentham made a generous donation to the Piha Surf Club of £4, a figure which in Depression times would have been the equivalent of more than a week's wage.

COURTESY NEW ZEALAND HERALD

RESCUE FROM AIR

SEAPLANE IN SURF

ORDEAL OF WOMAN

FOUR HOURS IN WATER

LIFE-SAVERS POWERLESS

KAREKARE BEACH DRAMA

The aid of a Fairey IIIF seaplane fro͞m the Hobsonville Air Base was ... the rescue of a woman ... nearly four

DROWNING GIRL.

RESCUE BY 'PLANE.

AFTER THREE HOURS.

SURF MEN'S PLUCKY EFFORTS

HELP FROM HOBSONVILLE.

After drifting backwards and forwards at the will of every current, some 400 yards off the beach in a heavy swell, beyond every effort of surf club members, a young woman, who had been swept from Karekare Beach in the surf yesterday, was rescued, after three hours, by a seaplane summoned from Hobsonville. The woman was Miss Hazel

AUCKLAND STAR

KAREKARE

My greatest passion

(Above) The Karekare Beach Races are an annual fundraiser for the local community, attracting widespread interest and publicity. (Opposite) Entrants in Round the Island race are hardy athletes who test their competitiveness in the boiling surf.

ARGUABLY it's the finest beach in the grandest setting within a day's drive of Auckland. I first saw Karekare as a boy of 14, cycling to Piha with a friend. I glimpsed it, as most people do, from the Piha Road, a black sand beach with a rocky island jutting from the surf offshore. When I got down to the beach, the local surf club was celebrating its 21st birthday, and I joined up on the spot. I spent my first day at Karekare then and in my heart and mind I've never left this place.

For years I've been hopelessly hooked into helping run the local surf club, enjoying every minute of it. I've never tired of the surf or the countless walking and running trails which criss-cross Karekare's headlands and valleys, nor of the after-patrol hours soaking and swimming in the cool, clear pools which flow down from the high fern-covered valleys surrounding this enchanted spot. Its hold on my life is unfathomable, except I'm not alone. Locals who have lived there all their lives feel the same way and a number of wise Aucklanders continue to be Karekare regulars.

A few Christmases ago, the milk truck rolled backwards off the Karekare cutting. As it plunged towards oblivion in the bush-clad canyon below, it landed squarely on the roof of a yellow Mini which had been lost for 20 years. In many ways that accident sums up Karekare. It's full of surprises. Harry and Norma Liddle lived at the bottom of the cutting for 40 years and they claimed there were half a dozen cars still down there, some possibly with the skeletons of passengers still inside, after failing to take a bend and careening into the green jungle which clothes the valley walls. My son, looking for a lost hub cap, came upon a BMW suspended and intact in a huge rata tree halfway down the side of the precipice.

The steep road puts a lot of people off Karekare. Known by the locals as the Cutting, it's one of the most hair-raising rides in the Auckland area. It's been blasted and chopped out of the sheer cliffs. The gradient is 1:14 and has only recently been sealed, to everyone's surprise. The Cutting carried the first tourists in touring cars, as well as artists to paint, and the famous for beach picnics. It still does.

About 1870, farmers John and Silas Shaw obtained land in the lower part of Karekare Valley and hills which reached to the sea, a very isolated and secluded spot at the time. The Piha Road offshoot was first cut through the bush by the Shaw brothers, to become Karekare's link with the outside world, and for years was little more than a bridle path. In those days there was a government scheme offering free land grants to foster settlement at Karekare and other west coast

HOMAGE TO THE BACH

Tin shacks in paradise

(Above) **This swingbridge at Karekare leads to a pottery kiln.**

ALONG the west coast for the last 60 years, Aucklanders and people from as far away as Wellington have bought a small section of bush, cleared a part of it and built a bach, often with a glimpse of the ocean, but most likely hidden away. My generation may be the last that still believes in 'roughing it' on the coast. The old furniture, the plates, knives and everything else we don't want at our city home finishes up at the beach. Despite the superior comforts of life in town, I'd gladly spend every moment at Karekare Beach.

Although the affluent speak of their weekend retreats as houses, and indeed it's creeping into the Karekare vernacular, it's still a bach to me, with a bench and enamel sink, and a stove that used to be at home. And out the back, up a steep and often slippery set of stairs, a wooden dunny with a corrugated iron roof, a wooden seat that doesn't quite sit on straight and a fearsome long-drop.

People who visit me at Karekare, who haven't seen a 'long-drop' before, ask what's down the bottom of it. There's a simple answer. The two water tanks seem to be the breeding ground for every mosquito north of Taupo, and although I've tried putting kerosene on the water, nothing seems to work and I've long since given up caring.

I've put a driftwood timber ceiling in the bedroom because it gives me something to look at when I'm thinking of how my life is going, on Sunday morning when the surf's too big to do anything and the west coast drizzle is coming in from the sea. As the family has grown, cabin fever has become a real problem, but I've resisted the temptation to modernise the place. To me, it's still a bach with creosote and white wooden joinery that always needs a paint. A place where there isn't a phone and I can have a snooze whenever I feel like it.

I tend to swim with flippers in moderate surf these days. My sons have taken over the more courageous parts of surf lifesaving. And that's all right with me, too. But when the surf season finishes and winter's on the land, I enjoy it most because I don't have anything to do down at the surf club, a place on the beach where I have known great happiness for so many years. These days I'm clubhouse director. It's the humblest role in the club. In my time I have been club captain and president, but now I'm just an ageing janitor if you like, responsible for fixing the broken windows after parties, for Kleensaks, and for ensuring the septic tank doesn't overflow after a heavy weekend. I seem to spend a lot of time with a shovel in my hand listening to turkeys half my age telling me how the new eco-toilet works.

However, in winter the place belongs to me. With the westerly gales blowing in, my sons Rupert and Fraser and a couple of mates will join me for a run from the Karekare carpark around the south rocks, following the old mill tram tracks, down to the Pararaha Valley and through the swampland, cold and always refreshing. It's one of the great runs in the world. There's no one for 30 km either way; even gulls will be huddled on Paratahi Island as the weather's often fierce.

Later in the afternoon I might start reading some council reports, making notes in the margins about whether I think it will go down with the ratepayers or not. Or I might write a bit myself, or draft an outline for some speech I might have to make. Or once again read a chapter from Herman Melville's *Moby Dick*, which is one of my other obsessions and on which I always convinced myself I could win *Mastermind* hands down. I've read so much of it to my kids that they know the first lines by heart:

> Call me Ishmael. Some years ago – never mind how long precisely – having little or no money in my purse, and nothing particular to interest me on shore, I thought I would sail about a little and see the watery part of the world.

They know who was the harpooner on the *Pequod* and what was the Spouter Inn. And I know there is no better place in the world to read this greatest of sea stories than here at Karekare on a stormy Sunday.

It's difficult when you're so spiritually attached to a place that you really can't bear to be away from it. So much so, that no other place has any real calling for me, neither Rome nor New York, nor Surfers Paradise nor Hawaii. But then again, I'm a man who's never played a game of tennis nor been to horse racing except on the beach at Karekare.

(Below) **The bach long-drop, open all hours.** (Lower) **Typical weatherbeaten coastal bach, used extensively in summer and infrequently during the stormy winter months.**

JENKINSON PHOTOGRAPH

Kare Kare. West Coast. Auckland. F.G.R. 5224.

(Top and Opposite Top) **Postcard images of turn-of-the-century Karekare featuring the beach trestle and Winchelsea guest-house.** (Above) **Karekare lagoon and surf club.**

areas, but many settlers were disheartened by the dense bush and soon abandoned their titles. The Shaw brothers battled on to clear their land and farmed it intensively.

The brothers also built the first simple valley homestead where the toilet block is today. The painting of this homestead by Charles Blomfield in 1873 records for posterity a tranquil valley with few trees, the legacy of the extensive Maori cultivation on the valley floor. To get their stock to and from Karekare, the Shaws hired a cutter from Onehunga to Whatipu. The beach was to be their only workable access, as the track up to the Piha Road could not handle cattle. The beach highway would be used extensively by millers, tourists and today, trampers.

John (Pa) Neal Bethell, before he moved up the coast to the beach that today bears his name, ran the mill store, cookhouse and butchery. Outside his cottage at the foot of Zion Hill he planted a mission fig from Bishop Selwyn's garden. Today there are two fruitful trees which grow there next to the Auckland Regional Council's toilets.

They say that some of the finest and largest kauri in the ranges grew on the Karekare hills. In 1878 the Guthrie & Larnoch Timber Company of Dunedin sent Mr Charles Primrose Murdoch to take over management of the coast bush mills. He replaced the Pararaha's bullock team with a bush and beach tramway and later began to extend this tramway towards Karekare where he planned to build another mill when the Pararaha area was worked out. On the morning of 25 March 1881 the Pararaha mill was destroyed by fire after a spark fell amongst shavings. As most of the millable timber in that valley had been cut, Murdoch

'WINCHELSEA' KARE KARE 116 (PROTECTED)

JENKINSON PHOTOGRAPH

decided to salvage the machinery, minus the oversize boiler, take it up the coast to Karekare and use it for the mill which he built near the Opal Pool Stream and close to the spectacular waterfall which drops from the Company Stream. Murdoch named the mill Karekau, and in full production it was cutting 100,000 super feet a year and employing 60 to 70 workers.

Murdoch's tramway traversed the sand-dunes to the Pararaha through the tunnel and then around the foot of the cliffs to Whatipu, crossing Taranaki Bay above high tide mark in a wide sweep to the south. The steel rails had a gauge of 2'6" (.8m). Today, all that remains are the rusted spikes embedded in the rocks, fixed in place with sulphur, which was used as cement in the 19th century.

It is not clear why the route across the sand was taken in preference to an existing road around the foot of the cliffs now called Pohutukawa Glade. This road, now a walking track, has always been known locally as Sandringham. The construction of the Karekare mill was started in August 1882 and completed in July 1883, but struggled to make a decent profit in the rugged Waitakere Ranges.

It was not economical, nor in many cases practicable, to build bush tramways to reach the bigger trees or to drag logs from the bush down to the mills. As an alternative they were 'driven' down the streams by releasing a wall of water. To obtain sufficient water for this purpose, dams were built at strategic places, usually where the stream narrowed and the banks were high and composed of rocks. There are several photographs of such dams in the Waitakere City Library

"Kare Kare" GUEST HOUSE T. McGUIRE Prop.

LEFT AND FAR LEFT: GODBER ALBUM, COURTESY ALEXANDER TURNBULL LIBRARY

(Right) **Main Road, Karekare, 1914. The conic wagon at left of photograph is now buried in sand on the beach. (Below) The grand drop into the Karekare Valley from the Piha mill. A load of sawn timber is eased down by the brakeman at the top of the incline. (Lower) Built in 1872, the first New Zealand-made locomotive was used by Charles Murdoch to haul timber from Karekare to Whatipu. It then became a landmark on Karekare Beach for almost a century. This photograph from the 1950s shows tourists posing on the old rusted boiler, which now lies beneath more than four metres of sand. (Opposite) Winchelsea House today.**

K. ABERCROMBIE COLLECTION, WAITAKERE CITY LIBRARIES

collection. Bush mill historian Jack Diamond describes the construction and operation of a kauri dam:

> Heavy baulks of timber, some as much as two feet square, were secured across the stream bed and on this solid foundation the dam was erected. In the face of the dam was an opening through which the water and logs escaped when the dam was 'tripped'. This opening varied according to the size of the dam but was usually about 10 feet [3 metres] square while the gate which covered it was composed of upright planks of timber. These gate planks – usually 12" x 4" [0.3m x 0.1m] – were wired side by side across the beam above the opening while at the base they rested against a beam let into recesses in the wall on either side of the opening. This beam was in two halves and a piece of timber called a "tom", about 4" square [0.1m] and varying in length up to 18" [0.5m] whose base was let into a hole in the floor of the dam, kept these in place. To complete the "trip mechanism" as this arrangement was called the tom was secured at the top by an iron hook called a "trip hook" which was hinged to the gate and from which a length of wire was taken to the top of the dam.
>
> When conditions were favourable for a drive, all that was necessary to trip the dam was a good pull on the wire which lifted the trip hook, allowed the top to come out of its socket and the gate to fly open releasing the impounded water.
>
> The length of time necessary to fill a dam depended not only on its size but on the rainfall. In some cases eight months or more might elapse before the dam filled and even then it was often necessary for the stream to be in flood to ensure a successful drive. To assist the drive, trees and shrubs on the banks were felled into the stream.[1]

The Murdochs lived at Karekare in rural splendour. The first house was lost in a fire, all inhabitants escaping injury. The larger second house, built in 1881, stands today. When the timber ran out, Charles went into growing flax for the rope and linen industry plus a woodturning operation in Freeman's Bay making spokes for the carriage trade. Murdoch's photographs of his wife and their family in the Waitakere City Library show a grand and idyllic lifestyle on the coast. A country gentleman and his large, handsome Victorian family. Charles was also

[1] A large, beautifully-built model of a bush dam can be seen at Rose Hellaby House on the Scenic Drive at Waiatarua.

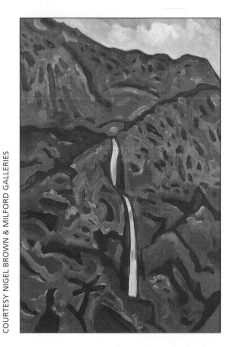

COURTESY NIGEL BROWN & MILFORD GALLERIES

(Above) *Falls at Karekare* by Nigel Brown, **1996. (Opposite) Above the falls you can still see remnants of the kauri dam and flume structure.**

a botanist, establishing around the Karekare homestead numerous rock plants, some of which survive to flower today during the summer months.

The ingenious engineering-minded Murdoch piped water from atop the main waterfall, the flow traversing the steep cliffs into a trough of five-metre lengths of jarrah 200 metres long, before finally plunging down a flume to drive a pelton wheel which generated power to operate his flaxmill. This innovative power supply was later used by the Farley family, subsequent owners of Winchelsea, to provide electricity for the house and for a lone streetlight by the wooden bridge. In this way, Karekare has the distinction of beating Auckland City (still on gaslight) to a power supply by 15 years.

The youngest of the Murdochs' nine children was drowned in the Karekare Stream and the family buried her at the bottom of the hills where she had played. They planted a Norfolk pine near the spot. Now over 100 years old, it still stands by Winchelsea House, stunted by the wind.

The Murdochs' second home was to become Winchelsea House, one of the great boarding-houses on the west coast. Passionate about the sea, Murdoch was one of the founders of the Akarana Yacht Club and was honoured by becoming the club's first commodore. He sold the Karekare property to Charles Farley, who chose the name Winchelsea after his home in England. Farley himself had an interesting life, being the first to establish a dairy factory in the Waikato, around 1882. Subsequently he was asked by the New Zealand Government to go to Italy and demonstrate butter-making to their dairy farmers. After completing his contract, he returned to farm at Mt Albert.

At the time Mr Farley bought the Karekare property and the grand house in 1900, the valley below Zion Hill was owned by Abel Lovett, who had it left to him by a Norwegian named Pedersen, who lived in a kauri cottage where the picnic ground is today. By the early 1920s, Winchelsea House had a reputation for fine accommodation, with its magnificent dining room, a staff of 15, a full-size billiard table, a tennis court and croquet lawn out front. The Farley family successfully ran it as a five-star guest-house for up to 20 visitors.

Weekend visitors got themselves to the Waikumete railway station by train and there transferred to a horse-drawn coach for the journey over the ranges. The coach left Karekare at 5 am, which meant getting up at 4 am. Breakfast was at 4:30 am. In winter this trip must have been a nightmarish end to a holiday. After a two-hour spell, fresh passengers were picked up from the train, arriving back at Karekare at 5 pm. The drivers were Harry Wilkins, Gill Wood and Wally Farley, names which are still familiar in the west. Carrier pigeons were released from the station by the coach driver with details of the guests and their care and food requirements. The Farleys believed in luxury transport for their guests and purchased first a Model T, and then the grander 1924 six-cylinder Essex 4. It was capable of doing 75 miles per hour, but as the difficult drive from Glen Eden took five hours, it was a painful slog.

Winchelsea House closed in 1942 for the full service and in later years the Karekare guest-house became a trampers' stopover, gradually falling into disrepair as succeeding owners lost interest and couldn't keep up its maintenance. In the 1950s, now known as the lowly "Cabins", it provided a convenient place for surf club members to accommodate their sweethearts, who were forbidden by the club to stay overnight in the bunkroom.

Today Winchelsea House is lovingly restored and renovated. A new section

Karekare Beach Races

Hoofbeats on the sand

U SUALLY held on a late summer Sunday on the lowest of tides, the Karekare beach races have grown steadily in popularity. As I am no expert on horses, I think most of them are ponies and mares, but they still seem to move quite fast at a gallop as the hard beach sand makes an ideal course for the enthusiastic horses and young riders. There is always a small betting tent and some spirited and biased commentary from volunteer local race callers, supplemented when things get serious by a real race caller who sounds just right and seems to know his stuff.

The whole day is about family fun and fund-raising for the Lone Kauri School, the volunteer fire party and the surf club. Everyone associated with the beach community takes an active part in selling sausages, raffles, plants and highly-prized race day T-shirts designed by local artists. Media celebrities are out in force on race days. It's a time for putting on the style.

The horses and riders are splendid at full gallop, against the backdrop of the surf. The weather is usually perfect for the day, not too hot, with a cool sea breeze. Racing generally starts at 11 am with the first event, the Pohutu-kawa Glade Stakes. The betting is often brisk and the races are named after Karekare scenic spots. There is no printed programme, but there are usually six races plus a couple of fun ones thrown in for good measure.

A few years ago, one of the horses threw its rider and took off around the south rocks on the low tide and galloped down to Whatipu, pursued by the Auckland Regional Council ranger and half the field. Thankfully, over the years there have been no falls and few injuries to horses and riders.

The steep road down to the beach is too narrow to bring the horse trailers down, so they trundle down the longer Lone Kauri Road. It keeps the traffic flowing, but be prepared for delays. Local papers carry the dates of the meeting and the race day organising committee spends most of the year gearing up for the event.

(Above, Below and Opposite) **The colourful coastal communities come out in force to enjoy Karekare Beach Race day.**

(Right) The untamed coast is a vast adventure playground for the young at heart. (Below) Travel by horseback has been the quickest form of transport on this coastline for more than 160 years.

has been architecturally designed in keeping with the character of the old building, by the owner, children's author Dorothy Butler. Over the wooden bridge, constructed by the Farleys from a large macrocarpa tree, a side road passes the original marae site of Te Kawerau a Maki. This site, known as Te Marae o Mana, leads to a surf spotters' lookout perch over Union Bay and the North Point.

A post office at Karekare was opened for a brief period, from 1 February 1885 to 30 April 1886, with Charles Murdoch as postmaster. There is no further record of postal service at Karekare until 21 April 1904, when an office was opened with Charley Farley as postmaster. At the same time, Farley took on the duties of mail contractor for the service with Waikumete (now Glen Eden), by horse, twice-weekly, collecting and delivering mail along the route. This early rural mail service was evidently not particularly successful.

A petition to the Central Post Office in March 1907 requested that the mail service be reduced to once a week from the beginning of June till the end of October, remaining at twice-weekly during the summer months. Among the 10 signatures to this petition there were eight members of the Farley family, including the postmaster himself.

Money-order and savings bank facilities were added in February 1909 and a telephone line extended to Karekare from Waikumete in June 1912. The telephone office was opened for service on 4 June of that year. By 1935 the population of the area had dwindled. On 31 January 1941 the post office was closed.

There's no beach on the west coast with more presence and more history than Karekare. It has charmed generations with its rugged scenery and quiet, tranquil glades, streams and waterfalls.

At the bottom of the hill there's McCready's Paddock, a small picnic area at the site of an early mill, once belonging to the West Coast Timber Company. Timber from this mill was transported down the present road by horse-drawn wagon on a set of rails. You can camp overnight on the cool grassy paddock by the Karekare Stream.

By 1997 there were about 30 permanent residents but the valley floor is still sparsely populated. Few ever sell a place at Karekare. That's something you just

don't do. I'm pleased to say that most people have built in harmony with the landscape, so Karekare has avoided the crassness of some of the holiday homes which have visually damaged Piha. Instead the land remains unconquered, having resisted the sawmillers' attempts to tame it with one of the most complex bush rail systems seen anywhere in New Zealand. Young kauri are once again flourishing in the bush. Already a group over 30m tall soar again in the valley behind the property of Everest climber and mountain photographer Michael Gill.

The Karekare Ratepayers and Residents' Association is probably one of the most effective on the coast. They have worked to keep Karekare and the environment well protected and these days usually have an excellent relationship with the Waitakere Council. It was not always like that.

In the past, the common enemy for this community was the environmentally insensitive Waitemata County Council, which, before the days of any decent environmental plan for the region, bumbled from one clumsy venture to another. I remember attempts to control the dust nuisance every summer on the Piha Road saw the council proceeding to mine the sand-dunes on Karekare Beach, maintaining that as the beach was a dedicated road it was theirs. Repeated pleas by us locals were ignored until television publicised the debate. The bulldozers and trucks were off the beach within a day and Karekare at last had a group of dedicated residents prepared to fight for preservation of the beach. But this battle is never over.

When you come down to Karekare you'll notice the first of two rustic wooden

(Top) **Strong onshore winds provide exhilarating sport for parapenters, hang-gliders and other birds of freedom.**
(Above) **Tragedy strikes as Atlantic Ocean rower Phil Stubbs crashes onto Karekare Beach, 20 December 1998.**

COURTESY KAREKARE SURF CLUB ARCHIVES

(Left) **The first Karekare patrol with their new reel and uniforms pose with the Governor-General Lord Galway. (Below) Relaxed ambience at Karekare. (Opposite) Lifeguards at Karekare Beach patrol from Labour Weekend through to Easter every weekend, saving around 100 people a year from drowning.**

bridges. The Waitemata County Council originally planned to replace this with a large, concrete National Roads Board structure complete with culverts and approaches like a motorway on-ramp. After months of angry protests, the original bridge, a very aesthetically-pleasing structure, was left intact.

Few old locals can forgive the cutting of a dozen hundred-year-old pohutukawas to form a new carpark in the early 1970s. The carpark was never built; the trees are lost forever.

There was a long and eventually successful battle by locals and the Auckland Regional Council to keep vehicles off the beach. To save the shellfish, paddle crabs and rockpool life, a rahui was placed on the beach by local iwi. The Department of Conservation and the locals gave full support. This has led to a rise in shellfish numbers. The ban will stay and may even be extended to the rest of the area's coastline. I hope so.

You'll have to walk to appreciate the beach. The carpark, known as the Green, has been levelled and grassed and locals have surrounded it with plantings of young pohutukawa. You'll need to jump or wade the stream and then it's a five to ten-minute walk to the water's edge.

Halfway down the beach towards the surf, the remains of the rusting girded trestle struts are all that's left of the bush railway which plunged over the Karekare hills to drop two wagon-loads of logs into the valley, and geared by a series of pulleys and ratchets, to pull one wagon from the Piha mill on the other side.

Dominating the surf seascape is Paratahi Island to the south. To the north is Union Bay, Tahoro, with its own rock sentinel called the Split Pin, Tokapiri. The hill behind keeps slipping. It buried a Maori fishing village in olden times, and in the 1950s a boat and shed under tons of rock, mud and bush.

On the main beach under the sheer towering rock-face of the Watchman Rock, Te Matua, is the Karekare Surf Life Saving Club house, the third to be built on the beach since the club was founded in 1935. The original clubhouse, situated in the tennis changing sheds above the beach, was known as the Grand Hotel. After a particularly wild night the Grand Hotel was burnt to the ground.

No surf club in Auckland has a more difficult beach to patrol. Twice, the club has won the New Zealand 'Rescue of the Year' Award, a prestigious honour in lifesaving circles. Both rescues have been made in the infamous Cauldron where boiling surf pounds against 70-metre cliffs to the north of Union Bay. In one rescue, local lifeguard Stephen Pye led a recovery of five board riders who had been swept into the Cauldron to certain death by drowning if the patrol hadn't braved the surf, assisted from above by the rescue helicopter.

(Above) **Bathed in a warm afternoon sun, the Lone Kauri Road winds down to the beach.** (Below) **Karekare Beach Races, a fun day for the whole community.** (Opposite Top) **Karekare Beach, looking south from the Ahu Ahu cliffs.** (Opposite Lower) **Pohutukawa Glade has been used for many films, most notably** *The Piano*.

A few years ago, a French television film crew, in New Zealand to shoot a commercial, stopped at Karekare for a quick swim. Ten were swept to sea within minutes. In the mass rescue that followed the alarm being raised, club members brought them all to safety. Jed Falby, the director on the assignment, later took the hat around in Paris and the resulting cheque bought the club's first inflatable rescue craft and motor, which has saved hundreds over the years.

On their annual club day, the club stages a two-kilometre swim around Paratahi Island, no mean feat in big surf. Or small surf, for that matter.

A stone shed in the centre of the beach was built by the club in 1937 for patrolling and gear storage, but over the years the sea has receded, leaving the patrol platform and the rock isolated. It is now almost covered by the shifting sand-dunes and the timber roof rises out of the dunes.

The Karekare Surf Club was the second lifesaving patrol to be formed on the west coast, the Piha Club beating them by a year. Both clubs bought reel and lines from the same Australian manufacturers for £100 apiece and started saving lives.

Elderly surviving members of the first club patrol still remember their most famous regular visitor of those days, the Right Honourable Viscount Lord Galway GCMB, DSO, OBE. Over the long summers of the 1930s, Governor-General Galway and his family would picnic regularly in Union Bay. Inevitably the grand Bentley would get

COURTESY DEAN BUCHANAN

(Top) *Two Rata*, by Dean Buchanan, 1991. (Above) **Karekare local and internationally recognised painter of the New Zealand bush, Dean Buchanan.**

bogged in the sand and the clubbies would be summoned to dig and push to get it on its way. The rewards varied from French champagne to English beer. Still prized in the clubhouse is a signed photograph of the 'Gov' and that first team and reel. At almost two metres tall, Galway dwarfs the original clubbies.

Although the club prides itself on one of Auckland's highest rescue ratings, don't count on it, as the beach can be unpredictable. Like all west coast beaches, Karekare must be treated with great caution. The northern point is one of New Zealand's top surfing spots. In a southwesterly swell, the waves are stronger and more powerful than at Piha or Muriwai. Union Bay and the North Point are becoming known around the world. Karekare was named one of the top ten beaches in the world by *Beaches* magazine, lauded for its isolation and rideable surf.

The lagoon on the beach is unpolluted, warm and shallow, a great playground for children. At low tide they'll also find a couple of large saltwater pools amid the North Point rocks.

Opposite the carpark is the weekend home of artists Peter and Sylvia Siddell. When Peter started to paint he used Karekare hills, cliffs and caves as the setting for his desolate canvases. Later, when he developed his themes of Victorian houses, the Karekare hills, tussock and flattened manuka were reflected in the windows and mirrors and gave his paintings a meticulous and surreal quality which has found a widening circle of patrons.

Sylvia Siddell is also highly regarded for her pencil drawings of tortured domestic objects. These days the Siddells spend their weekends at Karekare. He doesn't paint there much anymore, using the place purely for relaxation.

Across the main beach heading south, just before the high cliffs of Mount Zion, turn left into an enchanted valley which follows the cliffs through glades of pohutukawa and kowhai. Early photographs show this area had a cluster of mill houses and stables for the logging ponies. From this valley rises the Zion Hill track, a moderately steep but spectacular climb to view the whole beach, and from the top, the Manukau bar and the Pararaha Valley.

The track through Pohutukawa Glade (Sandringham) will take you back to your car but if you're feeling like a refreshing swim in the beautiful opal pools, walk a short way up the hill, passing on your left the group of white-painted houses, which were owned by the Browne family and originally served as the second accommodation at Karekare. In 1930 Ted Browne opened his place up for guests by erecting two bunk-houses, one on the area he had first used as a tent site, and the other on the house side of the Opal Pools Stream on the right of the track down to the stream.

The frame consisted entirely of kauri rickers and the walls and roof were corrugated iron. In its day it was a clean, dry place to sleep and that was all the Brownes wanted. Ted was encouraged to go into the boarding-house business by the number of young members of the Manukau Amateur Cycling Club, who went to Karekare requiring a place to sleep and three good meals a day. They didn't require luxuries such as silver service or tennis. Ted and his wife Stella were great hosts and very popular with everyone. They stayed until October 1936, when they moved to Piha, where they ran the boarding-house and local post office for many years. It is still on the hill above the Piha shop.

For the more adventurous, the track to the waterfall is easy to find. It leads to one of the most beautiful falls on the coast, Te Ahu Ahu, or 'the pendulous

white thread', which has been used for many television commercials. It's 30 metres high and falls into a large, clean, sandy-bottomed pool. Turn right and follow the Opal Pools Stream as you wind up the mountainside. You'll discover large and often very deep pools with shockingly cool, clear water. They say there were once 40 pools but now only 10 remain, the rest destroyed when the Lone Kauri Road was bulldozed through in 1947.

To return home, take the Lone Kauri Road. Although four kilometres further, the metalled road is less severe than the cutting. On this narrow but scenic road the author C.K. Stead and the poet Allen Curnow have had weekend houses for many years. Curnow has drawn on the darkness of the beach and bush for some of his most evocative poetic works. His 1982 poem *You Will Know When You Get There* may have a universal theme, but for me the images and moody feelings it conjures are of the untamed coastline, Karekare in particular:

(Top) *Nikau*, by Dean Buchanan, 1991.
(Above) **Poet Allen Curnow, author of *The Loop In Lone Kauri Road*.**

Nobody comes up from the sea as late as this
in the day and the season, and nobody else goes down

the last steep kilometre, wet-metalled where
a shower passed shredding the light which keeps

pouring out of its tank in the sky, through summits,
trees, vapours thickening and thinning. Too

credibly by half celestial, the dammed
reservoir up there keeps emptying while the light lasts

over the sea, where it 'gathers the gold against
it'. The light is bits of crushed rock randomly

COURTESY MARTI FRIEDLANDER

COURTESY RAY FORSTER

Glass and stone sculptures by Karekare
artists: (Top) **John Edgar with his** *Section*.
(Middle) **Ann Robinson at her studio.**
(Above) *Flax pod*, 1996, **Ann Robinson.**

glinting underfoot, wetted by the short
shower, and down you go and so in its way does

the sun which gets there first. Boys, two of them,
turn campfirelit faces, a hesitancy to speak

is a hesitancy of the earth rolling back and away
behind this man going down to the sea with a bag

to pick mussels, having an arrangement with the tide,
the ocean to be shallowed three point seven metres,

one hour's light to be left and there's the excrescent
moon sponging off the last of it. A door

slams, a heavy wave, a door, the sea-floor shudders.
Down you go alone, so late, into the surge-black fissure.

Once when I was running the Lone Kauri Road, wearing a New York T-shirt, I passed him with a sweaty "Good morning." A few years later I had cause to remember this chance meeting when reading one of his best-known works, *The Loop in Lone Kauri Road*. Still writing in his 80s, this great New Zealand literary figure swims in the buffeting surf most days over summer at the beach below his modest cottage.

Nearby, the large Lockwood on the top knoll belongs to The Rt Hon Jonathan Hunt, New Zealand's longest-serving MP, who has lived at Karekare for the last 30 years. It's his generosity and support that made possible the Lone Kauri Community School, which is built on his property. Locals raised the money, helped by an anonymous donation.

On the Lone Kauri Road the glass sculptor Ann Robinson and her partner John Edgar, whose stone sculpture and jewellery are widely sought, have their studio. Ann, the daughter of one of Auckland's most famous mayors (Robbie), is a craftswoman of rare talent. Her work with glass vessels, often weighing up to 50 kg, presents an enormous challenge in both technique and skill. The astonishing pieces of dazzling beauty which emerge from her kiln reveal the spirituality she brings to her craft and the understanding she has of her materials. Ann is a humble and unassuming artist who enjoys discussing the origins of glass and the new colours and designs she is using, influenced by the bush and the forms and light of the South Pacific.

John Edgar is a fascinating artist, with large innovative works in stone, metal and glass combinations. Size is no barrier, as he seeks new dimensions and interpretations of the landscape. An exhibition in marble and black granite suggested the shape of the west coast hills and headlands, merging the skyline with a hairline sliver of blue glass. The effect is a monolith creation as exciting as the earth itself. Like many coastal craftspeople, Ann and John are proud to show their work, but it is best to phone first.

Above the beach is the studio of renowned artist Dean Buchanan, whose early reputation was made on his bold, colourful canvases of bush and coastal landscapes. The west coast has given him an undeniable place in New Zealand art. Buchanan loves to walk and roam the ranges, sometimes seeking inspiration and adding to his extraordinary collection of found objects at the site of old farm and mill bush cottages, or with the occasional artefact discovered in a stream or watercourse. He has an amazing ability to spot the shape and contour

Sunset at Karekare 4 / Albrecht

of a lost and forgotten treasure. It must be his painter's eye. His bush studio, where he works and welcomes visitors, is never short of drop-in fans. Half an hour with this energetic and enthusiastic man, who knows every valley on the coast, will enthral you.

The lone kauri after which the road is named, is long gone. Felled in 1936, it featured on many of the early postcards of the west coast. In 1912, two bushmen, Moffat Byles and Tony Golter, gave a climbing exhibition for members of the Waitemata County Council and their wives. (There are local tales of the skeletons of other climbers who lost the rope, being found high in the branches when the trees were felled.)

These two human wetas climbed the 80-foot tree using boots with two-inch spikes protruding from each toe, and in each hand a hook that they used to walk up the tree. When at the top and into the branches, they unfurled a rope for the descent, but not before they had taken off their boots and leapt from branch to branch with an extraordinary display of balance and bushman's courage. The lone kauri's stump is still visible a few metres from the junction where you rejoin the Piha Road. It was felled not by the miller's axe, but by the Council's command, as the road was upgraded.

You will be leaving the sun behind you, and I hope a great day. You'll probably realise by now that Karekare is a beach for people who appreciate nature at its best, a place unspoilt and still untamed. Chances are, you will think of coming back. It isn't easy to let go of this place.

(Top) *Sunset at Karekare 4*, Gretchen Albrecht, 1975. (Below) *Inanga Rei*, 1993, jade, John Edgar. (Overleaf) The Watchman stands sentinel on Karekare Beach.

KAREKARE WALKS

Karekare Walks

1. Ahu Ahu Track

Take a right at the bridge by Winchelsea House. At the end of this short metal road a track to the right will take you up Mt Hikurangi, high above Mercer Bay. Geologists tell us that this bay is part of the eastern flank of an ancient volcano that was progressively eroded by the sea. To the Kawerau a Maki people, Mercer Bay was known by the beautiful name of 'Te Unuhanga o Rangitoto'. Allow two hours return, or another hour if you want to take in the very popular Mercer Bay Loop Walk, with its stunning views of sea, cliff and setting sun.

2. Karekare Falls and Opal Pool Stream

This walk takes a mere 10 minutes. From the parking area, head over the wooden bridge and 200 metres up Lone Kauri Road. The track leads down to the falls and a picturesque area ideal for a family picnic, with tables on a grassy flat bordered by pohutukawa and a grove of nikau. The Falls were sometimes referred to simply as 'Te Rere' or 'the waterfall'. However it was traditionally known by the poetic name of 'Te Ahoaho' or 'the pendulous white thread', being likened to the pure white fibres of muka flax swaying in the breeze. The pool at the bottom is safe for swimming. Alongside Lone Kauri Road, the Opal Pools flow through a series of small, clean and elegant pools, deep enough for a summer dip.

3. Zion Hill Track

From the carpark at the beach, cross the footbridge to Sandringham Valley, now called Pohutukawa Glade. Proceed through to ascend Mount Zion where the Murdochs' mill ponies used to graze. Your reward will be breathtaking views of Karekare Beach and the northern coastal headlands. At the junction of Zion Hill and Buck Taylor tracks you have the option of taking the Buck Taylor Track down to the Pararaha Valley and back along the beach, or you can continue on the Zion Ridge Track to the Lone Kauri Road, through a magical grove of ancient puriri. This walk is around two and a half hours.

GETTING THEM BACK ALIVE

Unsung heroes of the untamed coast

THERE is no more respected voluntary organisation in New Zealand than the surf lifesavers, and on the west coast beaches the job is long and arduous. Year-round, the surf is heavy and treacherous. These young men and women are well aware of the hungry shore break that can snatch the unwary swimmer. Every weekend from Labour Weekend to Easter and every day through the summer holidays, the lifeguards patrol these beaches.

Many of the modern rescue techniques of quick victim recovery now used internationally, were first tested on these beaches. The water patrols have long abandoned the wooden reel, line and canvas belt, for the much faster method of neoprene rescue tube and swimmer, backed up by fast, manoeuvrable inflatable surf rescue craft, powering to the spot in heart-stopping leaps over the waves.

The helicopter service, which was the first of its type in the world (and of which I was one of the founding team members), was developed as our west coast answer to the Californian concept of rescue from behind the breakers, using the piers that extend through the surf to give quicker access to the victim. For many years, we investigated methods of rockets or some other device that would get a rescue line quickly to the drowning victims. The helicopter idea came out of a workshop, and with the assistance of Radio Hauraki and a cigarette sponsorship, we were able to fund its first five years of operation. These days, it's almost obsolete. Club lifeguards need to move so fast in a surf rescue that the chopper cannot compete, although it is still useful for ferrying injured victims over the ranges to Auckland.

The clubs recruit them young – 'nippers' start to learn water wisdom at seven; junior guards at 12. A trained lifeguard averages 20 years of age, with swim fitness and reliability being the main criteria. There is fun and enjoyment too. Even when not on patrol, 'clubbies' often hang around their beach to surf or join in a rescue. Some clubs provide weekend accommodation.

Piha's surf club was founded in January 1934 by five young sportsmen from Auckland, who sat around a two-gallon keg of beer and a bowl of hot sausages and resolved to form the first club on the coast. These days the club averages well over 500 rescues a year. The Karekare Surf Club was founded in 1935. Muriwai's club followed, in 1939. North Piha and Bethells came next. North Piha became the United Club in 1968.

The west coast clubs account for around 2000 rescues a year in the changing rips and criss-crossing undercurrents of the beaches. It's a great service provided by dedicated, often hard-pressed and overworked young lifeguards free of charge to the swimming public.

COURTESY KAREKARE SURF CLUB ARCHIVES

COURTESY ROY NUDS

(Top) **The first wooden rescue surf-ski on the west coast, Karekare, 1938.**
(Above) **Lifeguards test strength, 1935.**

PIHA

A New Zealand icon

(Above) **Lion Rock sits majestically between the main beach and North Piha. It is one of the most familiar coastal landmarks of the Auckland region. (Opposite) Piha's international reputation for big waves attracts surfers all year round.**

THE coastal view from the lookout above Piha Beach is a dramatic and familiar image of New Zealand. It's been used on countless postcards, calendars and the Auckland telephone book. High above the beach, generations of surfers have stopped here to check out the waves. Visitors have paused to take the great holiday snap and to admire the view. These days the road is sealed all the way across the ranges from the Scenic Drive to Piha and after the lookout it drops very steeply down the great southern face of the Piha Valley.

For 80 years it was a place to stop after the bone-shaking metal and mud road over the ranges from Glen Eden. Standing sentinel on the beach below is Lion Rock, the colossal island fortress of the ancient Maori known as Whakaari. It too is known by generations of New Zealanders as one of the most definitive coastal landmarks in the country.

In 1939, before Judge Acheson, Te Kawerau a Maki fought to establish their continued claim on Lion Rock. Before the Court, four Maori on behalf of their iwi, pleaded their case and were successful. The evidence they produced was not contested, so the Court recognised their ownership of the island, as well as two large blocks of land close by. Unfortunately for them, the decision was overturned by later submissions and by the end of the Second World War, Lion Rock was in public ownership, as it still is in 1998, administered by the Auckland Regional Council. Their other island, Taitomo, which they also successfully claimed, sits alone, washed by the Tasman swells.

Every summer Piha Beach becomes a magnet for serious surfers and a temporary home for thousands. It is the most popular west coast beach in New Zealand, and its summer surf almost always lives up to expectations.

In the early part of the 20th century, Piha was shaped by the duplicity of Canadian-born, Chicago-educated Dr Frederick John Rayner, a well-married Auckland milling entrepreneur and dentist. His wealth was made from a dentistry complex, The American Dental Parlour, which stood on the site of the Civic Theatre. This booming business enabled him to develop a vast kauri logging enterprise at Piha, where his legacy is recorded by Rayner Road, the lack of any kauri trees and a long, cynical poem by Allen Curnow. Under Rayner's ownership, Piha was a hive of mill activity. Two hundred people lived and worked in this unsustainable coastal industry. Along the beachfront ran the bush tram pulling logs out from the Piha gorges and the Anawhata watershed.

The Piha Valley echoed with the sound of steam boilers, huge saws and traction engines. A wonder of the age was the giant rollercoaster tramway, plunging down the Piha hillside in a spectacular fall of 4.5:1 gradient. On the other side,

GODBER ALBUM, COURTESY ALEXANDER TURNBULL LIBRARY

GODBER ALBUM, COURTESY ALEXANDER TURNBULL LIBRARY

(Top) **The kitchen at Piha fed thousands of meals to mill workers over the years.** (Above) **A kauri dam moments after being tripped. Dams were often built above waterfalls to increase the velocity of the water flow down the streambed, which would carry all felled timber downstream toward the sawmill at Piha.**

dropping down to Karekare at a gradient of 2.5:1 to the mill, was a similar track. At the top of the Piha hill, a brakeman controlled the whole operation. Two fully laden mill trolleys pulled an empty one up from the other side.

On a calm day in 1915, a new attempt was made to transport timber down the coast by towing bundled and sawn timber through the breakers by means of a steam barge. It was too difficult. The transfer of the timber from bullocks into surf ended in failure and was abandoned after a month of trying.

The Piha sawmill flourished between the years 1912 and 1921, boomtime for the timber industry. There were now over 30 mill cottages in the valley plus a schoolhouse and a large dining hall. The mill manager, Mr Hans Peter Knutzen, appears in many of the early photographs of mill days. Always well-dressed, this Dane with a bristling moustache, a cane and a bowler hat, had arrived in New Zealand aboard the brigantine *Seagull* and came to the coast after doing a stint on the Northland gumfields. Knutzen spoke five languages and was Rayner's confidante and advisor in all things milling. He sits proudly in the bush tram cab as it chugs along the Piha flat, carrying a load of timber destined for the wharf at Whatipu.

The machine was a Dubs A-class locomotive built in 1873 at the Dubs factory in Glasgow, Scotland, for New Zealand Railways. The loco was shipped to New Zealand and worked around the mills and then later Timaru and the central North Island area before coming north. Its heyday came in 1912 when it was sent to Auckland's wild west coast. There A-196 (it was originally A-62) chuffed and puffed along the stretch of track laid on sand to serve the Piha timber mill. For 10 years, as the surf whipped at the lines high on the trestles above the

GODBER ALBUM, COURTESY ALEXANDER TURNBULL LIBRARY

windy beaches, A-196 could be seen, tides allowing, with smoke billowing from its timber-fired stack, carrying its load along the tramway track.

Horse-power was used to get timber from the mill to the foot of the incline. The 'Sandfly' took the load further down the coast. From the Whatipu wharf, scows took the sawn kauri blocks up the harbour to Onehunga, where they were used for building in the rapidly growing city (many of the shops going up in Queen Street were made from west coast kauri), or to Dunedin or Sydney.

And although we tend to romanticise the beach railway, the reality was somewhat different. It was a nightmare of damaged trestles, floods and washouts. The mill employed gangs permanently working on sections of the railway, which was often out of action for weeks at a time. Yet before the mill and bush tram were retired, 14 million super feet or 33,000 cubic metres (1100 big rig truck and trailers) of kauri had been run through the huge four-metre saws of the Piha mill. Then A-196 went to the public works department in Wellington and was used by the Stores Board. It ended its long career at the Otahuhu railway workshops, shunting in the sidings. In 1954, A-196 was put on a concrete plinth there. Apprentices remember sitting on the loco at the workshop while they munched their sandwiches. When the workshops closed, Jack Ryder of Avondale talked them into letting him restore it. It's still in his shed.

Rayner's company was taken over by New Zealand Railways just before the First World War, and by then the coast was 'free' of the kauri forest that had clothed the hills and valleys for a thousand years. Rayner, a remarkable business-man to the end, registered the Piha Development Company two years before his death in 1930. Before Rayner, a Dr Stockwell owned the Piha Estate, a vast

GODBER ALBUM, COURTESY ALEXANDER TURNBULL LIBRARY

(Top) **A-62, later A-196, is re-assembled at Piha after being transported in parts from the Whatipu wharf. Some 66 km of tramways were constructed to transport timber to the 23 sawmills which operated in the Waitakere Ranges at different times.**
(Above) **Kauri logs from Anawhata Valley were taken down this tramline, along the back of North Piha Beach, and up Piha Valley to the mill.**

(Right) *Mid-Beach, Piha*, a 1988 acrylic painting by Don Binney. (Below) Piha potter and surfer Zeke Wolf with friend. (Lower) Wolf uses coastal imagery and colours in his work.

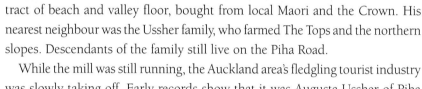

tract of beach and valley floor, bought from local Maori and the Crown. His nearest neighbour was the Ussher family, who farmed The Tops and the northern slopes. Descendants of the family still live on the Piha Road.

While the mill was still running, the Auckland area's fledgling tourist industry was slowly taking off. Early records show that it was Augusta Ussher of Piha Farm, who bought a section of bush which contains the beautiful Kauri Grove Track from the Sharp family of Karekare in 1886 and through it formed a new road down to Piha. Her idea was to open the Piha area for 'visitors'. The old road to the coast was always difficult for wagons and traps to negotiate. One of the reasons was that it first crossed a major swamp and later went up 'Breakneck' at the beginning of the Huia Ridge Track. It is still there today, starting just inside the Lone Kauri Road. Before the Piha Road dropped down to the Piha Valley, it passed the giant lone kauri which gives its name and legend to the road winding through the farm towards Karekare Beach. The Ussher Road to Piha also opened up the kauri to mill. These trees had never been logged because of lack of access to the valley below.

As milling commenced and the forest rolled back, tourists were invited to enjoy the healthy coastal air. 'Ozone blown from the sea' was a catch-phrase which worked well. To visit the west coast for recuperation was also considered to be compensation for the gruelling ride from Waikumete. In 1896, £400 was given by Government for the tourist industry. Visitors were invited to enjoy the great kauri forests of the ranges and the vistas of the coast along the way. Painters and writers journeyed to Piha, sketching, painting and versifying the glory of its many moods. In 1903 Augusta, in a generous moment, offered her block to the government, providing it was placed in reserve as a public park. The government of the time seized the opportunity, bought it for £90 and promptly forgot about it. It was not until 1905 that it was finally gazetted and then listed under the new Ministry of Tourism and Development. Not surprisingly, it was intended that Piha would be developed as a resort area for New Zealand. Piha was an acquired taste –

AUCKLAND ART GALLERY TOI O TAMAKI. GIFT OF MR E. VAILE, 1904

not everyone took to it. The seas were often high and treacherous, people got swept out, many drowned, and the accommodation house Ocean View, a part of which still stands at 167 Piha Road, by Te Ahu Ahu Road junction, was never five star.

The big attraction for the early tourist was the famous Blowhole. In Maori legend, the Blowhole and the Piha Gap were claimed in ancient times to be the lair of the fabled taniwha Kaiwhare. This massive sea creature was finally snared in the net by the warrior chief Hakawau, the thrashing about of its tail levelling the land between the Blowhole and Taitomo Island.

At Piha in 1910, the first boat launched on the coast was taken through the breakers by two venturesome youths, sons of the timber mill managers, Nicholas Gibbons and Henry Roe. It was reported in *The New Zealand Herald* that they attempted this extremely difficult feat and returned safely with a good haul of fish. The boat, a small wooden cutter, finished up its working life on the Bethells Lake, used by guests of the lodge. This coast is not for pleasure boating.

As more tourists came to visit the west coast, the enterprising Ted Le Grice, who owned a piece of land where the Piha store now stands, built a new boarding-house from timber salvaged from the derelict mill houses. The four buildings that made up the accommodation were given grand names – Regal, Roxy, Royal and Regent. The Brownes of Karekare moved to Piha, leased the block and did a roaring trade with tourists through to 1940.

The Piha Surf Life Saving Club was founded in 1934 with 12 members, including Frank Ross and Laurie Wilson and the brothers Bert, Stan and Cliff Holt. Within four years, it had grown to 35 members who had rescued 90 persons and delivered first aid to over 250. The clubhouse was built in 1935 on a section of beachfront sandhills donated by the Piha Estate. It was surfing which put Piha on the map.

(Top) *The Gap, Piha, West Coast,* 1904, oil on canvas by Frank Wright and Walter Wright. (Above) The Tasman swell surges into the Gap and lagoon beyond.

THE 1939 PIHA FIRE

A flaming con job

(Above) **An arsonist's weaponry.**
(Opposite) **The Piha fire made headlines in** *The Auckland Star, The Weekly News* **and in** *The New Zealand Herald*. **The media failed to detect anything suspicious.**

OF ALL the strange events on the west coast, the Piha bach fire is one of the most interesting. Many of the old-timers still recall the night of 11 February 1939 when the fire broke out. The bach, which stood at the corner of Sylvan Avenue and the Piha Road in the grove of puriri trees, was well ablaze when the members of the Piha Surf Lifesaving Club arrived to help. James Talbot, one of two Australians who had rented the cottage for the weekend, was racing around in great distress. His companion was inside and beyond rescue. Within minutes the fierce heat made a rescue attempt futile. It was soon a pile of hot embers and flat iron.

Naturally the locals were deeply distressed and as dawn broke on the morning of Sunday 12 February, the scene was truly tragic. A few bones were found but the fire had been so intense that fragments were welded to the bed in which his unfortunate travelling companion Mr Gordon McKay had apparently been burnt to a cinder. Talbot was able to return to Auckland later on the Sunday. He was given some money from a whip-around by the Piha residents. It was presumed that the fire was caused by Mr McKay smoking in bed or overturning a kerosene lamp. At that stage there were no suspicious circumstances, although Betty Hansen of Piha, who watched the fire, tells me that everyone was talking about the intensity of the blaze.

A coroner's inquest was held in Auckland on the Monday morning and after evidence had been heard, it was adjourned *sine die*. The human remains were buried at the Waikumete Cemetery. Only three people were present, including Mr Talbot, who carried a wreath and looked greatly upset.

Later news from Australia revealed the existence of insurance policies for approximately £40,000. The Auckland police began investigations at the request of an Auckland solicitor acting for Australian solicitors, who wanted careful enquiries made to ensure that Mr McKay had indeed been burned to death at Piha. Detective-sergeant F.N. Aplin went to Piha to investigate the fire and he was struck by the degree of burning of both building and body. As the building was only of asbestos sheeting with a corrugated iron roof, he became suspicious.

When sieving debris at Piha, Aplin found the remains also of many articles that had belonged to McKay including parts of a razor, suitcase hinges, a signet ring, buttons from his suit which had been made by a Sydney tailor, and other incidental articles.

The remains that had been found in the fire, supposedly McKay's, were exhumed and further examined by a pathologist. A small ball of cotton wool was found lodged in the palate bones. This indicated that the body had been laid out after death by an experienced person, and so certainly was not McKay's. The evidence also suggested that the remains were from a body which had been dismembered. The police obtained a list of persons who had been recently interred in the Auckland district. They then visited every cemetery from Helensville to Bombay, taking samples of clay from each recent grave.

On 11 March 1939, when the police opened the grave of Mr Patrick Henry Shine at the Waikumete Cemetery, they discovered that the body had been stolen from its coffin. This was the body which had burned in the bach at Piha.

Talbot was arrested by the police the same day as the exhumation, but it was not until 25 March that McKay was caught hiding in Grafton. He had attempted to disguise himself by growing a beard.

Brought to trial, both men were found guilty on charges of interfering with a dead body and of arson. The jury found them not guilty of attempting to defraud a Sydney insurance company. McKay was sentenced to four years' gaol and Talbot to two years. It had been alleged that they took the body in an attempt to report McKay's death and claim insurance on his life. Ironically, Patrick Shine was a New Zealander who had served in the Australian Army during the First World War. He was interred for the third time in Waikumete Cemetery, where his headstone can be seen today, close to the cenotaph.

COURTESY AUCKLAND AND STAR

BURNED TO DEATH.

SYDNEY VISITOR.

COMPANION SUFFERS SHOCK.

£233 IN NOTES DESTROYED.

A man was burned to death in a fire which destroyed a bach at Piha early yesterday morning, and a companion, who had to dash from the blazing building to save his life, suffered from shock. The victims were:—

Mr. Gordon Robert McKay, aged 43, married with five children, a fruit pre-
...Street, Burwood

FATAL FIRE

AUSTRALIAN VICTIM

COMPANION'S ESCAPE

DESTRUCTION OF BACH

£230 IN NOTES BURNED

An Australian visitor was burned to death in a fire which destroyed a bach at Piha early yesterday morning. He was a married man with five children, his family still being in Sydney. A companion, also an Australian, was unable to attempt a rescue and had to flee the blazing building to

COURTESY NEW ZEALAND HERALD

DEATH IN COTTAGE

Australian Visitor at Piha

COMPANION'S NARROW

An Australian visitor was burned to death in a fire which destroyed a bach at Piha early on Sunday morning. He was a married man with five children, his family still being in Sydney. A companion, also an Australian, was unable to attempt a rescue and had to dash from the blazing building to save his own life. The victim was:—

Mr. Gordon Robert McKay, aged 43, a fruit preserver, of 15 Selbourne Street, Burwood, Sydney.

Mr. McKay, who had been in Auckland less than a week, had taken £200 in Australian banknotes with him to Piha, and the whole amount was lost

At about ... awakened ... sound and ... need some ... other bed ...

When ... bot found flames ... through the panelling. Realising the need for quick action, he thrust open the door in the hope of dragging McKay to safety, but was immediately driven back by a wall of flame. The heat singed Mr. Talbot's face and cloth ing as he staggered back to safety, by the time he had escaped from the bach, a four-roomed wood and iron building, it was burning fiercely.

...To Ch...

COURTESY AUCKLAND WEEKLY NEWS

COURTESY AUCKLAND PUBLIC LIBRARY

(Top) **The Duke of Gloucester opened the Piha clubhouse, Christmas Day, 1935.**
(Middle) **Former ranger John Byers.**
(Above) **Piha takeaway king Bon Kryeziu.**

When the first American board riders, Californian lifeguards Rick Stoner and Bing Copeland, announced they proposed to ride waves on their nine foot long balsawood Malibu boards, the surf club got ready for a rescue, especially when they saw the visitors go under waves on their way out through the surf. Ridicule turned to astonishment when the two displayed how manoeuvrable their boards were with the rudder at the back. In the 1930s, surf club members had had plywood boards, and although they could stand on these, they could not control them. The surf-ski with paddle was developed by club member Don Wright, who was the national champion for many years. Rick and Bing started manufacturing boards from the surf club, while other boards were imported from Australia.

By the next summer, there were about a hundred boards around New Zealand. Piha club member Peter Byers bought Rick and Bing's equipment when they returned to the States, and made his custom surfboards at a workshop in Valley Road until the mid-1970s. This was when the craze of surf riding started in a big way. It was to grow with the years and the generations. The boards got smaller, the number of riders multiplied. On a good day, 500 surfers will be in the water, taking the left-handers off the Camel, for here in the small Piha bay the surf is truly magnificent. It is helped by the bar, a sand shelf which stands the swells up and rolls them shoreward. The swift Patiki Rock rip takes you swiftly out towards the big swells and a good board rider can easily paddle to the centre of the beach for a great ride towards shore.

The surf rescues are numerous and this club often holds the New Zealand surf rescue record. On a bad day, mass rescues are the norm. Now with the new clubhouse, their third in sixty-odd years, the local surf club goes from strength to strength. In the mid-1970s the helicopter service was trialled here at Piha Beach, starting with a small farm helicopter, modified so lifeguards (of which I was one) could plunge from the inflated pontoon into the surf below. You clutched a neoprene tube which you then affixed both to the desperate swimmer and to a rope dangling from the helicopter, before the pilot counted to 20 and lifted the patient and hopefully you, clinging to both victim and rope, towards the shore and safety.

A year later, with his aircraft fitted with strange-looking rear underview mirrors, the pilot could see the action in the water. It was the beginning of high-tech rescue work. Pioneering lifeguarding paid off. The rescue helicopter became a regional institution and sadly, because of cost with the new jet helicopter, no longer services the surf beaches except during major emergencies.

COURTESY AUCKLAND PUBLIC LIBRARY

At Piha, a rescue jetboat fleet was used for 10 years but proved unsatisfactory as it was too heavy to launch and chancy in big dumping surf. Now inflatable rescue craft can pluck a number of people out of the water within minutes. These boats are used extensively at Piha and along the coast, with 70 percent of all rescues.

As a teenager I spent many happy evenings at Piha. In those days there was a picture theatre, crowded on a Saturday night, no one paying much attention to the screen. The store, then the centre of Piha's community, still sells ice creams and beach supplies, and acts as a meeting spot for everyone under 20.

Piha is the Bondi Beach of the west coast. The rich and famous have their weekend houses there. No one talks of a bach at Piha any more. As the prices skyrocket, the old-timers either die or move out. It is a pity, but I'm sure before long the first of the top-class international resorts will be built here, a hundred years after the government thought it would be an ideal site.

In March, the marlin are running off Piha Beach. On one of his days off in 1992, Andy Pedersen, the local ranger, pulled in a 125 kg striped beauty, one kilometre offshore. Its massive mounted head dominates the staircase of the Piha Surf Club.

There's plenty more where that came from. Every year in late February the Counties Fishing Club, based on the Manukau, heads off over the bar for black marlin and yellowfin tuna. In late autumn, the surf off Piha can be as flat as Auckland's sheltered inner city beaches.

While I'm swimming out to sea with my mates off Karekare, enjoying the warm water, it's heartening to know that up to 200 anglers are into the annual shark fishing contest. In 1997 the winner was an 11-year-old with a potential world record haul of a 200.2 kg bronze whaler. From the top of Lion Rock, I've watched the birds and dolphins feeding on shoals of bait fish. To me, this always indicates that there are large fish underneath.

Nick Kinghorn, longtime surf lifeguard and now maitre d' and bar manager at the Piha Surf Club, heads out in his seven-metre runabout to pull in yellowfin tuna and the occasional marlin, to serve to patrons at the club restaurant.

In the summer, the water temperature off the west coast creeps up to around 20°C. Whales, dolphins and some sharks find it appealing. There is a deep trench off the Kaipara, but the coastline flattens closer to the surf break. I remember once jumping off a surf-ski onto the back of a basking shark. Dolphins, enjoying the small surf of mid-summer, will come into the rolling breakers and catch waves with style, just to show how it should be done.

(Top) **Camping out on Piha Domain, 1935.**
(Middle) **Piha author and activist Sandra Coney and her mother Doris Pearce.**
(Above) **Park ranger Craig Lupton.**

(Top) **North Piha Beach, looking south.**
(Above) **Remarkable rock formation in a
cliff-face at the southern end of Piha.**
(Previous Page) **West coast sunsets are too
often missed by day visitors leaving early.**

The camping ground and the tennis courts are a Piha summer institution, dating back over 60 years. The council has banned alcohol over the Christmas period, following three alcohol-related deaths of young people. For many years, drinking and hooning up has been part of the wild Piha nightlife. As for the holiday period now, it's become a real problem as fast cars and the closeness of Auckland's expanding western suburbs brings Piha a mere 20 minutes from Henderson.

Much of the social life is around the Piha Surf Club, with its legendary lifeguards and heroics in both surf and cliff rescue. It was here that Tom Pearce and his rugby mates, who played for Auckland in winter and became lifeguards in summer, brought the first surf boat to New Zealand. The Banana Boat, as it was called, was the forerunner of New Zealand surf boats, although more snapper were caught from the boat than lives saved. It started the sport of surf boat competition in New Zealand. The Banana Boat was bought second-hand from a Sydney club and served its purpose well, training the 'greats' of the Piha teams.

The Piha Surf Club boat crew won the first national surf boat championships held at Wellington's Lyall Bay in 1940. The winning team was Tom Pearce (steersman), Haydn Way (second oar), Ronnie Foubister (third oar), Eddie 'Tiger' O'Brien (stroke) and Max Cleary (bow). This amazing crew stayed together for 13 straight years. On the wall of the new clubhouse, one of the finest in the country, is a photograph of the surfboat leaping skywards through a monstrous Tasman roller.

The United Surf Club at North Piha also does great service every summer.

The club is an amalgamation of the old North Piha Club, founded soon after the war, and the now defunct Browns Bay Club, whose members were looking for a new home and bigger surf to keep them happy.

At the far end of the bay there are two large caves. They are dangerous because of falling rocks from the cliffs above, which have unfortunately taken the lives of three people over the years. There are warning signs posted, but from time to time they are burnt at beach parties, so it pays to be wary, particularly after rain.

The northern end of Piha has been the scene of many tragic and miraculous surf rescues. For the unwary swimmer caught in the rips that sweep out to sea, there is little hope of survival without flippers or the courage and strength to swim well out into the Tasman and then head for the safety of the main beach. It's best to take extra precautions on this section of the coast.

Les Mills, Mayor of Auckland and former champion shot putter, has holidayed with his wife Colleen over Christmas for the last 30 years in a small bach behind the surf club. There are two large carparks at the end of the beach and an excellent picnic area maintained by the council. It's a very accessible getaway, yet you can find seclusion and quiet without difficulty.

Over summer, Piha Beach is usually very hot and crowded, so you will probably want to escape to North Piha. Barnett Hall, the centre of this 'other Piha', was built by the North Piha Ratepayers Association, a hard-working group who also constructed the well-designed, unobtrusive surf club next door. For the last 50 years North Piha has used a communally-owned water supply for residents. Around 80 people and the camping ground draw from massive holding

(Top) **The classic view of Lion Rock as seen from Piha Road.** (Above) **North Piha Beach towards Te Waha Point in late afternoon, viewed from Lion Rock.**

tanks on a hill 53 metres above sea level. The original U.S. Army mains piping is starting to show its age. The water is taken from both the Marawhara and Wekatahi streams and over the next few years the community will upgrade their equipment as fires accidentally started by the large numbers of surfers and overnight revellers are a constant worry.

Barnett Hall holds all the surf parties over Christmas and a big New Year's Eve party. It was named after Tom Barnett, who owned a house in nearby Garden Road. No one seems to know how he came to have the hall named after him, as his reputation was earned growing gladioli and dahlias. Perhaps he is honoured because of the substantial financial contributions he made to the building project.

There has always been a bit of rivalry between the local ratepayers associations on the coast at Piha and in the early 1980s the two groups finally merged, which was a major event for the community. They now call themselves the Piha Community Centre Society. It is an impressive tag, but not much changed. They have taken over four years to select a site for the new toilet block and another two years to decide what colour it should be painted. There is one thing about Piha: nothing comes easy and the community always insists on having its say on all things big and small, to the bitter end.

I always enjoy the run up the Glen Esk Valley. It's a short drive or jog from the bottom of the Piha hill. The name derives from Glen Ness in Scotland, but apparently got mixed up. It often appears incorrectly on maps. The road finishes by the stream at a picnic area known as the Riverina, and is the scene every New Year's Eve for a traditional west coast ritual. For over 30 years the members of the Piha and Karekare Surf Clubs have met here for a drinking and initiation ritual, which goes a bit like this:

Junior club members were not permitted to drink until they were 18, when they took over full patrol membership, and not before they had shinned up a nearby cabbage tree. No women were ever permitted at Riverina, and nor are they even today. Every New Year's Eve the tradition continues. The tree is about eight metres high, and after a few drinks that is not easy. Over the years a few have fallen without injury to the bush below. Finally a large silver tankard appears which takes a pint and a half and does the rounds of the club members. Lately it's been in fashion to skull it naked, which would have horrified the old-timers. It all finishes good naturedly as the sun goes down.

If you are not into this kind of thing, the area leads to a beautiful track up the valley to the Kitekite Falls. Continue up this track, now named after the local Byers family, and soon you will reach the Piha Road, where you can either return on the same track, or walk the road back, enjoying the views of the coastline. It's a good hour and well worth it.

Piha Walks

1. The Gap

This is the attraction that made Piha famous. At low tide walk south along the cliff rocks of the beach till you arrive at the Gap. Wild weather guarantees huge ocean surf as the waves break through the entrance. The small rocky outcrop is known as the Wedding Cake. The lagoon in front was the home of the legendary Piha taniwha. At low tide you can also explore the passage beneath Taitomo Island and come out

(Above) **Lone bugler sounds *The Last Post* from Lion Rock at Anzac Day ceremony.** (Opposite) **Led by a pipe band, war veterans and visitors retreat to Piha RSA after the annual Anzac parade.**

(Top) **Taitomo Island with the Gap at centre left.** (Above) **United Club captain Mike Lake drinks from the captain's mug during New Year's Eve surf club ritual at Riverina.** (Opposite Lower) **Clubbie Trent Kinghorn up the cabbage tree.**

near the rock known as the Stack. Surfers and fishermen use this cave to gain access to the ocean.

2. Tasman Lookout

At the southern end of Piha is a breathtaking lookout over the Tasman, reached by taking the steep track which starts from the boulders rising from the ancient pohutukawa trees. The pathway hits the lungs, the thighs, and sometimes the nerves – but what a view from the top! It encapsulates Piha: the endless surf and its worshippers; the red and yellow surf patrol flags, the lagoon, the black sand, the bush-bound hills with the baches clinging improbably to the slopes, with the Tasman stretching to the horizon until the eyes ache. It's a 30-minute return journey to the lookout.

3. Lion Rock Track

This ancient pa site is worth the steep climb. The track is stepped and fenced to ensure safety to the top. Take care; it's not suitable for young children. Allow an hour there and back. An emotional place to visit on Anzac Day, when locals pay homage to veterans of the wars. A march led by pipers starts at 2 pm from the RSA to the Rock and back.

4. Horoeka Track

This beautiful, easy track drops off the Piha Road, 600 metres after the turnoff to Karekare Road, before the Te Ahu Ahu Road. It follows a steepish spur, initially in bush, down the northern side of the valley. Further on, the track

PIHA WALKS

TE WAHA POINT

LOOKOUT

NORTH PIHA

KAIWHARE POINT

NUN ROCK

TAITOMO ISLAND

TAKATU HEAD

Blowhole

THE GAP ①

② TASMAN LOOKOUT TRACK

PIHA

LION ROCK ③ TRACK

SURF CLUB

NORTH PIHA ROAD

WHITE TRACK

Site of WWII Radar Station

SURF CLUB

GARDEN ROAD

Marawhara Stream

LOG RACE ROAD

AHUAHU ROAD

PIHA ROAD

GLEN ESK ROAD

Piha Stream

HOROEKA ④ TRACK

KITEKITE TRACK ⑤

Glen Esk Stream

KAREKARE ROAD

KITEKITE FALLS ✕

⑥ PIHA VALLEY TRACK

TO PIHA GORGE

McKENZIE TRACK

offers wonderful views south over the Karekare Valley, Mount Zion and the large fortified cave of the early Maori above the Opal Pools. For this walk, allow about 30 minutes.

5. Kitekite Track

The awesome three-tiered Kitekite Falls drop 40 metres in a shower of spray – too high for the West Coast Timber Company, which built the Glen Esk Dam at the top of the falls. The drop over the falls damaged many of the logs. This popular, easy walk will take you 45 minutes one way.

6. Piha Valley Track

Piha rewards effort. Tramp, scramble, or stream-bash up the valley to a spectacular canyon of conglomerate rock soaring over 30 metres above the bushline! Beginning from the end of Glen Esk Road, this level track follows the right-hand side of the Piha Stream past the McKenzie Track junction for about 30 minutes, then the left-hand branch veers off into the lower end of the Piha Gorge, while the main track ascends sharply to Centennial Track and the remains of Black Rock Dam. Revel in the high cliff-faces, but watch your step on the rocks and in the stream. Allow two to three hours.

THIS SPORTING COASTLINE

Making tracks

(Above) **Style is everything in surfing contests. Piha delivers the waves.** (Opposite Top) **Crossing Little Huia ford in the Head-To-Head Triathlon.** (Opposite Lower) **Competition was brutal in The Ultimate Challenge.**

EVERY YEAR there are more sporting contests on the west coast, and more sporting codes. The surf and the bush trails offer infinite possibilities. After the no-contest counterculture excesses of the 1960s, the Christian surfers headed west to Piha in the 1970s to immerse themselves in the Easter swells. It was a celebration of the ocean and the surfing goodlife. Gone were the drugs and the booze. Instead here was a three-day homage to Good Clean Living. A huge striped tent dominated the camping ground and after two days of competition the Sunday service was a feast of music and prayer.

If the Piha regulars scoffed at first, they were amazed at the transformation this Christian revival brought to the coast. The first professional surfing circuit saw clothing and surf gear manufacturers courting a young market with money to spend on style, hero-worship and a sport that was more a lifestyle than simply a weekend pastime.

At Piha surfing contests are now regular events. You'll often see 150 competitors vying for honours, either edging out for the big ones at the back or catching the rides, peeling off from the Camel. It makes you long to be 17 again.

During the 1990s the Head-to-Head Triathlon grew in popularity. It's an epic contest that starts at the entrance to Manukau Harbour at Whatipu Beach. The first leg is a run over the saddle and down to Huia, where competitors take to their cycles for the slog along the Waitakeres to Christmas Beach on Herald Island. This is the changeover point, where they board kayaks or surf-skis for the leg down the Waitemata Harbour, under the Harbour Bridge to North Head for the final run leg to Narrow Neck Beach.

The race draws triathletes from all over New Zealand. I've had the honour of starting this race, but I've promised myself that when I get back into serious training, I'll compete instead of observing enviously.

On New Year's Day there is a race from Swanson that runs south-west. Known as the Waitakere Classic, it has a reputation as one of the toughest courses in the North Island. It's hell on the feet, a terrible grind over difficult tracks, but competitors still enthuse about it. There must be easier ways to enjoy the bush tracks than this.

For a number of years, the Karekare Surf Club promoted the Ultimate Challenge, a two-day event. The competitors biked the ranges from Swanson to Piha. When that was considered too easy, the Karekare incline was added to separate the sheep from the goats. The second day featured a swim around Paratahi Island followed by a run of around 50 kilometres of coastline tracks

(Top) **A break during the serious competition gives locals a chance to show off their strength.** (Above) **Kim Tunnell, gold and silver medallist, an outstanding competitor at many World Lifesaving Championships.**

to Muriwai Beach. Finally this race became too daunting and the event failed because of the unpredictability of the large surf off the island and the ever-present fear than someone would lose their life.

The Ultimate Challenge has been superseded by the International World Oceanman event at Piha, which brings together professional surf lifesavers from around the world. With a multi-million dollar budget, the 50 men and women compete in seven venues in four countries, in a multi-discipline event of beach sprinting, swimming, paddle boarding and kayaking. This event, the first on the circuit, is a true test of lifesaving skills and human endurance. It has a television audience estimated at over 500 million in more than 100 countries.

The Oceanman course on the beach and in the surf is daunting: 8.1 km for men and 3.5 km for women. The action is close to the spectators and in late autumn when the event is held, the west coast beaches are starting to feel chilly. In the inaugural race of 1997, a number of the competitors suffered from hypothermia, while others suffered cuts and bruises from rocks as they came to grief in the surf-ski leg.

The lifesaving clubs are regular competitors on the west coast. The IRB (Inshore Rescue Boats) Championships, where clubs show their skills in dismantling the motors of their inflatable rescue craft, then frantically re-assemble motor and craft to pick up a patient, is something worth watching. This event is held when patrolling has finished for the season. It is an example of teamwork under extreme pressure. In the face of sometimes colossal waves,

the driver must manipulate the boat, spinning it around to line up a stand-in victim who will be plucked on board if the bow-man gets the hold right. In a real-life rescue drama, this is the technique used to rescue swimmers, so it's in competitions like this that skills are fine-tuned.

The Super Dune, held annually at Bethells Beach, has to be one of the most gruelling events in the country. Organised by the Waitemata Canoe and Multisport Club, it starts at the Surf Club headquarters on a 42 km cycle around Te Henga Road and the Scenic Drive. Two loops, that is, followed by a 12 km run across farmland to O'Neill Beach and Lake Waimanu, where they complete five laps before sprinting for the tape back at the clubhouse. Held in April, this one is for the superfit, the best of who complete the course in a little over three hours.

The untamed coast offers challenging courses in wild New Zealand settings. Organisers have found locals willing to tolerate these sporting events, but the enormous amount of high-tech equipment and transmission gear that accompanies the major races, tends to make local authorities and the resident communities wary of too much of a good thing.

(Top and Above) **The 1997 inaugural World Oceanman Series had 50 of the best lifesavers in the world competing, including wildcard entrant Nathan Meyer of Australia, the 1996 World Ironman champion.**

TWO SMALL GEMS

Mercer Bay and White's Beach

(Above and Below) **Mercer Bay is visited only by the adventurous, on a precarious track down a near-vertical headland.** (Opposite) **Mercer Bay from Ahu Ahu Point. Ancient Maori pa site in foreground.**

MERCER BAY can be glimpsed from the north point of Karekare Beach. It is named after an early settler, slate-cutter Andrew Mercer, and not, as local legend would have it, after a honeymoon couple trapped by the tide. This small beach is reached by a looped track originating from Te Ahu Ahu Road, or alternatively, from the Karekare end up the Ahu Ahu track and down the middle of the saddle. The beach, almost covered by high tide, yields to the visitor only by way of an incredibly steep descent. So take care, first, to find the track; second, to stay on it. It can be dangerous.

It is best to take a route down the northern creek bed. Here a track follows the flax and scrub lava flow in the stream-bed at the end of the bay, close to Te Ahu Ahu Point. The old fishing track went down the centre of the bay. One section was an old wire over a rocky bluff. Scarcely stuff for the faint-hearted, this is now considered to be unsafe except for experienced locals. The northern descent takes about half an hour and is best attempted in summer, with the tide at its lowest and the stream dry.

Mercer Bay is a remarkable small gem of a beach, framed and buttressed by high cliffs at both ends. At the southern end, the high sea-carved rocks are home to a local shag colony and form the outer edge of Karekare's infamous Cauldron. The sea always seems rough, pierced by flat rocks rising from the

bull kelp. Large granite boulders fill all the small inlets; Mercer Bay, too small and closed out for surfers except for the odd day, is a beach-fossicker's paradise. Centuries of driftwood have accumulated in the gaps and crevices, and pieces of wrecks and the odd bottles and crabs can also be found.

The northern end of the cove has marvellous secrets to reveal. A large sea-cave, Te Ana areare, or "the cave with the cavernous or vaulted interior", perfectly tunnelled through the headland, offers a wonderful experience for the adventurous. To be entered only at extreme low tide, the black abyss eventually reveals a dull light and a concealed black sandy beach. High above are secondary ledges which were used by Maori in ancient times as a refuge. On one of these platforms in the early 1930s, Will Browne of Karekare found two exquisite whalebone combs. The year before, in company with the renowned artist and *Herald* cartoonist Trevor Lloyd, he had discovered in a cave at the Pararaha Valley one of the finest collections of fishing hooks and small stone sinkers in New Zealand, intact in a decayed flax kite. The collection forms a major part of the Maori fishing collection in the Auckland Museum display.

COURTESY HILLARY FAMILY COLLECTION

Do not attempt to walk this tunnel in anything but dead low water. At half tide, surges of high velocity pour through and endanger life, but at low water you may enter with relative safety and emerge at the other end inside the mammoth dome, holding inside its cavernous interior a hidden beach. This cave is as big as St Peters, and known as Cathedral Cave. It is one of the largest on the New Zealand coastline: 120 metres high with a perfect hole in its dome.

(Top) *Te Ahu Ahu Headland,* Jean Loomis, 1964. (Above) **Sir Edmund Hillary relaxing at the family bach above White's Beach, 1973. (Opposite) Rose Cottage is hidden amongst the Pohutakawa trees above White's Beach.**

Over the centuries, sand has filtered down through the roof hole to create a remarkable sand-dune within the interior. Unless the tide is right, you have to swim into Cathedral Cave, so a wetsuit is useful for buoyancy, warmth and protection against rocks. When exiting the cave hold onto the walls, and you'll soon be out on Mercer Bay beach again.

Above the beach is a beacon light which sweeps the sea at night. This was the site of New Zealand's longest-serving radar station, which operated from 1942 to 1952, with a range of 200 miles (320 km) out into the Tasman. The foundations of the many huts are a silent record of the 100 people, including my mother, who served here during the war. The huts of Piha No.4 Radar Station were demolished in 1956.

(Above) **White's Beach as seen from the Signal Box Lodge, Anawhata Road. The kauri signal box, which served Waitakere Station for 80 years, was used as a bach before its transformation into today's luxury accommodation.**

WHITE'S BEACH is named after early farmer, translator and author John White, one of the most fascinating characters of colonial New Zealand. White's Beach is tucked between Te Waha Point (the large ancient pa site to the north of Piha), and Fisherman's Rock on the south side of Anawhata.

It can be reached by the Rose Track, which branches from Anawhata Road down a concrete driveway on private property, or else by the Laird Thomson Track which climbs steeply up the headland from the northern end of North Piha. Thomson was a tramper and mountaineer and one of the leading spirits in a group of west coast walkers who called themselves the Sundown Strollers. He founded the Alpine Sports Club and later, with his neighbour Jim Rose (Ed Hillary's father-in-law), they bought land overlooking North Piha and White's Beach. In later life, they generously donated land on the peninsula which divides the two beaches. The steep and narrow Laird Thomson Track soon gives you not only a view of White's Beach, but one of the best views of the main Piha Beach and the northern bay, which on early maps is shown as Kohonui Bay.

White's Beach always works curiously on me. It's a series of paradoxes, accessible yet secluded, beautiful yet rugged, intimate and contained yet wild and free. Perhaps it's to do with the vegetation – hardy coprosma sculpted by the prevailing westerlies, toi toi, marram grass – that grips the steep descent to

the beach from Anawhata Road. Or perhaps it's the few beach houses. Diminished by the bush and the grandeur of the landscape, they hug the slope high above the beach, windblown and weathered. Prison escapee George Wilder, who held a New Zealand escape record, hid out in them, leaving thank you notes as he went. One is still preserved on a cupboard door.

The two headlands jutting into the Tasman provide views of the towering cliffs and the kelp beds which flourish below. The sea off the points is full of mullet and kahawai, which explains the profusion of gannets, shags, and black-backed gulls. The descent is not as arduous or nerve-wracking as at Mercer Bay, but it's still a long way down and back. Wear shoes with a decent grip. White's Beach is best at low tide. When the tide is high, it's better to avoid the coastal route and the shorter descent to the rocks from the Laird Thomson Track, in favour of going on up the ridge, meeting the Rose Track, then following it down to the dunes behind the beach. At the northern end, at dead low tide, a scramble round the rocks will reveal caves, one clogged with timber. It's possible to trek around the rocks to Anawhata. Take care, and check your tide-tables.

With luck you'll have the beach to yourself. Nowhere near Auckland is there a beach with clearer water or with a feeling of exhilaration so sharp and so pure.

ANAWHATA

The lovers' ladder

(Above) **High tide surges around Parera Point, framing Keyhole Rock in the distance. (Opposite) Isolated and pristine, Anawhata Beach can only be reached on foot by a steep track from the end of Anawhata Road, or by splashing down the Anawhata Stream.**

THERE is no road access down to Anawhata Beach. The winding, dusty metal road just stops. So climb over a wooden gate and walk down a long, steep but well-kept track to the beach below. You have to trudge back up again, but don't be put off; this small beach is worth every gasp.

Appearing on very early maps as 'Arawhata', it has a rich history. Dividing the main beach is Parera Point, a small headland that crouches into the surf between the small southern bay and the main beach. From the ancient Maori comes a very special love tale of this place. On the headland there stood a small fortified pa. Across the Mobbs Stream, which still keeps to the old beach-flow patterns, is a long line of shelter caves which were used for living and sleeping. Long ago, it was the setting for an elopement. A young Maori woman of this beach, forbidden to meet her lover from Piha, escaped into his arms by scaling a plaited rope that had been lowered to her from the cliff-top. It must have been quite a climb and some romance, as the cliffs rise up 40 metres or so from the beach below.

Some of these old love stories have a habit of ending somewhat less happily. Te Kawerau a Maki settled in this very fertile valley with the spectacular gorge beyond, but were later driven from their cave shelters and the headland pa by Ngati Whatua in a succession of 18th century raids. The survivors of these battles no doubt would return after a time of hiding out in the forest and take up where they had left off, although fewer in number. They were finally ousted by Turehu's Ngapuhi musket-wielding warriors about 1826.

In 1854 the Anawhata Valley and surrounding hills went as a land package to the Governor of New Zealand as part of the huge Pao o Te Rangi block, bought from a few displaced and disputed iwi for a mere £800 sterling. The new owners were settler farmers, who were granted land in allotments of 40 acres (16 hectares) for each adult and 20 for each child in the family. They in turn found the impossibly steep terrain overwhelmed their energies and resources and thwarted attempts to earn a living from the land. By the early 1860s, their labours exhausted, they had moved on.

Enter new landowners Francis and John White, who bought 600 acres (243 hectares) of land north of Te Waha Point, encompassing most of Anawhata. It seemed like better land, more sheltered from the westerly winds. Unfortunately this venture also failed and the family realised little from their investment, losing it in land mortgages to the New Zealand Mercantile Company, which then sold it to the McElwain family.

The McElwains, who knew something the others didn't, persevered with the

GODBER ALBUM, ALEXANDER TURNBULL LIBRARY

AUCKLAND INSTITUTE & MUSEUM

GODBER ALBUM, ALEXANDER TURNBULL LIBRARY

rugged land until 1917, accomplishing much in their time there. When they sold it to the Mobbs family, their legacy was some workable land, a woolshed, a three-bedroom house and some farm buildings. The Mobbs stuck it out for a mere six years. Before they left, they sold to Auckland University a piece of land for a tramping hut. This wonderful small hut still stands on the sheer precipice between White's and Anawhata, connected to the road by a small track.

A Mrs Harriet Colwill bought a large slice of the Anawhata property from Mr Mobbs in 1923. It was bounded to the south by the Anawhata Stream and to the north by Cannibal Creek. Mrs Colwill had a small concrete cottage built some distance up the Anawhata Stream, sheltered from the prevailing winds. Although larger and modernised, this cottage still stands, and is owned by the Forgie branch of the family.

Phyllis Rose (the mother of Louise Hillary) remembered a windlass worked by bullocks pulling the last of the timber out of the gulleys in the 1920s. The hill overlooking Piha was known then as Dead Horse Knob.

When I first went out to Anawhata in the mid-1960s, the land was again reverting to native forest. The buildings built by the McElwains were falling into disrepair and campers were using the old farmhouse for weekend stays. In the large beach caves, someone had fashioned sets of elegant furniture out of driftwood. Along the beach there was a string of army huts, used by holiday squatters. There is still a small cluster of them today. When their owners finally depart from this world, the huts will be removed for good.

A farmer, adventurer and crazy collector of vintage cars, Graham Craw, worked much of the valleys for 30 years. His passion for old Packards took him to every part of New Zealand and at one time he had assembled more than 50 of these gleaming monsters of the 1930s and 1940s, in a farm paddock above the beach. Later his museum on the Scenic Drive was a big attraction full of motors, machinery and junk. He sold a large area of bush high up the Anawhata Valley to a group of American truthseekers, the Laughing Man Institute, in the late 1960s. These good-natured people were intending to establish a retreat and learning centre on the block. But in the mid-1970s they were unceremoniously evicted from their holdings by the Waitemata County Council, who believed that the land should be returned to park status and joined to the Regional Council holdings. There is still some bad blood about the way this whole thing was handled.

The Anawhata hills above the gorge were considered by the millers to be difficult but workable, so large trees were designated for felling. The streams in the gorge were dammed by the mill companies. The trees were felled and rolled into more than a dozen holding and driving dams, the biggest in the ranges. Some of these substantial structures involved 50 or so bushmen in months of work before the dam was full of winter rain, then tripped to send the logs down the narrow gorge to the holding dam at the bottom of the Anawhata Incline. You can still find the remains of this holding dam about a mile up the gorge. Large holes were drilled and blown in the sides of the cliffs during construction of the dams. At Anawhata a bush tramway, built by New Zealand Railways, linked the Piha mill to the coastal milling network. It was a tough slog up the headland at North Piha. All the big timber was gone from Anawhata by 1916, so they settled for the smaller trees, cutting them at Burgeson's small sawmill until the late 1920s.

You may wish to check out the large caves high in the cliff-face. You will need some climbing skill, but they are of staggering proportion. You will find them at the back of the beach, up the main stream bed, about one kilometre from the cluster of huts. Here are two galleries, each 26m in length, situated one above the other, up on the 150m cliffs. The easiest way to approach these caves is from the stream below, but the ascent is almost sheer in places and the final narrow ledge that leads up to the lower gallery is not an easy climb. These caves must have been almost impregnable during the conflicts that raged through this area. They also have an advantage of being sheltered by the great waterfall, which tumbles to the valley below. There are many other caves in this cliff, but they can only be reached after a strenuous climb through tangled undergrowth, up the rock-faces. Here at Anawhata, you can get an idea of the harshness that would have faced Maori sheltering in these caves. Although these are not burial caves, which are always strictly tapu, they should be treated with great respect.

Pre-European New Zealand's largest pa site at Anawhata is known as Kuataika. This area is situated on a long ridge behind the Anawhata Beach, on a knoll, 264m above sea level. It is reported that in pre-colonial times, a track from Anawhata rose over the ranges to the Waitemata Harbour, following this ridge. No doubt the pa acted as an outpost for the settlement.

The two pa at Anawhata are smaller. Pukekowhai, a headland pa above the sea, is surrounded by steep cliffs on three sides. It must have been a fierce and daunting obstacle for warring factions. In the middens around the base, you will still find evidence of previous life on this site, but the earthworks of the defence have been all but obliterated by a century or so of farming.

(Above) **Anawhata Stream flows through a beach lagoon to the sea.** (Opposite Top) **Climbers bleed a kauri tree for gum, 1920.** (Opposite Middle) **Tripping of a dam on the Anawhata Stream unleashes logs into the gorge below. This was one of 91 kauri timber dams in the Waitakeres.** (Opposite Lower) **This 6 km tramline was built in 1916 to haul timber over the high ridge between Anawhata and Marawhara valleys to the mill at Piha.**

(Right) **Anawhata ceramic artist John Green of Fairygreen Studios has been crafting clay fantasies for 25 years.** (Below) *Biscuit chair*, **by John Green.** (Lower) *Jack*, **by John Green.** (Opposite Top) **Signal Box Lodge above White's Beach.** (Opposite Middle) **Old concrete cottage in a grassy clearing beside Anawhata Stream.** (Opposite Lower) **To reach the beach from remote Anawhata Gorge, a tramper wades around bluffs in the Anawhata lagoon.**

COURTESY HOWARD S. WILLIAMS

COURTESY HOWARD S. WILLIAMS

The other pa is Parera. Standing above the beach, you can still observe the terraces and pits with midden material on the site. As at all archaeological sites on the west coast, digging is strictly forbidden and these precious treasures should be treated with utmost care.

At Anawhata most weekends you will find no more than a dozen people on the beach. The surf here is often unpredictable and the rips can be hazardous. There is no lifeguard service on this beach. For many years there was a wooden reel and line under a cover on the headland, but vandals soon made this service pointless to continue by ruining the reel and using the cotton line for fishing. I used to take a rescue tube from Karekare each year and put it on a post for emergencies. Usually it disappeared within days and I finally gave it up.

There is still much to enjoy. It's a haven for day visitors who like solitude, spending their winter weekends walking among high cliffs and the raging westerlies.

Here at Anawhata, the beach and the bush remain places of unease. No one has lived in this place with comfort for long.

Anawhata Walks

1. Anawhata Beach Track
This short 700-metre track starts from the carpark, going over a gate and down a section of driveway to the track. Thirty leisurely minutes should see your way down to the beach, the last section being along the short creek-bed to the surf. Allow 40 minutes for the return. It's a steep metalled track, so award yourself a breather on the way up.

2. Rose Track
This excellent coastal track begins on a corner of the Anawhata Road, passing through private property down a concrete driveway. Branching right just before passing Rose Cottage, the track descends steeply to White's Beach. Cross the beach and continue to the northern end which leads to Fisherman's Rock Point. Two hours return.

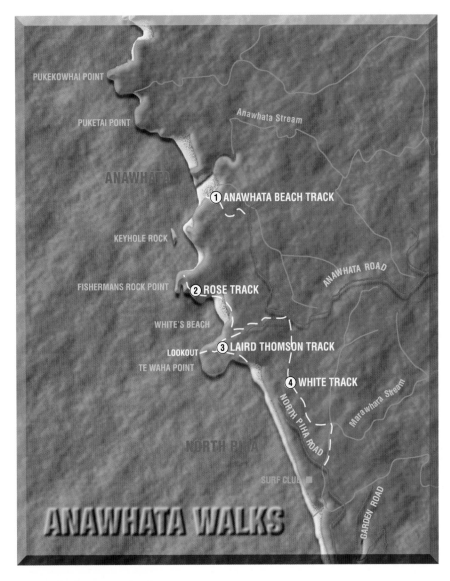

ANAWHATA WALKS

3. Laird Thomson Track

During the Second World War, as the Japanese threat loomed, the Anawhata hills were used to train commando troops. Headlands and beaches had dug-outs sandbagged, ready and waiting. Ken Hall of Swanson recalls the myriad of trails through the bush which were cut during four years of army training.

One trail is the Laird Thomson Track which leaves Rose Track, then briefly follows a private driveway before dropping down the ridge to Te Waha Point saddle. From here a short detour leads to a lookout over White's Beach. The main track descends steeply to the northern end of Piha Beach. Allow 20 minutes if descending, 35 minutes if ascending.

4. White Track

From the bridge on North Piha Road this steep track leaves the Marawhara Walk, and climbs above the beach through lush bush. The last section is up a private concrete driveway. Allow one hour to reach Anawhata Road. You could return the same way, or take the Laird Thomson Track past the seated lookout on Te Waha Point.

COURTESY RAYMOND SALISBURY

ISLANDS IN THE SURF

Lonely outcrops in the Tasman swell

(Above) **Whakaari or Lion Rock, Piha Beach.** (Right) **Paratahi Island, with Karekare Beach to left.**

THERE is always a fascination with islands. Although the islands off the west coast are often little more than rocky outcrops, remnants of forgotten volcanoes heaved from the ocean depths, they are still compelling. Pounded by the surf, they are a resting place for sea birds and for wintering seals. Some are covered in green, velvety moss and lichen, and in the crevices bloom the occasional succulents.

On this coast the sea has retreated from cliffs in relatively recent times. In the 19th century the Tasman roared into bays that today are peaceful glades of native bush behind the dunes. Taranaki Bay once had a number of rocky outcrops ideal for fishing and for gathering shellfish at low tide.

In 1865 an earthquake centred off the Waikato Heads may have sent tidal surges into the Maori coastal fishing settlements and kainga. The number of lives lost and the effects on the geography of the coastline were not documented by the early historians.

The rocky outcrops we call islands abound with mussels and other shellfish, unlike the rocks of the adjacent beaches, which have been stripped of their

bounty by the increasing numbers of visitors. On the islands, the shellfish float in beds of bull kelp with the exotic name *Durvillea antarctica*. Maori knew this kelp as rimurapa and used it both as food and as seasonal storage containers.

To reach the islands, you must pick the right day. The crumbling rock makes climbing dangerous. At Manukau Heads, the headland Paratutae (105 metres), is no longer an island as such, but you can climb its northern face, following the path that the signalmaster took to raise and lower the signal arms. Across the bay is our first island, Ninepin Rock, Toka tapu a Kupe, (5 metres), with a small shipping beacon atop. Cutter Rock is no longer an island, and has been used to teach abseiling. Now it is in the wetland area of Whatipu. At the base of the rock is said to lie hidden the *Orpheus* gold.

Paratahi Island (20 metres) lies a hundred metres off Karekau Point at Kare-kare. On the lowest tide, you can almost walk to the beautifully-shaped outcrop, surrounded by a deep channel, but you will still need a few quick swimming strokes in the channel.

The side facing the land rises straight out of the sea. The western face, hidden from view, is a large sloping shelf, great for fishing. The big winter surf cascades up and over the middle section of the island in big seas. Terns often nest here, while in winter, seals are seen sheltering on its northern foot. Often sick or tired, they're best left alone. An old leopard seal returned for a number of years, claiming the island as its own. Maori named this outcrop after the shark's tooth.

At Mercer Bay there are three rocky islands. The longest flat rock, off the Cauldron, has a beautiful sea pool on its top face. It provided a perfect landing for a hanglider pilot who missed a thermal and faced almost certain death from the surf. With the hanglider still attached, he clung to the rocky face until rescue came from the Karekare lifeguards, who swam the Cauldron and held him until the glider frame could be released. The rescue helicopter flew him and his rescuers to safety, while the rusting glider frame still rests at the bottom.

(Below from Left) **The Wedding Cake, the Nun, Taitomo Island, with the Gap at lower right.**

Closer to the cliffs is a beautiful outcrop that resembles the Sphinx, called Te Pungapunga. Up to the 1960s it had a large hole in its topmost crest, which has now broken away. It is the nesting place of the little shag and the odd muttonbird.

Taitomo Island at Piha is still in the ownership of Te Kawerau a Maki. Separated from land by the Gap to the north, this large island outcrop is the only remaining piece of coastal land of the Kawerau a Maki iwi, whose mana of the area is their heritage.

The Keyhole pierces Taitomo, the island known locally as the Camel, which can be entered and swum through on the right tide. Leaping thrillseekers have taken to jumping into the ocean from a towering rock called the Nun. On the right day you can have a choice of 5 metre, 10 metre or 20 metre ledges. There is a catch. There is no downward path from the Nun, so you must jump or spend the rest of your life marooned, albeit with a great view.

Piha's Lion Rock or Whakaari is a true island only on high spring tides. Over the years local councils have ensured the climb to the summit is a safe and pleasurable one, although it is still a tough slog. Some people have even been known to get married on its summit.

There have been several fires on the rock over the past few years and the tagger's mark is now evident here. Many people have been drowned while surf-casting from its base. A rockfall on its southern flank has somewhat marred its resting lion profile, which impressed the colonials enough to give it this name. Unfamiliar with lions, Maori saw the shape of a dying or crouching warrior.

(Below) **An ancient pa site, Parera Point at Anawhata was once an island.**

Parera Point at Anawhata, an ancient pa site in the middle of the beach, is no longer an island. Easy to climb, it is an ocean lookout and summer picnic spot.

Te Ihumoana Island at Te Henga is perhaps the most beautiful island on the coast. In private ownership now, this island was a fortified pa. The chief was killed close by, where the Waitakere River enters the Tasman Sea. His head was placed on a stake and subsequently his name Waitakere was bestowed on the river and ranges, and later the city and the parliamentary electoral district. There is no sign of the freshwater stream which is said to have flowed from the island in the past.

Kauwahaia Island lies just off the coast at O'Neill Beach, surrounded by turbulent surf. It is a nesting place for both terns and shag. From its sea face on the right tide you can collect abundant shellfish and cast for large snapper. Access to the island is dependent on the tides and surf conditions.

The islands at Bethells support colonies of grey-faced petrels. There are over 300 pairs. Mainland colonies on the west coast headlands have declined because of predation. The colony at Te Henga has been established for many years, and as access is extremely difficult, they get all the protection from people that they need.

Two islands at Muriwai are of major importance to the coastal environment and ecology. Motutara Island, separated from the mainland by a tidal moat, is one of 23 gannet colonies in New Zealand. All but three are on islands, with Muriwai itself being one of the exceptions. In the early 1980s, young birds from these islands spilled over to the adjacent mainland cliff-tops, forming two stable breeding colonies, overlooked now by two viewing platforms. The gannets cover the whole of the top surface with their nests and landing, feeding and courting strips. These magnificent birds are a joy to observe in their daily rituals.

(Below from Left) **Kauwahaia Island, Erangi Point and Te Ihumoana Island, Te Henga.**

Offshore is the largest island on the coast. Oaia Island is 30 metres high and is covered with a thick coating of bird droppings. Gannets also make their home here, sharing it with a large colony of seals who base their winter courtship and travelling cycle on this island. In the winter months, adults and pups are seen sunning or resting on the island. You'll need binoculars to see the wildlife, as the island is one kilometre from shore.

Oaia Island is the subject of Colin McCahon's 1972 painting *Moby Dick is sighted off Muriwai Beach*, a work inspired by the painter's response to the view out to sea from Muriwai, where he had a studio. This painting was featured on a New Zealand postage stamp in 1997, in a series honouring McCahon.

(Top) **Lone fisherman beneath the southern face of Paratutae Island, Whatipu. Ninepin Rock at centre left also marks entrance to the Manukau.** (Above) **Colin McCahon's painting *Moby Dick is sighted off Muriwai Beach* featured on a 1997 postage stamp.** (Opposite Top) **Keyhole Rock, Paikea Bay, Anawhata.** (Opposite Lower) **Oaia Island off Muriwai is the largest on the coast.**
STAMP REPRODUCED COURTESY NEW ZEALAND POST

CAUGHT ON FILM

Photographers of the coast

(Above) **Elle MacPherson on location, Karekare Beach, 1991.**

THE FIRST photographers arrived in New Zealand in the late 1840s. The process of getting an image onto a glass plate was protracted and difficult. Cameras were heavy, but there was great interest in the new technology because for the first time in history, the image of a person or a landscape could be captured as a permanent mirror image.

Yet few of these early photographers were interested in our landscape or even sunsets. Instead they set up studios, with painted backdrops, drapes and pot-plants, as there was money to be made photographing the wealthy, the fashionable and the famous. Like gypsies, they moved through the country towns recording the local dignitaries in a flash of magnesium.

As the towns grew into cities, photographers became a regular fixture in the main street and their subject matter broadened. The first great landscape photographers were the Burton Brothers, who had talked themselves into recording the surveying expeditions of the King Country, and photographed the Whanganui River and local Maori. The brothers recorded bush settlements, mills, farms and picnickers. Photography was coming to be regarded as a record of our memories, of good times and celebration.

In Auckland some of the early photographers headed west. In the 1880s Daniel Louis Mundy took his camera and chemicals and using his collodion and wet plate process, sensitised each negative on the spot, completing the processing later in his small, darkened tent. Mundy photographed the countryside, selling first edition prints of his plates which he either framed or bound into attractive hand-made leather albums.

From 1905 the entrepreneurial Frederick George Radcliffe toured the west coast, photographing streams, glades, houses and settlers. He sold large framed sepia first edition prints of these images. To the boarding-house proprietors at Whatipu, Karekare and Piha, he sold neatly-mounted postcard six-packs of the area. He was not beyond retouching water lillies or adding the odd flower to a hat. Radcliffe's legacy is an astonishing 7000 glass plate negatives of New Zealand scenic beauty.

Albert Percy Godber was born in Wellington in 1875 and spent all his working life with the railways, mostly at Petone. He was suited to higher office in the department, but as a mechanic there was no chance of promotion to management, so he devoted much of his free time from 1901 to recording the world of the steam engine. He took photographs of railway construction, interiors of the workshops, locomotives and rolling stock, lines and bridges, and bush railway scenes. As an employee of the Railways Department, he was able to travel cheaply, taking several holidays in the Auckland region.

COURTESY HISTORY COLLECTION, WAITAKERE CITY LIBRARIES

(Above) Olaf Petersen's classic award-winning photograph of the great sand-dune near Lake Wainamu, 1976.

Around 1915 he visited Piha and Karekare, recording the bush felling operations, timber dams, the west coast roads and the tramway. His photographs are among the best-known images of the area. Godber's love affair with steam encompassed the men who worked on the engines, who posed easily for him. The images are full of detail of brass, polish and steam. When he died in 1949, Percy Godber left his collection of rail photogaphy to the Alexander Turnbull Library.

Although still expensive and unwieldy, the camera became more widely available at the close of the 19th century. One who took up the hobby was Herbert Robert Arthur, born in 1875. An accountant with the Auckland Gas Company, Arthur was a man of some style and wealth. If the love of his life was the beautiful Rhoda Mowbray of Waiuku, his passion was photography. Following their wedding in January 1896, they travelled to Karekare with a tent and and a camera for their honeymoon. Over the next week, with his Newman half-plate camera and La Vern lens, Herbert Arthur recorded some of the most memorable images of the coast. The photographs which make up this collection show two young people very much in love, enjoying their first holiday together. The images include him shaving in the early morning and Rhoda tending a very smoky fire in the evening.

They returned to the beach in 1936 and compiled a second album, which

RIGHT & MIDDLE H. ARTHUR COLLECTION, WAITAKERE CITY LIBRARIES

shows an elderly couple still caring for each other after all those years. Both albums, which are now held by the Waitakere City Library's archive collection, also contain footnotes elegantly inscribed by them both. It is a window on a lost time and age.

Aircraft brought a new photographic dimension to the coast. Wally Badham and his flying mate Leo White were pioneers of the West Auckland skies. White later founded the aerial photography company Whites Aviation, after experiments pointing his camera earthwards as he flew over the beaches.

At Te Henga in the late 1940s, Jim Foley, a brilliant pianist, started photographing the coastline and the locals. Foley, a bachelor who worked in the textile industry, would spend 30 years recording people and events at Bethells. I got to know him well as he visited the beaches over many summers, photographing anyone who caught his eye, processing the pictures for his collection in the darkroom of his house at Waiatarua. Tragically, most of his images were lost in a fire following his death in the mid-1980s.

Christchurch-born Brian Brake made his name as a photographer working for Magnum in Paris. His work appeared in *Time*, *Life* and many other leading publications around the world. By the time he returned to his homeland to build and live in Titirangi in 1976, he was internationally recognised as one of the leading photographers of the 20th century. Brake's images of Picasso at the bullfight and the timeless image of raindrops on an Indian woman's face in his Monsoon assignment for *Life* magazine had made him a celebrity, but later in his life he wanted to return to photograph his own country. He was a regular visitor to the west coast beaches, with his camera following a cloud or a ray of sunlight in the bush.

Although trained in portraiture and documentary film production, he had a remarkable 'eye' for bringing a landscape to life. In April and May 1989, Brian Brake hosted 169 photographers from around the world, the largest group of international photographers to visit this country. They gathered to share experiences, to photograph and to attend lectures by the inventor of the Hasselblad camera Ernst Haas, as well as Chris Rainer and other photographers from the Brookes Institute. The tour was called Focus on New Zealand, and their first assignment was on Auckland's west coast. They were awed by the landscape and the surf. Their hundreds of images of the area offer many highly personal interpretations of the coastline, showing what the eye often misses, or sees without registering. I remember listening to Brian Brake's comments on the photographs, as we looked through this impressive collection of 'foreign' images of the familiar winter coastline.

Olaf Petersen spent his life at Swanson, where he first came to know one of New Zealand's finest Edwardian photographers, Henry Winklemann. In his retirement Winklemann bought a small poultry farm in the foothills of the Waitakeres. Petersen couldn't have had a better tutor. For over 60 years Olaf captured Te Henga in sharp, crisp images for the *Weekly News* and other publications. A regular exhibitor in the photographic section of the Easter Show, Petersen often carried off the trophy for best landscape in black and white. Through the camera lens he saw the shadows, the grasses and the contours of the sand-dunes. His most famous photograph is of the

COURTESY ISAMBARD PRODUCTIONS LIMITED

(Left and Below) **The television series** ***Black Beauty*** **and** ***Black Stallion*** **first took images of the untamed coast into the world's livingrooms.** (Lower) **Early camera.** (Opposite Top) **Karekare locals were cast in** ***The Piano*** **alongside the film's star Holly Hunter.** (Opposite Lower) **Photographer Herbert Arthur and his bride Rhoda honeymooning at Karekare, 1896.**

COURTESY ISAMBARD PRODUCTIONS LIMITED

great sand-dune at Te Henga after a storm, with human figures dwarfed by its cathedral proportions. Patron of the Auckland Photographic Society and a stalwart of the Ornithological Society, he died in 1994.

The untamed coast is now often used by fashion photographers, catalogue advertisers and the film industry. International audiences saw the west coast at its best in the television series *Black Beauty* and its sequel *Black Stallion*.

Crowded House filmed their acclaimed music video *Together Alone*, with its dazzling helicopter sequences, around Karekare.

Photography is now so inexpensive that you can buy a disposable camera to record your visit to the beach, and even a cheap waterproof camera can be tucked into your togs as you leap into the surf. I wonder if the pioneers of west coast photography would approve.

Notes for photographers

Most landscape photographs in this book were taken with a Bronica SLR camera with a 75mm or 40mm lens, producing 40x60mm transparencies. Most people photographs were taken with a Canon EOS using 20mm, 50mm and a 100-300mm zoom lens. Transparency film used was Fuji Provia 100 ASA, and for colour prints, Fuji and Kodak Gold III 200.

For anyone interested in photographing this type of landscape, here are a few tips. For beach locations, beware. The worst environment for cameras is the beach, where there is a salty atmosphere and lots of abrasive sand blowing around. Always keep your camera covered until ready for use, then clean with a soft damp cloth on returning home.

For the dense New Zealand bush, the main problem facing the photographer is the variation in the light, which makes it much more difficult to set optimum exposures. The best time to photograph is on overcast days. This reduces the extreme contrast between the highlights and shadows of bright sunny days. If you are really keen, use a tripod and long exposures. A flash unit can help, and if the camera is hand-held, use 400 ASA film.

BETHELLS TE HENGA

Beach dreams and swamp music

(Above) **The gigantic black sand-dunes of Lake Wainamu.** (Opposite) **Surfers head for the waves, O'Neill Bay, Te Henga.**

BETHELLS, or Te Henga, is the grandest of the west coast beaches. It is awe-inspiring and dramatically beautiful. To me, its splendid isolation and its sense of history are quite overwhelming. To walk the Bethells dunes, to swim in the freshwater lakes and to run the high hills is to absorb the essence of the west coast.

Te Henga has warded off civilisation well. Its landscape makes no concessions. Its surf is often very dangerous and it is addictive. It has become an all-season favourite with many people, who return again and again to seek a special solitude, its healing spaces, its great sense of place. If the beach is special, so are the people. They are the most clan-like on the coast and like all isolated communities, they are not likely to welcome intrusion or new ideas for their beach.

The Bethell family has lived in New Zealand for six generations. Francis and Mary Bethell and their seven children of Welsh origin sailed for the new country in 1858, on the 1842-ton sailing ship the *Kingston*. The century-and-a-half saga of the family's life in New Zealand is lovingly recorded in the book *The Bethells of Te Henga* by Mary Woodward. It is a 'must read' for anyone interested in this wonderful beach and the Bethells dynasty.

(Above) **Te Henga: splendid isolation and a sense of history.**

Francis and Mary Bethell were granted 225 acres (91 hectares) on the northern slope of Anawhata Valley but Francis had no liking for farming, choosing to remain mostly in Newmarket to ply his trade as a wheelwright, while his two sons, Robert and John Neale, cleared the Anawhata land and started to farm it. From an early age John used to climb to the top of the range which separated Anawhata from Te Henga and look down on the wide expanse of coastline, dreaming of someday making it his own.

It was to be many years of working bullock teams and trains of packhorses carting provisions to the timber camps, of gathering and trading kauri gum from the gumdiggers, and of farming in the Piha Valley before his dream was realised. In 1894 he purchased 1000 acres (405 hectares) from the lawyer and landowner E.T. Dufaur, who had bought it from Maori some years earlier. John used the name Te Henga and successfully farmed there, introducing buffalo grass which stabilised the foreshore dunes. He raised a large family and eventually became well-known in the area as Pa Bethell, dying in 1942.

The Bethells community is still there on the southern road, nestling in a grove of pohutukawa above the small Lake Waiataru, affectionately known as the Duck Pond. The Bethells household used to have a small schoolhouse, where young children from as far away as Piha made up the daily roll. Because the children stayed during the week at the Bethells' farmhouse, the school was probably New Zealand's first and smallest boarding school.

At Te Henga you are conscious of the massive sand-dunes that sweep up this vast valley towards Wainamu, an exhilarating freshwater lake, imprisoned by the build-up of sand over the centuries. Although suffering badly in recent years with weed, the lake is superb for swimming and boating. Wainamu is one

of three lakes, the others being Kawaupaku and Waiataru. Lake Waiataru's meaning is unclear, but could possibly mean the lake of Taratuwhenua, an important Maori of the area. Lake Wainamu has been in public ownership since 1979. It was thanks to the Waitakere Ranges Protection Society and the Queen Elizabeth II National Trust that the lake and the bush area of 333 acres (135 hectares) came into public ownership. Its access is either on foot from the parking area before you drive on to the beach via the Waiti Stream, or over the sand-dunes from the beach. I would recommend you walk the stream, have a swim in the lake and return via the dunes.

In the Bethells dunes you'll find the New Zealand pipit, a small brownish bird rather like a skylark, but more approachable and displaying the distinctive habit of often flicking its tail up and down. On the beach itself are the odd variable oystercatcher and an occasional Caspian tern, while white-fronted terns fly offshore, searching for small fish.

Te Henga was probably continuously inhabited by Maori for several centuries and today the area still contains the largest concentration of archaeological sites of any district in the Waitakere Ranges or on the coast. Some 75 sites have been recorded by archaeologists. These include numerous pa, pits and terraces, rock shelters and a remarkable rock wall formation. The area also contains the best-preserved examples on the coast of an island pa site, Ihumoana Island, where tradition records that the Maori chief Takere was murdered.

Here in the adjacent Te Henga swamp, Te Kawerau a Maki built a large pa, elevated from the water. Although the exact location is now lost and subsequent archaeological expeditions have failed to find trace of it, it is thought to have been opposite Parawai Pa Point. Records from the 19th century show that this

(Above) **Members of the Waitemata Rugby Club train in wet sand at Bethells.**
(Overleaf, pages 164-165) **Lake Kawaupaku, hidden in the bush above Te Henga, is held sacred by Maori.**

(Above) **Te Henga, with O'Neill Bay to the north, from the lookout point.**

large pa was situated in a bog of raupo and had been built on tall totara posts. The fence surrounding the pa (the palisade) was built on a platform of split wood tied with torotoro and was immensely strong. This fencing was continued all around this platform and down through the mud to solid ground, so no enemy could penetrate the barricade.

The pa was sacked by Kawharu, the warrior chief, and the Ngati Whatua, during the wars of the coast, probably around the year 1700. The invading warriors waded and swam out to the pa during the night and at sunrise took the inhabitants by surprise.

This wetland is the largest of its type in the Auckland region. It is the only freshwater coastal swamp of any size within 200 km. Here you will find pukeko, black swan, shoveller, paradise ducks and introduced mallards. One of the most interesting residents is the endemic fernbird. These small birds are poor flyers, entirely dependent on the area for feeding and breeding. Their character-istic 'tick' duet, in which each member of the pair utters one syllable of the call in strict sequence, can be heard in the swamp at dawn and dusk.

Another special bird is the threatened matuku or bittern. This is a heron which has adapted to living in swamps and is extremely well camouflaged by the reeds. Its presence is often only revealed in spring by its booming call, a low and mechanical sound. Its name is commemorated here in Matuku Reserve, a 100-hectare sanctuary of the Royal Forest and Bird Protection Society, incorpor-ating a large area of the wetland as well as adjacent bush slopes. It is one of the few places in New Zealand where large cabbage trees can be seen growing in their natural habitat, a swamp forest.

COURTESY HISTORY COLLECTION, WAITAKERE CITY LIBRARIES

(Above) **Also known as Cormorant or Shag Lake, Lake Kawaupaku, photographed by Olaf Petersen, 1968. Ross Bethell is in the canoe.**

As you cross the small wooden bridge to enter the beach area, at the junction of the two streams, you will see the site of the old Waiti settlement, which housed the Kawerau descendants up until around 1912. With the building of the Waitakere Dam, the Waitakere River ceased to flow with any strength. In the early days the Bethells swamp could be navigated by canoes from its outlet to the sea. Eels, native ducks and freshwater lobster were abundant in the swamp and they were a prized food source for Maori. Te Henga must have been a paradise for food gatherers and the generations of Maori who lived there. Today the swamp is still vast and in winter you can, with some difficulty, manoeuvre a canoe down the main centre channel. Early photographs from the turn of the century show a thriving community with clear stretches of water right back into the hinterland.

Like many ancient Maori campsites, Te Henga has magnificent groves of old karaka trees. It is thought they have grown from the rejected stones of the karaka berries that were collected by Maori for food.

Tree-carving by Maori was relatively unknown on the New Zealand mainland, except for here at Te Henga, where there are a number of trees that still bear the signs of ancient carvers.

The Bethell family had a close association with Maori and Pa Bethell knew, but kept it a secret, that local Maori continued to bury their dead in the sand-dunes near Lake Kawaupaku. This is the main reason why this lake's access is still restricted.

Harding and Billings Tourist Guide for 1912 mentions the Bethells hostel, but glossed over the jolting 16-kilometre boneshaking cart ride from Waitakere

(Top) **O'Neill Bay, looking south towards Te Henga.** (Above) **The Waitakere River meanders through swamp and rich farmland.** (Opposite Top) **O'Neill Bay can be reached from the Te Henga-Goldie Bush Walkway, or along the beach from Bethells.** (Opposite Lower) **Whakatu Bay, between Te Henga and Anawhata, was named by legendary Polynesian navigator Kupe. Locals know the bay as McGaffries.**

Station. Frank Bethell, Pa's son, was still running an accommodation house by Kawaupaku up until the 1930s. He called it "The Trampers' Rendezvous."

The accommodation house took up to 60 guests and over the Christmas holidays every bed was spoken for. The tradition of hospitality remains. Excellent short or long-stay accommodation in the cottages Te Turehu and Te Koinga is provided by John Paice and Trude Bethell-Paice. It is also a spectacular venue for weddings, under an ancient pohutukawa tree overlooking the expanse of the beach. Four-wheel bike tours and horse trekking are popular with visitors. Te Henga continues to draw its admirers back, time after time.

Around the turn of the century a real hard-baked old pioneer named Houghton lived near Lake Kawaupaku in a hut with a huge chimney where a great log burned day and night. The log was simply pushed into the fire from outside the hut, burning as it went. Houghton is remembered in the track and gully which bear his name.

In early colonial times, settlers were aware of an old Maori named Pareoha, who lived by himself for 50 years in a cave behind a wild and lonely bay beyond the southern end of Te Henga. He cultivated a garden and dried his own fish. His isolation gave rise to tales that he had eaten human flesh and been expelled from the Waiti settlement, so settlers named the stream that flows over the cliff-face Cannibal Creek. It is now recognised that Pareoha was not a cannibal but a tohunga, a man of spiritual wisdom, whose chosen life of isolation and contemplation caused others to regard him with fear and mistrust. Even in death he was an outcast. He was not buried in the local tribal burial ground, but on the flat at the entrance to the beach, by the bridge over the stream.

COURTESY DON BINNEY

(Right) *Te Henga*, Ruth Cole, 1994. (Below) *Swoop of the Kotare, Wainamu*, 1980, Don Binney. Perhaps more than any other artist, Don Binney focused popular attention on the west coast landscape and birds with his brilliant colour palette.

The sweep of Te Henga Beach is divided by Erangi Point. This headland is named after a young Maori woman, in honour of her famous swim to Puketotara, a distance of three kilometres, with a baby on her back, to meet her lover. It would have been quite a swim. She is acknowledged as the Hinemoa of the west coast, swimming to her local Tutanekai. From this sandy headland crossing, you can walk down to the beautiful O'Neill Bay. This beach, Kauwahaia, is excellent for surfing. Right-handed waves peel off, caused by the irregular ocean floor. Offshore, there is a large mussel reef known by its ancient name, Maukuku. The bottom is strewn with boulders, which makes surfing at low tide rather precarious. You'll see small groups of pied stilts huddling together on the sand in this bay.

I don't surf at Te Henga. When I was 22, in 1962, we were called from Karekare to assist in a rescue on the main beach. By the time we drove to Bethells, 14 people had been swept out to sea in an attempt to save two young girls who had got themselves into difficulties earlier in the afternoon. It was a tragic and terrible afternoon for us all, with no local surf club in those days on patrol duty.

The Air Force had been alerted to the impending tragedy and had been able to get an aircraft in the air. While low-flying the surf line, they were able to toss inflatable rafts from a rear door to the many would-be rescuers now drifting well out to sea. Many survived by climbing into the life rafts. When we arrived about one hour after the raising of the alarm to find three bodies on the beach, we knew it was going to be a day we'd rather not remember. Locals were attempting to reach swimmers by tying tow-ropes together, with little success. We quickly retrieved many exhausted swimmers and the rafts brought in the rest, but five people, including the two girls, had drowned. This horrific experience put me off swimming at Te Henga and although I have competed at surf carnivals there over the years, it has been with some reluctance.

In the centre of O'Neill's is a large rock column known as Tikinui, a tapu sentinel three or four metres high. At the base of this rock, the Maori chief Taratuwhenua speared a young man who was secretly courting his daughter while lying concealed under layers of bull kelp. Taratuwhenua plunged his taiaha into the young man's heart while addressing his daughter, who was sitting by the pile of kelp. The rock bears silent witness to this tragedy.

(Left) **John Paice, knifemaker.** (Below) **Trude Bethell-Paice and John, at home at Bethells Beach.** (Lower) **Lucy Lawless, homegrown star of the television series *Xena, Warrior Princess* on the set at Te Henga.**

From Te Henga you can take the coastal national walkway up over the O'Neill's cliff towards the rolling tablelands that lead you to Muriwai Beach. It will take you around two hours to do this enjoyable walk. It is safe, but strong footwear is essential. Looking down on the beach from this vantage point, you can take in the grand wind-blown landscape below. On a big surf day the waves are awesome. I recall two small children vanishing on this beach on a summer day, and a lone surfer trapped beyond the big surf calling out for help as night fell.

Te Henga also had a noteworthy wreck when in September 1853, near the mouth of the Waitakere River, the 265-ton barque *Helena*, Hokitika-bound, struck the westerly spring squalls. After battling winds and swells for 11 days, a decision was made to try for the Manukau. When this failed, the next plan of action was to beach the ship in Waitakere Bay. It was a plan doomed to failure. The rolling surf broke the ship in two and as the vessel turned in the waves, the captain and six of the crew were drowned. The captain was buried in the Bethells sand-dunes, the bodies of the crew lost to the surf.

The Bethell family still has a large influence on this coastal settlement, and I enjoy meeting

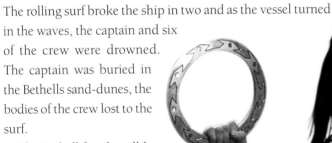

GEOFF SHORT/PACIFIC RENAISSANCE PICTURES

with them and talking not only about the past but their future aspirations. Bethells Te Henga, because of its proximity to the expanding Auckland metropolitan area, is feeling the pressure of weekend day-trippers.

The Waitakere River is also the boundary between Waitakere City and Rodney District. Few locals seem to be aware of this, and to me Waitakere City, in the amalgamation process of 1989, should have continued up to Helensville.

The other important historic boundary is Taupaki, inland from Te Henga. The word translates as 'a line in the sand', and was the Maori boundary between Te Kawerau and Ngati Whatua, which was drawn to signal the tribal limits which should not be broken. Taupaki is depicted at the base of the great carving at the Arataki Visitor Centre. At the feet of the first figure, by the giant toes of Te Hawiti, the line of demarcation is gouged out of the wood.

The Waitakere City Council has embarked on an ambitious programme with locals to try to minimise the negative effect of increasing tourism. Code-named The West Coast Plan, it will be a long process extending into the 21st century, working with the communities to develop a plan for the whole coast. At Te Henga, meetings have dealt with how large numbers of day visitors can be handled. It is no easy task to balance conflicting demands. Some local residents are enthusiastic about the employment potential of visitor activities. Movie and television commercial film-makers regard the Bethells Te Henga area as a useful and versatile location.

Hercules: The Legendary Journeys and *Xena: Warrior Princess* are examples of major American television productions using this area for colourful backdrops and unusual landscapes. Many of the local farms are used extensively as locations for feature films. *The Piano* production team built a cluster of cottages at Te Henga and the lakes feature in many local television commercials. There is a growing fear among locals that over-use by the film and television industry could harm this wonderful asset.

In the meantime, come and enjoy this wonderful beach, but remember that this fragile environment is in your care while you use it.

Te Henga Walks

1. Te Henga-Goldie Bush Walkway
The Te Henga-Goldie bush track, part of which is administered by the Department of Conservation, offers serious walkers a bracing workout. It starts from a carpark off Bethells Road, skirts round the headland behind O'Neill Bay, then follows coastal cliffs beside Te Waharoa Bay before finishing at Constable Road, eight kilometres and five hours later. Please respect the private land you pass through, which is closed for lambing during August and September. A good option is to begin from Constable Road at Motutara Scenic Reserve, walking the 4.5 km and three hours to Mokoroa Falls. You'll be doing a lot of stream-jumping and boulder-hopping, so be prepared to get your feet wet.

2. Lake Wainamu and Houghton Tracks
The best approach is via Henderson and Swanson off the Northwestern Motorway. The Houghton and Lake Wainamu Tracks at Bethells lead inland, working their way around the area behind Lakes Kawaupaku and Wainamu. In winter the slippery conditions require strong shoes or tramping boots.

(Below) **On the Goldie Bush walkway, the Houheria Stream drops into the river below Mokoroa Falls. In the pool at the base lived the legendary taniwha Te Mokoroa, killed by Taiaoroa.**

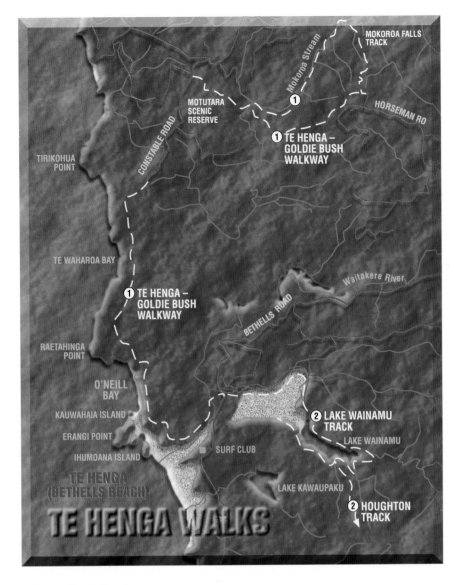

MOKOROA FALLS
TRACK

Mokoroa Stream

1

MOTUTARA
SCENIC
RESERVE

HORSEMAN RD

1 TE HENGA –
GOLDIE BUSH
WALKWAY

TIRIKOHUA
POINT

CONSTABLE ROAD

TE WAHAROA BAY

Waitakere River

1 TE HENGA –
GOLDIE BUSH
WALKWAY

BETHELLS ROAD

RAETAHINGA
POINT

O'NEILL
BAY

2 LAKE WAINAMU
TRACK

KAUWAHAIA ISLAND

LAKE WAINAMU

ERANGI POINT

IHUMOANA ISLAND

SURF CLUB

TE HENGA
(BETHELLS BEACH)

LAKE KAWAUPAKU

2 HOUGHTON
TRACK

TE HENGA WALKS

(Below) **Illustration of coastal birdlife
by John Walsby.**

3. Long Road Track

Formerly known as Sheeplands, Turua and the Wadhams Block, this walk is now one of the best in the Te Henga area. Purchased from the Wadham family, it constitutes a 320-hectare section of the Cascade Kauri parkland. The traditional Maori name for the land is Pae O Te Rangi. To reach this new park, drive up Long Road to the top and you will see the sign. The Long Road Track was established by the Walkway Commission; climb it until you see Auckland City in the distance. If you wish, follow this route through the ranges to Fence Line Track, which will bring you to the top of the Waitakere Dam. Allow three to four hours. (See map, page 20.)

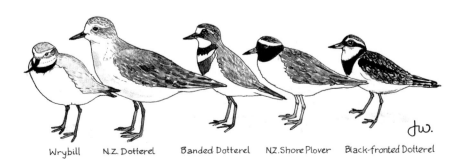

Wrybill   N.Z. Dotterel   Banded Dotterel   N.Z. Shore Plover   Black-fronted Dotterel

MURIWAI

The untamed coast

(Above) **Gannet nesting above the raging Tasman Sea. (Opposite) A lone gannet circles above as a breaker slams into Flat Rock. (Overleaf) Muriwai gannet colony is home to around 2000 birds.**

HALFWAY between Te Henga and Muriwai is a small waterfall which plunges over the cliff and is picked up by the southwesterly wind and turned into spray. Along this stretch of the coast, below the high cliffs, are the once abundant fishing and gathering rocks of the coastal Maori, who for hundreds of years used this area for the replenishment of seafood stock such as kina, paua, mussels and crayfish. Although many of the rocky outcrops are now fished out for paua, crays and mussels, there's a good catch to be had from the points that jut out into the surf.

Getting down the cliffs is the problem. From above these headlands you can see the great stretch of black sand which is Rangatira Beach, these days known as Muriwai, heading north through the haze to the Kaipara Heads. It seems to go on forever, a coastline always floating in a sea-mist or enveloped in sea-fog.

As the road drops past Maori Bay towards the distant sand-dunes, you become aware of a small settlement. This is Muriwai, meaning backwater or lagoon, but traditionally known as Te One Rangatira, or 'the Chiefly Beach'. If it is summer, the sea and sky will be crowded with gannets. The Muriwai colony is not large, at around 2000 birds. The national census carried out in 1981 recorded 56,000 gannets, so the Muriwai population represents only about four percent.

The gannet is one of the longest-living sea-birds known, living as long as 30 years. The ones you will see at Muriwai between July and December are between two and five years old. They will have made only one migratory flight to Australia, and for the rest of their lives they will stay around the New Zealand coast. Above the Tasman coast they wheel sharply then plummet, guided missiles slicing through the air into the surf below.

The attraction of the winged visitors to our shores is the big tourist drawcard at Muriwai and the ARC park headland. The colony includes a very narrow rocky offshore pillar known as Motutara. The island, 30 metres out in the Tasman, literally teems all summer with the nesting birds. In pairs or singles, the birds court, rest, squabble, and delicately land in a slow motion, precisely manoeuvring as they descend into their own small space. It is an exercise in territorial positioning and is fascinating to watch.

At Muriwai you will find people heading off from the carpark with huge surfcasting rods for Flat Rock, almost directly beneath the gannet colony. It's one of the west coast's most famous fishing spots.

The cliffs above Maori Bay are of geological significance. Pillow lava are massive cooled lava blocks, uplifted from the sea. For the more erudite rockhounds, the scientific descriptions are lensoidal piles of andesite pillar lava flows. Amongst

(Right) **Park Ranger Dave Beattie and son Tom at Muriwai Information Centre.** (Below) **Stuart Houghton, whose family have farmed Houghton's Bush for three generations.** (Lower) **Glen Houghton makes earthbricks for rammed earth houses.**

these grand phenomena are fossils that indicate that they were once on the sea floor between 1000 and 2000m on the outer slopes of a volcanic island to the south-west. These rocks indicate it must have been some volcano.

The carpark above Maori Bay makes a year-round viewing platform of these rocks and the beach below. The walk down to the beach takes about five minutes. From sea level you will appreciate the full grandeur of this unusual formation.

Here at Muriwai the Waitakere Ranges cease to be rocks and lava flow. The cliffs turn into sandstone, the surf endlessly pounds the beach and the dunes rise and fall, obeying the dictates of the prevailing winds.

Muriwai has one of the most extensive earthworks of the ancient pa sites on the west coast. Known as Korekore or Oneonenui and locally as Whare kura, it is one of the most documented pa sites in the Auckland region. You can see it from all of Muriwai. This grand, green headland cuts into the sand-dunes about two kilometres from the Muriwai settlement. Until the 1930s, it was one of the best-preserved sites in New Zealand. It is now grassed and many of the extensive subterranean storage chambers have been blocked up, which is a pity. But the huge defensive earthworks, some up to 20m across and 8m deep, have been only partially filled in, to provide tractor access to the western section of the pa. This was an impressive and apparently impregnable structure.

Unfortunately, the coastal weather has all but obliterated the magnificence of the sites. Yet to walk over it today, you can still have a sense of Maori life on the coast, the brisk winter climate and the splendour and isolation of these fortified headland pa. You can still see carvings on the side of a large storage pit, which is situated on the ridge which runs south-west from the main pa.

The beach is extremely long and has always been daunting to walk. In 1821 the Rev. John Butler, the first ordained clergyman in New Zealand, walked from Muriwai to Kaipara with a group of local missionaries including Samuel Marsden. He describes the coast and their ability to walk a considerable distance, heavily clothed, in the summer heat:

Sunday, Noon 12th December 1821. We rose very early, performed Divine Service, and proceeded; we arrived at the head of the river about ten am and after that,

COURTESY HISTORY COLLECTION, WAITAKERE CITY LIBRARIES

walked twenty miles in the course of the day. The land we passed over this day is not very good. A little before the going down of the sun, we reached a small village on the west side, near the sea.

These people had never seen a European, and the younger of both sexes were filled with wonder and astonishment. When I pulled off my hairy cap I travelled in, they shouted aloud; I apprehended they conceived my hat formed part of my head. The old chief made a long speech, and said he dreamed white men were coming to see him, the night before. We spent the evening among them in the usual way, in prayer and praise, and conversation, and were treated in the kindest manner possible. We slept among the trees, and in the morning, after many a hearty good wish for our welfare, we departed. This place is called Moodewye. There is also a fine waterfall, fifty to sixty feet deep. The chief's name is Homi-hamoo.

The natives accompanied us over the sandhills to the seashore, and then bid us good-bye, and returned. We walked on the sea beach upwards of twenty miles. This was a very fatiguing march on the sands; and also, we suffered a good deal from thirst, as the day was hot and windy, and no water to be had for sixteen miles. The sandhills reach for sixteen miles to this coast, and very much resembles a deep snow in winter. You behold an immense tract of sand, with a stunted shrub here and there growing through it. The wind whirls about the sand like a cloud; and it is almost impossible to stand or face it in a windy day. In passing along, I sat down on a small, sandy eminence to rest a while, being hungry and thirsty, and no water to be obtained among these barren sands. All our people, except Mr Shepherd, lagging a long way behind, I was led to contemplate a little while on the 42nd Psalm, and I can truly affirm I never felt the force and excellence of those pious words of the psalmist in such a manner before, "As the deer panteth for the water brooks, so longeth my soul after Thee, O God. My soul is athirst for God, for the living God; when shall I come and appear," etc, etc. 1 v. and 2 v.

I thought our situation was very peculiarly interesting: on the very verge of the world, or at least on the farthest shore that is known, and nearly the Antipodes of England; the tremendous roaring surf, which is seen and heard on this sandy coast many miles; the barren sand hills; the dreary wilderness of New Zealand;

(Top Left) **Pheasant hunters, Oaia, 1925.**
(Above) **Environmental activist and owner of Oaia homestead, Anna Mason.**

COURTESY HISTORY COLLECTION, WAITAKERE CITY LIBRARIES

COURTESY MURIWAI BEACH PROGRESSIVE ASSN.

(Top) **Motorcycle races on Muriwai Beach, 1926.** (Above) **An early land yacht waits for wind, circa 1914.**

surrounded by cannibals; exposed to the heat by day, and the cold dews by night. On reflecting on the dangers we had already passed, and the goodness of the Lord in preserving us amidst innumerable perils, my mind was filled with an awful sense of the majesty of God Who is everywhere present, and fills the universe with His presence. But how comforting to think that he is everywhere present for the comfort and support of His people!

We arrived at the place where we had to turn off inland about four o'clock, and, walking a little way, we halted in a valley between the sand hills, where we found water, and a few heath shrubs with which we made a little shelter for the night. Here we offered up praise and thanksgiving to our adorable Redeemer for all His tender mercies. I rested during the night but very little; I believe through weariness. Mr Puckey was attacked with rheumatic pains, in so much that in the morning he was obliged to be carried by natives; however, we had but a short distance to go, say about eight miles, which we accomplished before breakfast.

When we reached Kapooah, a settlement on the banks of the Kepero River, and the residence of the great chief, Teenana, we were received, as at every other place, with every mark of kindness and attention.[1]

Local tradition also records that the moa was caught in the area, although it had become extremely rare by the end of the 16th century. A Kawerau waiata refers to the existence of 'kuranui' or the moa in the district, and the traditions of this iwi record that it was referred to locally as 'Te Mana Pouturu', or 'the bird on stilts'. Ngati Whatua tradition records that moa were caught in some numbers in the southern Kaipara until the mid-17th century. It is also recorded that as late as 1700 a moa was sighted and pursued in the sand-dunes in what is now Muriwai Regional Park.

For those curious about the ancient bird life of the area, it is of interest to note that a locality on the high country north of Muriwai Stream was known as 'Te Hokioi'. The existence of the New Zealand falcon is commemorated in the

From *The Journals and Correspondence of the Rev. John Butler*, compiled and published by his grandson The Rev. John Gare Butler in 1893. John Butler was the first ordained clergyman in New Zealand. He travelled widely throughout the country between 1819 and 1850 and is credited with converting Te Kawerau a Maki to Christianity.

COURTESY MURIWAI BEACH PROGRESSIVE ASSOCIATION

traditional name for the ridge east of the Muriwai Golf Course, which is known as Karearea.

The 'musket wars' had left the tangata whenua of the area devastated. In 1839 Reverend James Buller, the Wesleyan missionary based at Tangiteroia at the head of the Northern Wairoa River, began to visit the southern Kaipara. By 1841 he was making an impact in the area, and in April of that year he baptised Te Otene Kikokiko, the leading rangatira and tohunga of Te Taou, so that by 1845 the majority of the Maori inhabitants of the area were practising Christians.

Between 1870 and 1871 most of the customary Maori land in the Muriwai area was surveyed and investigations of title were undertaken for each block. Certificate of Title to 'Oneonenui' and the blocks lying north of the Muriwai Stream was awarded to rangatira representing the wider Te Taou hapu who occupied both southern Kaipara and Tamaki. Titles to 'Muriwai' and 'Kahukuri', the two blocks south of the Muriwai Stream, were awarded to the Ngati Te Kahupara.

The 1870s and 1880s brought major change to the Muriwai area as a European settlement began. In 1870 John and Annie Foster established a flax mill at Okiritoto on the Muriwai Stream. Flax from throughout the Muriwai area was harvested and taken to the mill for processing. However, it did not operate for long, as much of the flax on the Muriwai block was destroyed by fire.

The 1890s saw the sale of much of the remaining Maori land in the Muriwai area. In January 1890 Motutara was sold to Andrew Stewart and Richard Garlick, who had leased the land since 1884 for mill pohutukawa and other timber.

In the early 1900s the Motutara area remained isolated, with access being along a 'bullock road' that was impassable in wet weather. It was not until 1914 that a road to the area was formally surveyed, and it was to be another four years before it was formed.

Mr Hugh Boscawen of the Department of Lands inspected the area in 1908. He reported that up to 120 campers were using the block each summer, and

(Top) **Start of the 50-mile New Zealand Motor Cup race, 1922.** (Above) **After the arrival of the motor vehicle, Muriwai Beach became a popular venue for speedsters, resulting in damage to the toheroa beds.**

COURTESY HOUGHTON FAMILY COLLECTION

COURTESY MURIWAI BEACH PROGRESSIVE ASSOCIATION

(Top) **John Ingram and Mary Bethell's Muriwai boarding-house, 1925.** (Above) **Before the ban, the toheroa season lasted six weeks.** (Opposite Top) **Wreckage of the** *May*, **1902, included 180,000 feet of timber.** (Opposite Middle) **Crowds watch as** *Faith in Australia* **goes nose-down while on a joy-ride, 1934. This Avro 10 aircraft later carried the first trans-Tasman airmail to Sydney.** (Opposite Lower) **Beached blue whale, 1922.**

that Motutara's "great charm, was the pohutukawa trees and its wild state". He recommended that the land be formally reserved, and on 17 December 1908 the 'Motutara Domain' was gazetted by the Crown as 'a reserve for recreation'.

Many of those who visited Motutara Domain at the time were holidaymakers staying in the two accommodation houses that had been established. A large guest-house had been built on the Muriwai Block near Lake Okaihau by the Ingram family in 1912. It had been developed as a sanitorium for the treatment of TB patients, who it was thought would benefit from the ozone-rich sea air and immersion in the hot black sands of the nearby dunes. The sanitorium operated for only a brief time until it became the Ingram family home, and later Ingrams Guest-house. Managed by John and Mary Ingram, it was modelled on the successful guest-house operated by Mary's family at Te Henga.

Muriwai Beach does not have perhaps quite the historic richness of other beaches along the coast. Nevertheless, it commands a position of great interest, drawing large numbers of visitors to walk the well-signposted headland tracks to the gannet colony. It's also a great place for kites and land yachts.

When I was young I would go with my family to Muriwai in late autumn to dig for toherora. The season would be advertised, and thousands of Aucklanders would drive at low tide down the beach, stop the car and go for their quota. It was great fun. You were not permitted to use any metal instruments for digging, as it was thought this would damage the fish and possibly poison the shellfish bed. Marine inspectors cruised the beach, as there were plenty of people prepared to beat the system, concealing bags under their cars or in the upholstery inside.

WINKELMAN PHOTOGRAPH/COURTESY WAITAKERE CITY LIBRARIES

COURTESY ALLEY COLLECTION

SOUTHERNWOOD PHOTOGRAPH/COURTESY HELENSVILLE HISTORICAL SOCIETY

It was always believed they were never permitted to search females, so the women concealed bags in their clothing. In the mid-1960s the toheroa beds were depleted and officialdom closed the beach until the shellfish recovered.

The toheroa population has been monitored by the New Zealand Marine Department (now the Ministry of Agriculture and Fisheries) since 1927. In 1962, the beds were estimated to contain 5 million and rose to 10 million in 1964. From then, it was a serious decline. The last tally was in 1986, when it was estimated that there were fewer than 100,000. So where have they gone? It is thought that climatic effects, combined with food availability, are the main problems. These days, on some weekends, 800 to 900 off-road vehicles may traverse the beds. The toheroa ban is still in place, and for many of us they are but a distant memory, a tasty treat from old New Zealand.

It was the roar of the high-powered motorcar that brought the crowds to Muriwai Beach in the 1920s. The first vehicle to venture onto Muriwai Beach was a 'Velie', driven by local farmer William Jones in 1918. It became stuck in sand and needed to be pulled out by horses. Racing motor vehicles became extremely fashionable following the First World War. Muriwai was ideal and the track laid out on this grand beach at low tide in February attracted competitors from Australia and New Zealand. Some 6000 people attended the 1925 Saturday championships. Many of them had camped out in the sand-dunes to see the next day's attempt on the Australasian five-mile speed record. During the night a westerly gale drenched the campers. High winds tore down many of the tents but didn't seem to daunt the crowd, which later saw a Sunbeam break the 100 miles per hour record. The record-breaker, C.W.F. Hamilton, who would later develop the Hamilton jetboat and pioneer adventure tourism in this country, needed a three-mile accelerated run to achieve top speed.

These events, which went on right through the 1920s, were organised by the Auckland Automobile Association and were first conceived by Bill Miller, as a promotional scheme to sell cars. He had been involved in the early days of flying and with his mate Jack Gillett, Buick agent for New Zealand, they put a plan to the AA, whose early members were motor dealers, and the first meeting was organised for 21 March 1921. It was part of a trade promotion in which prominent motorists would take the seldom-seen car to northern New Zealand to try and interest farmers and land agents in this new means of transport. On the last leg of the tour, the group detoured to Muriwai Beach and went for a fast drive along the Muriwai Straight. So the idea was conceived to stage races on a regular basis. It is reported that the 60 car enthusiasts stayed at Muriwai House and went toheroa digging in the evening.

In 1928 toheroa diggers damaged the track by digging hundreds of holes in the sand on the morning before the race. It was a bumpy start to the day's racing. Events in the six-race programme ranged from a five-mile ladies' race to the 50-mile New Zealand Motor Cup. This race included a five-mile straight so the big banger Sunbeams, Stutz and Armstrong-Siddeleys could show their best turns of speed.

Unfortunately for the Muriwai fans, even the best viewing spot in the sandhills behind the judges, soon lost the Bugattis and Buicks as they vanished in the spray-hazed distance. Spectators were continually getting in the way and although no lives were lost, there were some very narrow misses as the cars spun out into the crowd, breaking a few legs and arms. No one seemed to get

(Below) **Boating on the freshwater Lake Muriwai. (Lower) Muriwai House, once a private hotel, now serves as a shop.**
BELOW: COURTESY MURIWAI BEACH PROGRESSIVE ASSOCIATION
LOWER: COURTESY WAITAKERE CITY LIBRARIES

(Left) **The Muriwai Beach patrol tower is operational all day during summer holidays and weekends.** (Below) **Muriwai's Flat Rock is a favourite fishing spot.** (Lower) **Giant sea caves are south of the main beach.**

too upset. The competitors and the spectators rated the Muriwai races the most exciting free entertainment around Auckland.

The finishes were thrilling as the huge cars raced at fearsome speed, scattering spectators at the finish line. Competitors in the cars or in the motorcycle races endured the treachery of the Muriwai quicksand, which even today still traps vehicles if they stop and are hit by an incoming wave. Although there were plenty of spectators to push any car that got stuck, three cars were lost to the encroaching sea during these races.

Former long-serving Auckland mayor Sir Dove-Meyer Robinson told me how on one of his many honeymoons, he had taken his new wife camping at Muriwai Beach for a few days, where he could take part in that summer's motorcycle racing. Dove held a number of New Zealand records with his brothers. At the 1925 motorcycle championships, Coyle and Gardiner, astride their 600cc Nortons, were bowled over by the sea, only 400 metres from the finish of the championship race. In 1926, sidecars were included in the motorcycle section to add to the entertainment.

By the end of the 1920s, Muriwai as a motor sports venue was coming in for criticism. They said there were unruly crowds and that the surface was not up to standard. Often tidal rips would scour out sections of the beach and turn it into a judder hell, snapping axles. Getting there was still a problem. The long, dusty, potholed roads did not please the more sophisticated Aucklanders, who arrived tired, dirty and hot.

In 1928 the *New Zealand Motor Journal* described the journey to Muriwai as probably unparalleled for discomfort in New Zealand. At the beginning of the 1930s, with the depression looming, the Muriwai races lost their popularity. Fewer people had the time or money for luxury car racing. Another group of motor enthusiasts advocated a fast track at the back of Mangere. Some 9000 spectators and 2000 motorcars turned up to the opening of this new speedway. The introduction of this dirt track racing was more convenient for Aucklanders, who could get out there by tram to Onehunga and a short walk to the track. Save for the odd hill climbs, there were to be no more races at Muriwai.

At Muriwai in 1922, Sir Edward Edwin Mitchelson built his great wooden

(Above) **Parapenters and hang-gliders soar off the southern headland.** (Below) **Horse trekkers set out along Rangatira.**

mansion Oaia, named after the island which it faced. It commanded an impressive view, although it is now obscured by a belt of trees. From Mitchelson, an MP, former Mayor of Auckland City and Chairman of the Harbour Board, the government purchased 30,000 acres (12,400 hectares) in a controversial sales deal which caused a scandal at the time, as it was claimed that Mitchelson had ripped off the Crown with the price of this block. Critics said the government had paid too much for it and that it was not fit for the soldiers' proposed settlement purposes. The government had embarked on a programme of rehabilitation of many First World War returned soldiers, who were looking for work on the land. The scheme failed and the land, known as the Motutara Block, is now in three or four coastal farms, weekend baches and housing for the growing number of rural lifestyle seekers. All have paid more than Mitchelson did for his property.

My wife's family owned a magnificent wardrobe made from New Zealand timbers, given by Mitchelson to the family. It was commissioned by him and built at the timber company of Henderson and Pollard in Mt Eden. Its velvet-lined drawers and great inlaid doors are on display in the Auckland War Memorial Museum and Institute, an excellent example of wealth and Edwardian taste in bedroom furniture.

The Muriwai Surf Club was founded in 1942, going into recess during the later war years. It was reformed by the Waimauku stationmaster, who had got into difficulties while net fishing with friends. The clubhouse, now under the large sand-dune by the carpark, was built by voluntary labour and furnished from cast-offs from the Oaia homestead. Despite a constant battle with moving sand-dunes, the Muriwai Club in their new clubhouse on the domain is one of New Zealand's strongest patrols. Lifeguards have made some outstanding rescues after duty hours, as the beach often develops large holes close to the shore.

The beach has a history of visitor drownings. To the unwary, the flat, calm sections in the surf can seem inviting. They are in fact deep tidal holes and escaping from them is rare without assistance. These 'rip holes' offer the board surfer a channel back to sea. Swimmers caught in the rip must chance their luck by swimming across the hole, or if they are strong enough, by swimming out to sea, into the breakers, with the hope of getting back further along the beach. Extreme care while swimming without lifeguards on duty is always advised.

This is New Zealand's most popular surf beach, but it is also a designated public road to the Kaipara Head. It's a pity that every summer, hundreds of cars weave their way along this beach through the swimmers and picnickers. Why the entrance to this beach cannot be further north, I do not know. It would save a lot of problems. There has been a move to exclude cars from the beach, and I

would applaud any such initiative. Although there haven't been too many accidents on the beach at the Muriwai end, further north there are a number of wrecks in the sand, testimony to years of vehicle strandings by the tide.

Muriwai residents are rightly concerned about permission for the controversial technique of 'powerhauling' that the Ministry of Fisheries has granted to fishermen. Powerhauling catches grey mullet in the surf by dropping a 600-metre net out into the surf, off-loaded from an inflatable boat. A long drag line is then run from the net, up the beach and back. All of this gear is then winched in by a four-wheel-drive vehicle as it heads up the beach. Because the mesh of a mullet net is the smallest allowed under New Zealand fisheries law, by-catch is practically unavoidable. Banned in Australia, powerhauling over the years could strip this coastline of fish.

Surfcasting is still good on the Muriwai coast but care should be taken in driving the beach, particularly at night, as axles, winches and other solid objects from shipwrecks and car strandings are marooned in the sand. In 1963, a mysterious wreck emerged from the sand-dunes after a big winter blow. Ribs of pohutukawa beams and fluted bronze spikes gave a clue that it was probably a coastal trading cutter. The timber still bore the marks of axe and adze and marine historians decided that it had been built locally. Never authenticated, but widely debated, it might have been the ill-fated *May*. It is still there today, 40 km north of Muriwai.

Often the Muriwai surf will produce prolific schools of mullet in the holes scoured out by tidal rips. A group of friends and a surf net is all you need. Sustainability on this coastline has been a big issue for the locals who fought a hard-won battle against mining interests from New Zealand and international corporations in 1989.

This beach has been the scene of many dramatic surf rescues off Flat Rock. There have been countless drownings of careless fishermen in heavy weather gear who haven't had a chance when swept off their feet by breakers. The surf here can be fantastic, both on the main beach and at Maori Bay, probably one of the most inviting surfing spots on the whole coast. The bay can be surfed even by novices in almost all conditions, but I've seen huge surf here at times.

The sandbars create a small surf, ideal for learners and stunt surfers. It's a place to show off your style, and therefore it tends to be shunned by the more experienced surfers, who prefer Piha, Karekare and Raglan.

Moving sand is a real problem at Muriwai. There's a lot of it around – 16,000 hectares, in fact. Nowhere in coastal reserves has it been more out of control than at the Muriwai Beach Domain. The rising sand has now even threatened to engulf the picnic ground. In the last few years it has risen at Muriwai often

(Above) **Woodhill Forest pine plantation now covers most of the Muriwai sand-dunes.**

SWIMMING FOR YOUR LIFE

Two short tales of the sea

(Right) Volunteer coastguard crews like this one near the Manukau Heads have saved many lives on this perilous coastline. (Below) Westpac rescue helicopter on another emergency mission across the water.

COURTESY CLAYMORE SALSBURY

BEING a longtime swimmer, I've always been fascinated by the prospect of survival in the surf over a long period. It's not a pleasant thought to contemplate being caught by a rip and taken out to sea, although fortunately it rarely happens. Most people who perish, do so in holes quite close to the beach, within a toehold of safety.

Two outstanding swims on this unforgiving coast often come to mind. The first is the remarkable swim for safety and survival by 19-year-old Walter Dunn of the barquentine the *May*. Laden with 180,000 feet of sawn timber, the *May* was caught in a howling gale off the Kaipara Heads. Watti, as he was known, and the rest of the seven-strong crew, prayed for survival as they lost their line to the under-powered pilot boat and faced certain death in the mountainous waves. Broadside on, the cabin and crew were washed overboard, and Watti decided that he would chance the three-kilometre swim to Muriwai Beach. As the *May* broke up in the surf, Dunn tied his swimming medal, won at the Wairoa Championships, around his arm and leapt into the boiling surf. He battled towards the shore for two and a half hours, cheered on by the Russian crew of the barque *Concordia*, stuck high on the beach waiting for a favourable tide and a refloat.

The huge October surf was cold, but through this ordeal, Watti Dunn first survived by clinging to a piece of the mast and then to a hatch cover. When he lost these in the surf, he struck out for the distant beach, and crawled exhausted through the surf, clutching his precious medal. Refusing comfort and warmth, he walked the seven kilometres to Helensville for clothing and support from his friend and mentor Captain Cox, whose ship the *Waiwera* was moored at the township. Here he had his wounds dressed and at last rested from his ordeal.

It was a remarkable swim, given the appalling conditions. Watti Dunn never worked at sea again. He enlisted for the First World War as a private in Te Hokowhitu a Tu, the pioneer Maori Battalion in the fourth Maori contingent. His occupation is given on the army records as a rafter on the Hokianga. Upon his return from the war, Watti helped bring the logs down from the dams to the Hokianga harbour mouth using long poles, clearing the jams as he went, sleeping in makeshift whares. He died an old man of 86 in 1967, still remembered for his heroic swim.

When two fishing friends Douglas Prior and Adrian Larking set out for a day's fishing in their six-metre Bonita runabout the *Starfish* off the Manukau Heads in June 1990, their thoughts were on catching some deepwater snapper in the Tasman and being home by dusk. It was not to be. Sometime during that day, something went horribly wrong. Swamped by a wave off the coast, the *Starfish* foundered, leaving Douglas and Adrian to drift in the Tasman. Well-equipped for sea survival, but without a distress beacon, the two men, like Watti Dunn almost a century before, now had the unenviable task in the winter surf of making a beach-head. Wearing lifejackets and wetsuits, the pair strung extra lifejackets together to provide additional buoyancy and set off towards the distant coastline. Meanwhile, as night fell, their families on shore became more distressed and prepared to mount a full-scale search at first light.

(Above) **Piha surf lifesavers on patrol.**

Over the next few days the search became a nightmare of bureaucratic stonewalling and desperation for the families. The official search was abandoned after two days, on the assumption that both men must have been dead. Evidence clearly shows they were not. Caught in a northerly drift towards the Kaipara, they were not seen by spotter planes, nor were they picked up on radar or by the Coastguard who concentrated their rescue efforts around the Manukau bar. The fishermen would have been tiny dots on the heaving Tasman. Their families, knowing their fitness and that they would be wearing full-length protective wetsuits, organised six private search aircraft. The Muriwai bombing range formed an impossible search corridor and a restricted flying zone along the Muriwai coast. Co-ordination was also a problem between Search and Rescue, the Manukau Coastguard and police. The two friends were still alive, though quickly losing strength.

The difficulty for rescuers was that no wreckage was visible. The *Starfish* had disappeared without trace, and only frustration and despair remained. Five days later, Douglas Prior attempted to swim through the breakers of the Kaipara Heads. Weakened by his unbelievably heroic attempts to make it ashore, he died after struggling ashore below the Poutu lighthouse. The body of Adrian Larking and four lifejackets were found on Muriwai Beach.

The tragic death of these two men raised many questions about search and rescue co-ordination and safety. Their epic swim and their will to survive against all odds is one of the great dramas on the untamed coast.

(Above) **View north towards Muriwai from the Te Henga Track, a link in the national walkway, shows transformation of coastal headlands to farmland.**

by as much as eight metres a year, while the winds continually take all the newly planted vegetation from the surface. Planting continues, although it could mean the walking public will have to be excluded from access to the dune area for five years or so to enable the marram and other grasses to stabilise the dune system.

The Muriwai Golf Club is one of the finest in New Zealand. Built on a sand base, it was originally the site occupied by the U.S. Army Mobile Company, which practised beach landings for their upcoming Pacific campaign. It is estimated that over half of the soldiers who were housed at Muriwai lost their lives in the Pacific war. The golf course borders the sand-dunes with 64 hectares of undulating fairways and greens. With the roaring surf as a backdrop, this is a course to remember.

The large carpark in the Muriwai Domain usually fills most weekends, especially over the summer months as many Aucklanders flock to the beach and gannet colony, which is one of the most popular visitor attractions in New Zealand.

An interesting Maori name for the area by the Muriwai Stream is Paengatohora, which literally means 'the stranding place of whales'. Numerous strandings have been recorded during the 19th and 20th centuries. In 1840, six whales were reported as having beached and in 1928, the rare Shephard's beaked whale was found by the creek. In 1944, five sperm whales; in 1958, 13; and in 1983, four massive male sperm whales were buried by Muriwai rangers. In October 1974, 72 sperm whales stranded and died, unable to be rescued. Forestry

(Left) **The Muriwai golf course is playable all year because of its sandy fairways.**
(Below) **Pillow lava formations, Maori Bay.**

workers, using chainsaws, massacred the dying whales for their teeth and jawbones. The carcases stayed on the beach for three weeks before being buried. I remember visiting the sad sight of these whales, in a 10 km line, putrefying in the hot sun. The most recent stranding at time of writing was July 1997.

The Air Force has a bombing range 20 km up the beach and it is clearly marked with skull-and-crossbones signs, so you can't be under any illusion if you suddenly have the urge to sunbathe. The ageing planes still can pack a punch as they fire weaponry and drop bombs into designated target areas in the sand-dunes.

There is a real feeling of remoteness here. The colours seem to be forever changing and you notice this if you are taking photographs or walking this stretch of beach. Not only is there is a sense of vastness but a distortion of distance. I've walked this beach only once, on a two-day hike, camping in the dunes and then continuing in the early morning. I remember clearly the frustration of feeling I was getting nowhere. The landscape simply dwarfed me. The poet A.R.D. Fairburn wrote: "Hard, clear light revealing the bones, the sheer forms of hills, stone and scrub."

The light here is certainly harsh, the surf menacing and indifferent. I would hate to be lost on this stretch of the coast. You see a speck a long way off. It's a car roaring towards you. Eventually, it becomes blurred faces staring at you. In the moment of passing, you know they think you're crazy to be walking here.

Years ago, I was driving at night towards the Kaipara Heads with an ornithologist. We were going to check a gull colony at dawn. The pinpoints of light indicated a far-off vehicle heading towards us. For what seemed like hours, it got closer and closer. When we finally passed each other at speed, our wheel-mounts slit the other vehicle like a tin can. Neither of us stopped.

Behind the dunes is an exotic landscape of wetlands and small lakes. It was thought this area contained quicksands, and there were warning signs posted for years, but not any longer. Pick a low tide and a hot day and enjoy the thrill of a mountain bike ride along the hard sand. It will take you four hours, or you can overnight in the dunes as I have done. Take time to look at the sky at the end of the ranges. Without the hills, it's vast, and in summer streaked with high seascape clouds.

CLAIMED BY THE COAST

Shipwrecks and maritime disasters

(Above) **Beauty of the Whatipu wilderness masks its tragic past.**

I N THE 19th century, the ports of the Manukau and Kaipara harbours were busy gateways to New Zealand's finest natural resource, the native timber forests. To imagine these booming coastal seaports, think of busy settlements, wharves crowded with travellers, piles of merchandise stacked for delivery waiting for steamers, cutters, and the sailing of the next barque.

Both the Kaipara and the Manukau harbours are renowned today for their terrifying coastal sand-bars, but for captains of sailing ships and coastal navigators, traversing these obstacles was part of their job. The possibility of shipwreck must have haunted their lives. Newspaper reports of the time frequently listed missing or overdue vessels. Many ships destined for the ports on the west coast would arrive days or weeks late.

Wreckage would be sighted and investigated on deserted coastal strips or beaches, bodies buried where they were found and relatives on the other side of the world notified six months later. In its short history, New Zealand has had its full share of shipwrecks and maritime tragedies.

The west coast offered little hope for vessels blown off course, storm-damaged or lost. Many simply disappeared. Yet many boats and their crews survived shipwreck. Rescue was often impossible and survival marginal. Off the west coast today the lights of fishing trawlers blink in the darkness. Coastal cargo vessels still ply the Manukau, and the magnificent rescue teams of the Manukau Coastguard, on call day and night, are responsible for saving lives on the Manukau and out in the Tasman.

Big game fishing off the west coast is now popular, with charter launches leaving in late summer from Cornwallis and Huia. It will mean extra precautions for all concerned as this coast is notoriously unpredictable.

From the wreck of the *Orpheus* to the lost Swedish ammunition carrier *Svenborg Guardian*, the untamed coast has played a major role in the history of this country's coastal navigation. On Christmas Day 1866, the *Cambodia* had arrived on the 'wrong' side of New Zealand, using a chart which showed Auckland on the west coast. One hundred and twenty-one years later, the master of the *Svenborg Carrier*, using a school atlas to find his way into 'Auckland Harbour', found himself crossing the Manukau bar with a cargo of highly dangerous munitions for the New Zealand armed forces. How many others came to grief near the entrance to this harbour, we will never know. The following is a list of known shipwrecks and disasters on the coastline from Manukau to the Kaipara.

1840	April	AURORA	Brig or schooner. 550 tons. A total wreck at the Kaipara Heads. No lives lost.
1840	June	SYREN	Brig. A total loss at Kaipara coastline.
1841	September	SOPHIA PATE	Brig. A total loss at Kaipara. 21 lives lost. Stranded on sandbar at the harbour entrance. One passenger, the ship's master and crew member escaped in the ship's boat.
1846	February	LADY OF THE LAKE	Sailing vessel. Beach head at Manukau – stranded.
1848		ORWELL	Barque. Manukau Head. Total loss. Crew saved. Loss of vessel plus 164 cattle and 200 sheep.
1851	June 3	L'ALCENE	French corvette. Three-masted; 36 guns. Twelve lives lost. Vessel wrecked Kaipara. Beached on the heads coastline. 192 survivors.
1852	October 15	MAORI	Schooner; government-owned. Capsized in the Manukau, near present airport runway. Three lives lost. Two Europeans and 20 Maori left the wreck and swam to shore.
1853	September 20	HELENA	Barque; 265 tons; on Te Henga beach. Seven lives lost. Broke up in heavy surf with all hands being swept overboard.
	September 21	POSTHUMUS	Barque; 600 tons. Crew saved. Ship a total loss, breaking in two on the Tory Shoal on the Kaipara bar.
1860	July 25	UNION	Schooner. Total wreck. Karekare Beach. Four crew lost with no trace. Also lost cargo of coal.
	August	EMMA	Brig. Total wreck on the Manukau bar.
1862	July 14	ABEONA	Schooner; 44.5 tons. Lost off Manukau Head. Crew of five lost.
1863	February 7	ORPHEUS	Steam corvette. 1706 tons. Total loss. 189 lives lost. New Zealand's worst sea disaster. 252 feet; 20 x 8" guns. 60 cwt and one pivot Armstrong 110 pounder. 4 boilers. No guns have ever been recovered.
	September 15	SALCOMBE CASTLE	Schooner; 225 tons. Total loss. Kaipara bar. All crew saved. The captain ran the vessel on the beach but seas still broke over ship.
1864	August 6	ADVANCE	Cutter. Reported ashore on the Kaipara coast.
	August 13	LOTUS	Schooner; 90 tons. Struck tail end of Kemps Channel, South Spit, Kaipara. Loaded with 60,000 feet of timber. Known as the Pride of Kaipara Harbour.
1865	January	MAID OF KENT	Schooner; 50 tons. A total loss off Kaipara Beach.
1865	March 28	PETREL	Cutter. Driven ashore on Muriwai Beach after battling heaving seas. No casualties.
1865		THE ABE	Schooner also known as *Nebuchadnezzar*. Total loss off the Manukau Heads, with all crew drowned.
1865		ALLIANCE	Schooner; 73 tons. Total loss. Crew saved. Manukau headland beach.
1865	October	ELFIN QUEEN	Cutter. Wrecked off Manukau bar. The vessel drifted ashore and broke up to reveal captain's body. Five lives lost at sea.
1866	April	QUICKSTEP	Cutter. Cargo of potatoes. Total loss of ship and crew. Manukau Heads beach.
	May 19	PROGRESS	Cutter. Off the Manukau Heads. Two lives lost. One survivor. Cargo of timber and bricks lost with the ship.
	December 24	PIONEER	Steamer. Carried out to sea off the pilot station. Manukau Heads. No loss of life.
1866	December 25	CAMBODIA	Barque. 811 tons. Struck Manukau bar. Refloated but became a total loss at Huia. No loss of life.
1869	February 28	LITTLE FRED	Schooner. 131 tons. Kaipara. Total loss. Crew saved.
1870	March 13	CHALLENGE	Schooner; 57 tons. A new vessel with a load of timber lost the wind while crossing the Manukau bar. Total loss.
1871	December 14	MIDGE	Schooner; 92 tons. Total wreck. Pilot error off Pouto Point while entering the Kaipara Harbour.
1874	February 2	FLORA MacDONALD	Cutter; 18 tons. Capsized on the Manukau bar after losing her steering gear. All crew and passengers drowned. The eight bodies were never recovered.
1874	March 23	HERCULES	Brigantine; 139 tons. Carrying a full load of kauri from the Aratapu Mill on the Kaipara. A complete wreck, outward bound on the Kaipara bar.
	April 18	ALBION	Brig; loaded with 6000 sleepers. Stranded at Kaipara Heads with a broken back. A total loss.
1875	September 4	TAWERA	Schooner; 55 tons. Dismasted and stranded off Kaipara Heads. All five crew lost.
1876	January 15	MELAINE	Schooner; 136 tons. Stranded Kaipara Heads. A total wreck. All crew saved.
	June 23	WILLIAMETTE	Cutter; 28 tons. One of the Manukau lifelines driven ashore just south of Manukau Heads.
	July 2	LADY FRANKLYN	Barque. Stranded when the cable parted. Unable to refloat, she became a total wreck in the Kaipara Harbour.
1877	May 16	FERONIA	Barque; 329 tons. Stranded inside the Kaipara Heads. A total wreck. Caused by the master standing too close to the beach under sail without due cause. All hands saved.

1880	January 3	PRAIRIE	Brig; 139 tons. A failure of the wind left vessel stranded on the Kaipara bar. A total wreck.
	October 9	JAMES A. STEIRART	Brigantine; 170 tons. Outward bound with kauri. Ashore on the Northern Spit, Kaipara Heads. All hands lost.
1881	August 12	RONA	Schooner. Lost with all hands at South Head, Kaipara. Captain was unable to find the entrance and came too close to the coast bar; the vessel was lost in the surf. Maori burned the hull.
1882	March 29	VINDEX	Barque; 290 tons. Grounded in the channel while leaving the Kaipara Harbour and became a total wreck. No loss of life.
1883	January 19	MARY MILDRED	Barque; 460 tons. Stranded at Taihou Creek, Kaipara Harbour. Developed leak; total loss.
1883	March	CLARINDA	Schooner. Foundered off Manukau.
1885	January 2	ANNABELL	Brig; 348 tons. On Tory Shoal, Kaipara Heads. Total loss at sundown. All saved.
	January 17	WAVE	Brig; 174 tons. Total loss. Caused by master's error of judgement.
	February 20	MARY ANN ANNISON	Barque; 279 tons. North Spit, Kaipara Heads with cargo of kauri from Tauhoa. Total loss at nightfall. Crew and passengers landed safely.
	March 26	MATHIEU	Barque; 367 tons. Total wreck at Kaipara Harbour entrance, North Beach. All hands saved.
1886	May 19	STAR OF THE MERSEY	Brig; 255 tons. Cargo of 130,000 ft of bulk flitch timber out of the Kaipara. Total loss, but timber recovered. Bound for Dunedin, vessel started leaking after crossing bar. Crew saved.
1887	August 24	RECAMIA	Ketch; 69 tons. At entrance to Kaipara Harbour. Lost on Tory Shoal during southeast gale. Sank in 15 fathoms. All five crew lost.
1890	February 7	SPLENDID	Barque; 358 tons. Total wreck after stranding in Kaipara Harbour. Vessel rotten – unable to bear the weight of loaded timber.
	May 8	WILD WAVE	Brig; 173 tons. Stranded on North Spit, Kaipara. Carrying 144,000 ft of timber from Helensville. All crew saved. Vessel total loss.
1893	March 16	NORTHERN STAR	Barque; 338 tons. As a result of a collision with another vessel off the Kaipara Heads. This wreck remains a mystery.
1894	May 30	EMMA	Cutter; 21 tons. A total wreck on the Kaipara shore, though her cargo of 135 sheep was saved.
	July	PAKU	Cutter; 33 tons. Wreckage found at the Manukau Heads. All crew lost.
1899	March 21	CATHONA	Barquentine. Fully laden with a load of timber. Stranded on North Spit, Kaipara Heads. The vessel became a total wreck. All crew saved.
1900	October 2	LORD OF THE ISLES	Barquentine; 208 tons. Came ashore north of the Northern Spit of the Kaipara Heads, carrying cargo of bone-dust. Although the vessel was breaking up, all crew made it ashore.
1901	February 25	LADY SAINT AUBYN	Schooner; 161 tons. On the Northern Spit of the Kaipara as a result of a wind drop. All crew were saved.
1902	September 23	CONCORDIA	Barque. With a load of timber, ran ashore on Muriwai Beach south of Kaipara Heads. Russian crew landed safely except for the steward, who fell into the surf.
	October 17	MAY	Barquentine; 237 tons, built of oak. Carrying a cargo of timber from Pouto. Lost off the Muriwai coast. The vessel capsized in the surf. All were drowned except champion swimmer Watti Dunn, a 19-year-old Maori.
1904	November 15	KINCLUNE	Barque; 741 tons. Iron clad. Came ashore on Muriwai Beach, a total wreck. The crew landed safely. She stayed high and dry for years.
1905	May 14	NEPTUNE	Barquentine; 684 tons. Broke up after hitting the bottom and spilling the ballast on the North Spit, Kaipara bar. All crew saved.
	June 15	EMERALD	Barque. Wrecked on the beach of the Kaipara Heads. Driven ashore in a gale, the crew landed safely in the longboats.
1908	May 7	WARKWORTH	Cutter. Stranded and lost 15 miles south-east of Kaipara Lighthouse on Muriwai Beach.
1909	January	RIO LOGE	Brigantine; 241 tons. A new mystery of the Kaipara bar. Sailing en route for Dunedin, was last seen taking the bar. No trace was ever found.
1914	September 26	ANGLO-NORMAN	Barque; 762 tons. Norwegian-owned. Ashore in a fierce squall on the Northern Spit, Kaipara Heads. Total loss. All crew landed safely and walked to the Pouto lighthouse. The Northern Spit is known as The Graveyard.
1916	September 28	ALBANY	Steamer; 10 tons. Wrecked by the Muriwai Creek, Muriwai Beach, not far from the present camping ground. She had suffered an engine breakdown and headed ashore but was lost while being towed out through the surf.
1921	November 22	CYGNET	Steam launch; 3 tons. Destroyed by an explosion and fire outside the Manukau Harbour.
1933	February 3	SEABREEZE	Oil engine vessel, destroyed by fire, Kaipara Harbour.
1953	July 13	THISTLE TWO	Fishing boat. Lost at Manukau Heads. No survivors.
1968	May 11	CALLIE	Diesel launch. Last to carry fare-paying passengers on the Manukau Harbour. Wrecked on sandbank off Heads. No casualties.
1974	May 5	MOORINA	Wooden fishing boat. Lost on the Kaipara bar. All three crew lost their lives.

1981	October 6	**BROTHERS DIESEL**	Fishing boat. Capsized and sunk by huge waves off the South Head, Manukau.
1983	June 19	**EVIAN**	Cargo vessel. Man swept overboard in heavy seas.
1987	June 28		Six metre runabout, unnamed. Hit log in the Manukau with two of the three occupants losing their lives.
	December 23	**BLUEFIN**	Launch. Assumed to have hit a log in the Manukau with two fatalities.
1990	June 11	**STARFISH**	Six-metre runabout. Sunk without trace off Manukau bar with loss of two lives.
1994	September 3		Unnamed dinghy carrying four people on a scalloping expedition. Sunk 200 metres off French Bay in the Manukau Harbour with the loss of two lives.
1995	January 20	**BUCCANEER**	Fishing boat. Lost steering and ran aground while entering the Manukau Heads. Vessel a total loss but no loss of life.
	January 21	**TE IKA NUI**	Fishing charter boat. Lost in Kaipara Harbour after structural failure, with two fatalities.

As Herman Melville said, the sea is an endless mystery. After storms and tidal washouts, wreckage of past disasters is often uncovered. The finest reference to early shipwrecks is *New Zealand Shipwrecks 1795-1936*, which can still be found in better antique bookshops. It provides a wealth of information, culled from newspapers and shipping records.

Although the picture recorded by these shipping tragedies seems in this day and age to be horrifying, it should be remembered that literally thousands of ships made tens of thousands of safe crossings of the harbour bars.

Between 1840 and 1981, 38 vessels of large tonnage and significance were lost on this section of coast. In the 1880s, the Kaipara and Manukau harbours had 30 ships plying their waters and the bars of both entrances were continually being crossed.

COURTESY T. FAIRBURN

THE MIGHTY KAIPARA

Explorers and comets

(Above) **The Kaipara still offers excellent fishing.** (Opposite) **The treacherous Kaipara bar lies at the entrance to New Zealand's largest harbour.**

JAMES COOK got his first taste of the west coast weather in a "roaring gale and a high rolling sea" on 4 January 1770, standing off a coast too dangerous to approach. Cook spied through the heaving seas a "desart coast". This was the Kaipara coastline. He wrote later that day, referring to it as False Bay. By the time the storm had abated, the variable winds had left the coast behind and a gentler summer in New Zealand waters ensued.

In 1854, in a Batavian warehouse, a battered copy of Abel Tasman's journal revealed that more than 200 years before, the Dutch navigator sailed along the west coast of the North Island on his voyage of discovery. On a balmy December evening, three miles from the shore on the sea which now bears his name, he briefly records the sighting:

> This coast extends south-east and north-west, high in some places and covered with dunes in others, without reefs or shoals.

In the early part of the 20th century, Jane Mander set her feminist novel *The Story of a New Zealand River* on the Kaipara, this magnificent inland sea, the second-largest harbour in the world. The River, as the Kaipara was referred to in colonial times, was once a thriving commercial harbour, busy with ships of all sizes, trading from the multitude of settlements and mills that dotted the coastline of this vast waterway. Around this great basin were hills of virgin forest. Mander, herself a bush-miller's daughter, spent much of her formative years in the Henderson Valley homestead where her ears would have been ringing to the sounds of the axe and the crashing kauri. Her novel catches the majesty of the primeval forest before the settlers' onslaught:

> With a catch of her breath, Alice saw towering up out of the green depths on either side of that open way, row upon row of colossal grey pillars, seemingly as eternal as the hills, losing themselves above in a roof of impenetrable green. The pungent smell of the innumerable little cones mingled with the heavy smell of banks of moss upon their roots. A faint sound of the morning breeze stirred in their top most fringe of leaves leaking downward...

Today the South Kaipara Heads are reached by a long winding road from Helensville, or along the 65 km highway of sand that is Muriwai Beach. With a coastline extending for more than 3200 km, and a wide and graceful opening of around 7.5 kilometres, it is indeed a mighty harbour.

(Top) **Sunlight on the sandbar, South Head.** (Above) **The late lamented Rena Hinemoa Bycroft, shown here in 1997 at Haranui marae, near Parakai, campaigned against mining of the Muriwai coastline.**

In 1878 the brief notes on the Admiralty charts described a great "bottomless pit" of ocean and a vast, troubled stretch of water, the Kaipara bar, extending six miles (10 km) to sea. The early missionaries noted that Maori living on the coast used the lagoons which formed a long line of fresh water behind the dunes as their traditional fishing ground for the celebrated eels of the area, and that "the natives" of Kaipara had a legend that the sand-banks on the bar were once dry land, upon which their forefathers had lived and cultivated. This story pre-dated the similar tale of the Manukau bar, which also offered an expanse of dry land, suitable for the gathering of sea-bird eggs and abundant fishing.

The early missionary Samuel Marsden, on one of his three journeys through Northland in 1821, wrote in his diary that here the sand-dunes "stretch further than the eye could see, with rivers running from the interior into the harbour."

Maps from the 1840s approved by the Surveyor-General of New Zealand, Felton Mathew, show the spelling of Kaipara as Kai Para and a large patch of dry sand at the entrance. By 1860 this had vanished. Extensive surveys were carried out to find the safest navigable way into the harbour. The cast of captains is noted. With his schooner *Prince Regent*, Captain John Rodolphus Kent, who had made the maiden voyage through the Hokianga Heads, was unsuccessful in attempting to become the first European into the Kaipara. He tried for a number of years, but was unable to find an entrance through the bar. The mystery surrounding who was the first European to enter the Kaipara is the subject of a splendid book by the maritime author T.B. Byrne. In *The Riddle of the Kaipara* Byrne meticulously traces these early attempts to cross the bar of the Kaipara and claim the rich bounty that lay beyond. The honour went to Captain Thomas

Wing, who later ran the Manukau signal-station. On early sailing ships, instructions for entering the Kaipara were full of dire warnings:

> The Kaipara entrance may be known by the sand hills at the North Head, being 200 feet higher than along the beach before the sand cliffs recede inland, leaving an extensive level of sand and swampy ground. The breakers will be gently seen from the masthead long before the distinctions in the land are visible. The whole extent of the outer limits of the surf is eleven miles, in a semi-circle form. There are at present four channels, the northern is very narrow, and has from two-and-a-quarter to three fathoms and should never be taken except under difficulties, or when a vessel standing too far over has been drawn into the channel by the tide.

In 1840 the *Aurora* was lost at this spot. The south channel is narrow and not well known. The *Sophia Pate* was wrecked here in 1841. On the tidal charts, the notes are equally alarming:

> The tides in the Kaipara vary in strength according to winds. The ordinary springs run five miles an hour, enduring strong gales or freabes of seven miles. Vessels leaving the Kaipara should be within three miles of the heads at the first of the ebb, if it is intended to beat through and is possible for a smart working ship to do so. If a fair wind is necessary, it must be remembered the morning winds will rarely carry a vessel clear of danger, and will probably leave her becalmed amongst the breakers.

(Top) **Inland from the coast, the Kaipara farmland has well-drained sandy soils, excellent for sheep. (Above) Parakai reforestation advocate Elon Bycroft at his plant nursery.**

(Top) **Teatree Island, Kaipara Harbour.**
(Above) **Kaipara farmer and local identity Eric Leighton with his dog Bruce.**

And indeed they did. From the Kaipara Heads many magnificent vessels were wrecked. Given its notorious profile and its navigational hazards, the Kaipara was still seen in 19th century New Zealand as being a major port of entry for the colony.

With the developing trade the harbour started to boom. Although figures for the movement of coastal vessels were unfortunately not officially recorded before 1873, we know from early records that in 1867 no fewer than 110 vehicles had cleared the port and £13,000 of planing and sawing machinery had been cleared by Customs, indicating the extent to which milling, one of the most important industries of the time, was being established on its shore.

Jane Mander's novel gives us a clear picture of the Kaipara area in the 19th century. Its watery fingers reach nearly to the Waitemata and to the north as far as Dargaville. Its tributaries, creeks and streams number in the thousands and its sea change at the bar entrance presents a colossal churning of tidal currents.

The Kaipara was surrounded in those days by magnificent rich kauri forests that were situated in the tapu bush area at the head of the Hoteo River, about seven miles north of Wellsford in the Awaroa Valley, and in the Makarau Valley and other tributaries. In 1856 Captain James Stanaway assumed the role of harbourmaster. It seems that Stanaway had appointed himself the unofficial pilot and harbourmaster a few years earlier. He cited the reason for his self-appointment as the loss of the French corvette *L'Alcene* in 1851 and in 1853 the 600-tonne barque *Posthumus*. Fifty-two boats were wrecked during the history of the port of Kaipara.

In my early twenties a fishing trip for shark out of Tinopai went terribly

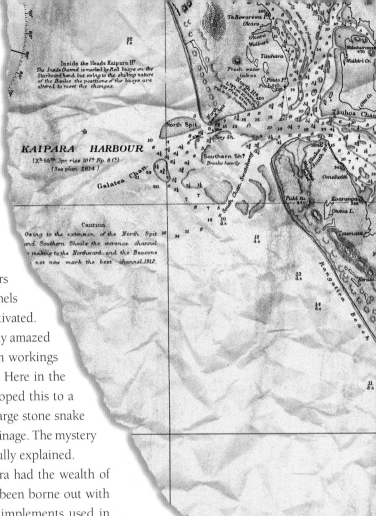

wrong as we became hopelessly lost in the myriad of shoals during the night. Although I was with seasoned Kaipara boatmen, I recall the fear and apprehension as our small craft moved cautiously through the sand-bar area on the darkest night of my life. Dawn found us still lost, but miraculously safe. Others have not been so lucky. It was a sobering warning. This harbour has taken so many lives. Often the careless pursuit of a dinghy, failure to wear a lifejacket, or a slip from a boat when the tide is running past the points and over the sand-bars can be fatal. The odds are strictly against you.

The Maori history on the Kaipara dates back 1000 years or more. There are extensive and fascinating irrigation channels in the swamps, indicating that this area was extensively cultivated. The structure of the channels and their size and complexity amazed early archaeologists, who compared them with the Mayan workings to drain and cultivate the basin that is now Mexico City. Here in the South Pacific, ancient Polynesian peoples had also developed this to a highly sophisticated level. To compound the enigma, a large stone snake sculpture formed the centrepiece and focal point for the drainage. The mystery and the origin of the Kaipara channels have never been fully explained.

I have long been interested in the idea that the Kaipara had the wealth of natural resources to sustain a large population. This has been borne out with the discovery in fields and farms of a large number of implements used in cultivation, fishing and hunting. In 1859, when the early settlers were arriving, they found the local Maori Ngati Rongo, a branch of the Ngati Whatua, making their seasonal fishing expeditions on the beaches of the Kaipara. On the beaches were thousands of shark (mango) and stingrays (roha) ready to be placed on drying frames made of manuka poles. The travellers were struck by the large number of blowflies, but strange to say they reported the drying fish were seldom struck.

The historian John Wright reports that in 1859, only 500 Maori were living around the lower half of the Kaipara, and much of the land had already been cut into vast holdings by Europeans, including the Rex family at the mouth of the Helensville River, Stanaway at the Aotea and Marriner on the Wairoa. The land was being cleared and although it would prove not great for farming, the days of the Maori settlements were numbered.

In the 19th century there were a number of schemes proposed to link the waters of the Waitemata with either the Manukau or the Kaipara by canals. The Kaipara scheme had the most interesting linkage investigated. In 1866 the Auckland Provisional Council engineer-in-chief decided to commission a report to estimate the cost of the best means of communication between Auckland and the Kaipara. Long before the interesting but difficult task of linking the Manukau with the Waitemata through the Portage inlet at New Lynn was contemplated, it was decided to look at the progress there to ascertain the best means of communication between Auckland and the Kaipara. The provincial superintendents had in mind the possibility of constructing "a canal to connect the headwaters of the Waitemata at or near the point where the navigation ceases in Brighams Creek, with the headwaters of the Kaipara."

(Top) **Section of map drawn in 1904-1905 showing detail of Kaipara Harbour entrance.** (Above) **The Kaipara has its share of colourful identities.** (Overleaf, pages 202-203) **Images of the Kaipara.**

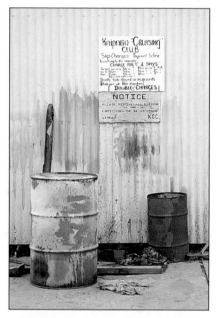

Brighams Creek is at the headwaters of the Waitemata and a giant canal was considered feasible, with a dam and locks across the mouth of the Canal Creek. At the junction of Brighams Creek they would form a basin for vessels to lie in when not travelling. The report went on to detail that 12 locks, having an average lift of 10 feet (3m) between high water mark in Canal Creek and the junction of Kumeu Creek, would do the job. But it would also mean that several cuttings, in order to straighten, widen and deepen the natural channel from the mouth of Canal Creek to the summit reach, with some other cutting beyond and down to Kumeu Creek, would be needed. It must have been daunting in 1866 to realise that this would involve 250,000 cubic metres of earthworks. It is a very comprehensive report and extremely ambitious. The minimum width of waterway in the canal was to be 24 feet and the size of the locks would be large enough to accommodate a boat 45 feet (13.7m) long with a 10-foot beam.

At the point where the canal would have intersected the Great North Road near Whenuapai, a bridge would have had to be built. Two bridges were costed in this grand plan, plus the removal of the Maori settlements. All of this would have been linked by a railway to Helensville. With contingencies, this grand scheme was quoted as costing £58,644 13s 4d, an exact amount for sure. But the engineer-in-chief, William Weaver, finally gave the programme the thumbs down. His report to the government stated that a railway line from Auckland to Kaipara would cost fully £10,000 less. They went ahead and built the rail line and dropped their grand canal plans.

In 1887 the Kaipara became the home of seven large ostrich farms, and the first 48 ostriches, valued at £10,000, were unloaded. For a while, ostriches were considered to be the next big idea. Almost a century later, in the mid-1980s, a consortium of New Zealand, Chinese and later French investors developed a prawn farm. Like the ostrich farms, the enterprise collapsed after two unsuccessful attempts to establish the industry, leaving the companies to be wound up amid widespread legal recriminations.

In the late 1890s the depression struck the Kaipara and the coastal trade fell off. In the first few years of this century and following the First World War, competition from railways and road transport saw a decline in the timber industry, as the pastoral economy, based on the fertile areas of the hinterland not dependent on water transport, started to rise. In 1896 more than 50 percent of freight on the Kaipara was timber, but by 1921 timber had declined to 25 percent and a few years before the Second World War it was down to 10 percent. The river trade was no more. Shark fishing had a brief run in the 1960s until traces of mercury were discovered in the fish and that industry also collapsed.

Recreational fishing trips and tourism have now become important business on the Kaipara. Tour operators depart from the beaches and wharves of the inner harbour, stopping on the other side at Pouto. Some cruise leisurely down towards the bar, lingering at favoured fishing spots out from the area known as the Graveyard.

If you are into running or motorcross, the sand-dune forest area behind the northern end of Muriwai Beach is for you. Forestry has given the area a superb venue for motorsport, publicised by television coverage of international motor rallies. You can enter the forest for a day's trail-blazing via Rimmer Road, three kilometres from Helensville township. There is no beach access except for four-wheel-drive vehicles.

(Above) **Kaipara gardener, philanthropist and pioneering industrialist Sir Tom Clark.**

Behind the now-forested dunes on the way from Helensville is a thriving local community whose activities include art and crafts, deer farming and macadamia nuts. Helensville still offers a number of hot pools with friendly service. Although they are not as popular as they once were, for a good winter soak, they can't be beaten.

Rimmer Road leads you to a vast pine plantation, where you can spot the odd deer, and if you like, surf some of the best waves on the coast. The beach at the end of the carpark walkway is sublime when an accessible left-hander, big and heavy, breaks in spring and late summer.

The Kaipara area is now attracting artists and investors. Jeff Thomson, the corrugated iron artist, has moved his studio to Helensville where he creates tin and iron stand-up animals and exotic sculpture. On the south head, Anthony Keidis, drummer in the California-based band Red Hot Chilli Peppers, owns a 100-hectare farm block. Sir Tom Clark, founder of Ceramco and one of the prime movers in taking New Zealand to the forefront of world yachting, and his wife Trish open their spacious house and splendid garden to raise funds for charity twice a year. Sheltered from the westerly wind, the hilltop farm garden is an example of what this remarkable climate can nurture.

Across the Kaipara Harbour at Pouto is the three-tiered, stately wooden lighthouse, no longer operational, but beautifully restored by the Historic Places Trust. This lighthouse, which once housed a 360-degree beam to warn shipping of the dangers of the Kaipara, sits high on a massive sand-dune, a silent sentinel to the maritime past of the harbour. Moved to a higher site, it has attracted a cult, following a radio documentary on psychic phenomena of Pouto, which sits on the junction of a line of both latitude and longitude.

Many visitors to the lighthouse and workers from the Department of Conservation and Historic Places Trust, have reported seeing boats below the lighthouse and mysterious visitors stepping ashore on the beach. In 1986, painters and carpenters working on the lighthouse saw a ship's longboat rowing into shore. Within seconds it had vanished. The observers all seemed reasonable individuals and not into ghost stories.

A few years ago I camped behind the lighthouse, and in the morning, after breakfast, I was aware a number of people had arrived at the lighthouse as I caught glimpses of colour through the dense trees. I thought it sounded like a family out walking, and I remember putting on some clothes in anticipation of their arrival through the grove. They never did. For the first time in my life I felt strangely aware and absolutely convinced of the presence of unseen visitors. Cross the harbour and investigate it yourself. You can see the lighthouse clearly from South Head.

This untamed coastline is also a changing landscape. The sand on the Muriwai side of the harbour continues to move. Between 1942 and 1983 the South Head spit extended eastward approximately 1500 metres, and this was quite extensive, enough for the spit to be recharted in the early 1990s. The sand build-up now meant that the bar was rapidly forming a new shape.

I am fascinated by the science of dunes and their movement. Most people wouldn't give it much thought, but here on the Kaipara these massive forms are pet projects of geologists. They chart them, like the derelict hulks of forgotten wrecks drifting up and down the coast. Over the years the dunes are measured for height and often given names and numbers as they continue their transformations, enlarging and falling away, ever-changing. For some of us, dune watching probably sounds as exciting as watching paint dry, yet for people interested in coastal movement, erosion and build-up it is an exact science of nature's hand on the changing landscape.

It is on the sand-dunes that we finish our journey. It is too far to swim this great stretch of water, and more than a month's walk to the other side. There the land shimmering in the haze seems more gentle, less troubled and tamed. More of a wasteland than a landscape with a story to tell.

Over the years this coast has offered me many gifts. Ocean and beach, tokens of great discovery. Rewards, if you like, for patience and perseverance beach-combing these watery margins. Like pieces of decking and spars from the *Orpheus* washed up after storms, and the four or five glass fishing floats festooned with barnacles, from the days when Japanese trawlers worked the coast. A number of sea-horses, dead and drying in the sun, ready to be hung up in the bach kitchen. More recently, on a chilly winter's morning, walking with a group of Maori whose ancestry links back through time on this coast, the discovery of a large live snapper at my feet as the tide receded stopped me in my tracks and filled me with the wonder of the endless possibilities of this place. Whether it was the company I was keeping on this occasion, or a profound revelation, is something I often find myself contemplating.

(Above) **Jeff Thomson is famous for his witty corrugated iron sculptured animals.** (Below and Opposite) **The dinghy is an essential part of the Kaipara lifestyle.**

I have silently acknowledged such gifting by simply returning to walk this coastline to experience its many moods. As my life moves through its stages, I have come here with changing needs. At first, I came to this coastline to enjoy its physical pleasures – its surf and its sunshine. I stayed to speak with a voice of protest against development and coastal mismanagement. Today, older and hopefully wiser, I'm using other tracks to continue exploring my love for this place. If I can't remember each and every day when I have enjoyed catching perfect waves, then it's just that they blur into one perfect sweep or curl. They are part of the memories of a lifetime.

My unreasonable and very all-consuming passion for one place, Karekare, has now extended to much of this coastline. I have come to know the beaches, the mysterious headlands, the caves and some of the history. They have all inevitably had other names in the past, and I would think, many more in the future. What they are called now and on the old maps is perhaps of no great importance. Their lasting significance is in the power of their beauty and living presence.

I am interested in the coast dwellers and what brought them as far as they could go. They didn't land on this coast, either in a waka or a longboat. They came by choice from other places, from placid harbours and seaports on the other side of New Zealand. They crossed the ranges, journeyed down the valleys and selected a fertile home place to make their own. They became absorbed and possibly even possessed by their surround-ings. The ruggedness of the place and the spiritual nourishment that the sea air and atmosphere provided had a way of bonding the settlers to the place. In turn, they took on characteristics that somehow expressed this unique place. Coasters always do.

These settlements still need their own history to be recorded. The schools, post offices, mills and stores, the fragments of their times are to be found in personal diaries, journals, land deeds and maps. When pieced together, they

(Top) **No longer a busy port, Helensville wharf is a tranquil haven in the early morning.** (Above) **Pouto Lighthouse at North Head, Kaipara, has been restored by the Historic Places Trust.**

form a rich tapestry of colonial life, far away from the growing towns that sprung up in the closing days of the 19th century. The old families on the coast mention place-names that were never recognised on a map. Hills that were burnt off each summer. Rivers that flow no more, and paper roads that were never built.

While writing this book, I spent a great deal of time following leads on many long-forgotten legends. It seems that time confers a blending of local stories and anecdotes so that fact and fiction merge. I believe it is important that these tales are passed on to future generations as living history. One way to come to terms with all this was to go and camp in the sand-dunes and think about the past. Lying under the stars on this coast, with the surf crashing and echoing off the cliffs, you realise that history takes on a new dimension.

Hale-Bopp, the three-tailed comet, made a fleeting but glorious appearance over Piha. It appeared in the western sky a few minutes after the sun dipped. For the three nights it was visible, I stood with a telescope on the Te Ahu Ahu hill lookout with my youngest daughter. Below is the site of the radar station where my mother spent four years of her life, watching for a Japanese invasion that never eventuated.

I couldn't help but think that on this headland, other people had stood watching for many hundreds of years, for coastal invaders, intruders and yes, even comets. That starry messenger of 1997 will not return for 2000 years. I wonder what the Untamed Coast will be like then.

REFERENCES

Suggestions for further reading

THIS JOURNEY has taken me to many sources to research the history of the coastline and with each interview or publication, the subject became larger and more fascinating. You may also wish to know more, so here is a guide to the untamed coast.

Books

Wing of the Manukau, T.B. Byrne, pub. T.B. Byrne, 1991

The Riddle of the Kaipara, T.B. Byrne, pub. T.B. Byrne, 1986

The Orpheus Disaster, Thayer Fairburn, Deed Publishing, 1988

West Auckland Remembers, Volume I, West Auckland Historical Society, 1990

West Auckland Remembers, Volume II, West Auckland Historical Society, 1992

The Bethells of Te Henga, Mary P. Woodward, Eureka Research, Sydney, 1988

The Kaimatura Camp-mate, S.B. Fletcher, Wentforth Print, Huia, 1985

The Piha Tramway, David Lowe, Lodestar Press, 1985

Te Hokowhitu A Tu, The Maori Pioneer Battalion in the First World War, Christopher Pugsley, Reed Publishing, 1995

Working the Kauri, Duncan Mackay, Random Century, 1991

Shipwrecks, New Zealand Disasters, 1795-1936, Dunedin Book Publishing Co, 1936

New Zealand Shipwrecks, 1799-1975, C.W.N. Ingram, A.W. Reed, 1977

Kauri Timber, J.T. Diamond and B.W. Haywood, Lodestar Press, 1980

Waitakere Kauri, J.T. Diamond and B.W. Haywood, Lodestar Press, 1980

Kauri Timber Days, J.T. Diamond and B.W. Haywood, Bush Press, 1991

The Turners of Huia, Alan Kirk and Harvey Turner, Institute Press, 1966

The Story of a New Zealand River, Jane Mander, Godwit Publishing Ltd, 1994, quote from p.39, Chapter IV

Fire on Clay, Dick Scott, Southern Cross Books, 1979

Once the Wilderness, John Diamond, Wilkinson Press, 1955

Once the Wilderness, J.T. Diamond, Whitcomb and Tombs (2nd Edition), 1966. Pictorial Edition, Lodestar Press, 1977.

Out of Auckland, Hawkins, Pelorus Press, Auckland, 1960

The Cyclopaedia of New Zealand, p.56: Trips for Visitors

New Zealand Sensations, Rex Monigatti, Reed, 1962

Turton Land Transaction: The Old Land Claims in New Zealand, 1877, Volume 1

Turton Land Transaction: The Old Land Claims in New Zealand, 1882, Volume 2

Silhouettes of the Past: A Century Ago: Published Lyceum Club Auckland, August 1939

Tangyes Limited General Catalogue, Pocket Edition, 1884.

Piha, Sandra Coney, Keyhole Press, 1997.

Newspapers

The New Zealand Herald

The Western Leader

The Weekly News

The New Zealander

The New Zealand Free Lance

The Western Sun (Incorporate *The Piha Post*), December 1964, Piha 8 o'clock, October 1964, United Surf Club

The Roundabout, September 1996, Huia Settlers Museum (Norm Laing)

The Roundabout, June 1997, Huia Settlers Museum (Norm Laing)

Piha Community News, Published Mary Dobbie, November 1995, No. 54

Piha Community News, Publ. Mary Dobbie, August 1996, No. 58

Papers

A few notes about Te Henga or Bethells Beach, Auckland Historical Society Newsletter, February 1965

Archaeological Sites of the Te Henga Districts, Waitakere Ranges West Auckland, Bruce W. Haywood and John T. Diamond, 1977

Whatipu, Its Past, West Auckland Historical Society, Bruce Harvey, June 1996

The Whatipu Sands, Graeme Murdoch, ARA Regional Planning, 1989

Soil and Water Volume 7, September/Fore Dune Stabilisation, P.J. Jew – A.R.A.

Waitakere National Park, E. Earle Vaile 1939, published by
The Waitakere National Centennial Park Citizens Association
A Retrospective view of Planning for the Waitakere Ranges
and Coastline – background p.1 – McAlister – Waitakere City
Council
A Physiographical study of Recent Sand Dunes on the
Auckland West Coast, R.N. Brothers, Volume 10, 1951
A Short History of the Ranges, E. Earle Vaile 1939,
Waitakere Library
The Maori in the Waitakere Ranges, John T. Diamond,
Waitakere Library
Titirangi Primary School Centenary Publication, 1972
A Century of Water Supply for Auckland, New Zealand. C.W.
Firth, Auckland Regional Authority, 1967 (a revision of the
original Auckland City Council publication, 1958)
Insects of the Waitakere Ranges, Dr Peter Madison
Birds and Forest Plants of the Waitakeres: Some Relationships,
John Staniland, 1997

Journals

New Zealand Motor Journal, 1920 – Muriwai Beach Races
The Piha Calendar 1996 – Text and Notes – Piha Tennis Club
and Sandra Coney, 1995
Centennial Memorial Park Golden Jubilee Edition, 1940-1990,
Auckland Regional Council Parks Department, 1990.

Manuscripts: Reminiscences

Anawhata Memories – Merle Ussher
Karekare Diary Notes – Mr Ray Gribble
Karekare Sea Rescue 1935 – tape interview Margaret Clarke –
Hamilton
Karekare Sea Rescue 1935 – Mr Stan Holt
History of Waitemata County, Eugene C. Grayland
(unpublished manuscript), 1963
Piha Fire – Doris Pearce – Piha 1995
Piha Fire – correspondence, Mr John Oxspring – Piha 1990
A History of Waitemata – Gary De Forest – (unpublished,
commissioned by Waitemata City Council) 1987
Karekare, An Album of the Past, Rae Westbrook, Lodestar
Press, 1976
Iron Bound Coast, Wallace Badham, (unpublished memoirs)
1976
From Windermere to Titirangi, an Atkinson family history,
Gillian Denny, 1995

Correspondence

Journal and Correspondence of Rev. John Butler – Turnbull
Library, Wellington and Hocken Library, Dunedin
Correspondence – Merle Usher – History of Anawhata
Correspondence – Inquest and Evidence, on deaths of Douglas
Prior and Adrian Larking on Muriwai coastline, June 1990
Proceeding Decision on TITLE – Piha Islands (Lion Rock) –
Judge F.O.U. Acheson – 24 October 1939 – Auckland Court
(letters)
Royal New Zealand Air Force Museum – Karekare Seaplane
Rescue 1995
Anawhata memoirs – Anna Kronfeld, Henderson, 1997
The Aviation Historical Society of New Zealand (Inc.) –
Squadron Leader L.M. Isitt's logbook

Institutions Visited Personally

The National Maritime Museum: Greenwich, Wreck of the
Union 1860
The Auckland War Memorial Museum – Wreck of the *Union* 1860
The British Library London – Wreck of the *Union* 1860
Alexander Turnbull Library – Wellington – Piha, Muriwai,
Kaipara, Karekare
Domain Museum Library – Wellington – Manukau, Kaipara,
Karekare

Personal Interviews

Margaret Clarke – Piha and Hamilton
Mr Harry Liddle – Karekare and Manurewa
Mr Basil Fletcher – Huia
Mr Ray Gribble – Karekare – Karekare guest-house
Mr Alan Gribble – Karekare – early settlers Karekare
Mrs Trudie Bethell-Paice – Te Henga Bethells Beach – Bethell family
Mrs Mary Woodward – Titirangi – History of Bethells
Mrs Jean Fairburn – Titirangi 1920-1940
Mr Thayer Fairburn – Titirangi and Blockhouse Bay – *Orpheus*
Mr Pat Shanahan – Karekare – History of Karekare Surf Patrol
1935-1940
Mr Michael Shanahan – New Lynn – History of Karekare Surf
Patrol 1947-1953
Mrs Betty Hanson – Piha – Piha Fire 1939
Mr John Oxspring – Piha – Karekare Sea Rescue 1935
Mr Wallace Badham – Howick – flying on the west coast, 1930s
Mr Dudley Badham – North Shore – Karekare guest-house,
1920-1935

ATTRACTING BACKYARD WILDLIFE